D0558561

THEY MAKE IT DAMN TOUGH FOR WOMEN
WHO ARE DOCTORS . . .
The surgeons who are condescending. The patients
who hate being treated by a female. Doctors' wives
who think of them only as threats to their mar-
riages.

But to Dr. Phyllis Donnan the struggle was worth
it. Worth the lousy hours and the horrible illnesses
she had to deal with. Because beneath the layers
of disease, beyond the shrouded secrets of her
sexuality and her own needs as a woman, was the
practice of medicine—still the most noble calling
of all . . .

WOMAN DOCTOR

Florence Haseltine, M.D.
& Yvonne Yaw

BALLANTINE BOOKS • NEW YORK

Dedicated to our friend
PATRICIA GERCIK

Library of Congress Catalog Card Number: 76-26539

ISBN 0-345-30150-1

This edition published by arrangement with Houghton Mifflin Company

Printed in Canada

First Ballantine Books Edition: September 1978
Fourth Printing: April 1981

Acknowledgments

We thank Mary Halperin, M.D.,
Luke Gillespie, M.D., Terry Kohn, Ph.D.,
Alan Chodos, Ph.D., and Jonathan Galassi,
our editor, for their help.

Contents

PART I

July and August

Private Medicine

1

"Now if you'll just disrobe and lie down, I'll do your breast exam, Mrs. Black, all right? Just like you do at your checkup. Climb between the covers so you won't be chilly."

The woman was beautiful. With dignity she moved to the bed, turned her back, and slipped her soft gown from her shoulders. Then she turned and lay down, covering herself with the hospital bedclothes.

When I uncovered her upper torso, what I saw nearly made me faint.

It was the first time I had seen a radical mastectomy—the breast and all the surrounding tissue removed. Although I was now an intern, somehow I had never seen what it looked like. Now I wished I *had* seen it before. It would have prepared me. But I had to conceal my shock from the patient. I had to approach her smoothly. I had to examine her, to find out whether there was more cancer to be found —by touch.

I glanced at her eyes. She was watching me carefully. Her face was not relaxed, but she wasn't frowning either, or blushing, or crying. Then I turned my own eyes to her body and began to examine her.

She was a slim, though well-nourished, forty-two-year-old woman. The one breast she had was small and firm. The dark red nipple had tightened momentarily with the chill of the air but now it was normally soft.

On the left side of the chest there was no flesh at all, only skin. The long, white, cross-hatched scar ran straight from the shoulder across the chest almost to the center of the body below the breastbone. It looked like a zipper that had been opened to let everything be scraped from the soft white leather before it could be zipped up again. There was no nipple, no breast, no fat, no muscle—no tissue at all, only skin covering the left ribs.

I had to feel along the bones of each rib and between them to make sure that no cancer had remained or recurred. Fortunately it was all bare. The skeleton here was intact.

Just a half-hour ago I had been in the fifth-floor conference room routinely working on my discharge summaries and my beeper had gone off. It alerted me to dial 3894 for the information I would need. When I did, the nurse told me, "Dr. Donnan, Mrs. Stella Black has arrived in 647 for admission. She's Dr. Speir's patient."

I gathered up my papers, walked to the stairs, and climbed to the next floor. I already knew a few important things about Mrs. Black. She was in one of the larger, better-furnished private rooms, and so she had to be wealthy. It was likely that if she was Dr. Speir's patient, she had cancer. As the intern, I was to admit her, take her medical history, make sure of her chemotherapy, start the intravenous line, give her her medications, and do the routine medical supervision. When I saw her chart and the diagnosis—metastasized breast cancer—I realized that she might be dead within the year. Once cancer has spread from its original site, control is difficult and must be attempted by general body therapy; that is, radiation and chemotherapy.

I knocked at her door. At her call I entered. In the comfortable chair by the light of the window, the woman sat reading a book. Dressed in a long silky gown of delicate greens flowing like watercolors into one another, she had looked up and quietly watched me enter. Her hair was a cap of dark waves. When I saw her closely, I noticed her irises were unusual, a

4

light brown rimmed with black. Subtle make-up on her beautiful face almost disguised her pallor and the shadows under her eyes and the beginning pull of pain. I thought she looked as though she had stepped out of an expensive, romantic movie. She smiled.

"I'm Dr. Donnan, the intern on your case, Mrs. Black."

"My name is Stella," she answered. Her voice was low and pleasant. "If you don't mind, please call me that. I find Mrs. Black too formal for a situation like this."

I continued, "As your intern, I need to take your history. While you're here, I'll try to make your stay as comfortable as possible. If you have any problem, please ask the staff nurse to call me."

"Of course," she smiled. "Fine. What questions do you want to ask?"

I drew up a chair, and prepared to jot down anything she said that could be useful. I always asked one particular question first, since my phrasing always seemed to win a patient's cooperation and participation: "Why did you come to the hospital?"

She looked at me gravely, with a faint smile, and said, "I came to the hospital because I am dying of cancer, which they will attempt to treat here." It was almost as if she were trying to break it to me gently.

I was startled.

She went on. "I'm trying to admit that I'm dying so I can come to terms with the fact."

I thought there was something contrived—bald and self-dramatizing—about her reply, as if she really were an actress from a soap opera. I went on. I was supposed to ask questions not only about medical problems but also about personal history; it was important to know as much about the patient as possible. I always enjoyed this part of the workup, for it gave me insight into the patient's real life. I asked, "Have you traveled anywhere?"

She hesitated just a fraction of a second, then said,

5

"To almost every country one can name. I think the place I'll return to at last, however, is Greece."

"About your children?" This was an important question because it let you learn the medical history of the family. She knew just what I wanted. She told me she had two: the elder, twenty years old, was a son who had had medical problems all his life. She could describe to me all the medications he'd received and the dosages. She had not had her next child for ten years, obviously because of fear. The girl was perfectly healthy. Her husband had never been sick a day in his life. They had been married for twenty-two years. He had been a successful industrialist and was now a state senator. He had been called away for hearings two days before she was expected to come in to the hospital.

Finally, after many other questions, I said, "Tell me the history of the disease that brought you here."

She paused, as though she preferred talking about her family to telling about herself. Then she launched into her story with the same command of detail she had shown about them.

She had always scrutinized herself very carefully for any unusual lumps. She characterized herself as having been cancer-phobic, and had always sought medical advice when she'd felt a roughness on the neck or dermatitis of the hands. She had been especially careful about checking her breasts, more than once a month, and five years ago had thought she detected a lump. A mammogram had showed nothing. Then, just a year ago, a slight thickening in the area around the nipple had sent her to her gynecologist. A new mammogram had shown a suspicious area near the ribs. Before she went under for the biopsy, she gave them permission to perform the radical mastectomy. When the biopsy showed the tumor to be malignant, the surgeons immediately performed the radical. They found that her cancer had already spread to the axillary nodes, the lymph nodes in the armpit.

Most lumps in the breast are benign: fewer than

10 per cent are cancerous. If treated early, a patient with breast cancer can usually live another five to ten years. But for some reason Stella's disease had spread quickly.

After removing the breast and nodes, they had given her a very guarded prognosis. Six months later she developed a lump in her side that upon removal was found to be the same type of cancer. Soon after she began to feel pain in her arm, and was readmitted to the hospital. The tumor had spread to the spine, where it was eating away bone and causing pressure on the nerve to the arm. Radiation had relieved the pain somewhat, and now, after a two-week rest, she was back to receive chemotherapy that would attack and kill the cancer cells in her spine.

She must have known that the cancer was spreading everywhere, and that it would not only kill her but also cause a great deal of pain before she died. Throughout her recital she was aristocratically calm and precise. Then, after I had efficiently entered all the relevant data, I rose and said, "Now I need to examine you, please," and asked her to lie down on the hospital bed.

That was when she had disrobed, and, lying there, had revealed to me the most shocking sight I had encountered so far in my smooth medical career: the bare, sliced, and scraped skin of a starving child where a beautiful, vibrant woman's breast should have been. It was incredible that I hadn't seen it when I was a medical student, but I just hadn't, and none of the diagrams had prepared me for the reality.

Then, of course, I had to touch it, feel it thoroughly, and let no revulsion or horror show to the patient. I was tracing the skeleton in a way I hadn't done on a cadaver cold from its refrigeration or on a live patient. The first time any of us had put our hands on a patient the temperature difference had been startling. Since we Americans do so little touching, many of us had difficulty learning to touch, but I had easily adjusted to the warmth and the sensation. Now, however, was the first time I had combined the cadaver and the patient by outlining the warm bones, and it was naked death that I felt with my fingers, more real and appalling because of its faint warmth.

I finished that part of the exam. On private patients the pelvic exam is deferred. She got dressed. Then, after I checked on the dosage, I started her intravenous line and medication. She glanced up at the bottle, smiled, and settled down in bed with a little sigh, as if she were as contented as she could be.

"Please hand me my book, will you, Doctor?"

I hung around the nurses' station until it was time to remove the line. My patient was dozing when I came back in, but she awakened to watch me remove the IV.

"I'll come again with your medications tomorrow, Mrs. Black."

"Please," she frowned at me. "Stella."

"Of course. Have a pleasant evening."

When I got down to the coffee shop, I suddenly realized how tired I was. I'd been on since Saturday morning at 8:00, was supposed to go until 6:00 P.M. Monday, and here it was only 5:00 P.M. on Sunday. I thought of all the admissions I would still have to do this evening for Monday-morning tests or operations. I groaned. The evening would be chaos. Why don't people come in when they're supposed to on Sundays instead of waiting until the last minute? I complained to myself. I wolfed down a BLT and some coffee and was just starting a dish of ice cream when my beeper went off again, startling me half off the stool.

When I finally had a chance to get to bed, at about midnight, I didn't go home to my apartment, of course, but slept in the on-call room, where the interns who are on duty sleep between calls. There were two sets of metal bunk beds side by side in a small room, and hooks on the wall for clothes. I always slept with all my clothes on, however, except for my shoes. All the interns on duty on this part of the service had to sleep in this room, and it was assumed that they were all male.

My sleeping here bothered the men more than it bothered me. One guy glared at me every time I stumbled in for a nap when he was there. He looked like murder was in his heart. He mumbled about how his wife wouldn't like this. Once, as I fell onto the cot, I said, "Don't worry, I wouldn't rape you. I'm too tired."

I don't know whether he ever got any sleep. I was too exhausted to notice, and was always out like a light.

This time, though, I couldn't get to sleep. I had been on straight since Saturday morning; here it was Monday, with never more than two hours of sleep at a time in between; I had to be up bright and early for rounds that morning; all my duties on Medicine for the first three weeks had flooded me with fatigue —and I couldn't afford not to sleep. I turned from side to side, squeaking the cot springs, trying to find a comfortable position, hearing the heavy tired breathing of my friend Ted Gilman and then his beeper going off and him getting dressed in the dark. I couldn't sleep. When I finally gave up trying, I just lay there and thought in a confused reverie about everything that had happened to put me here on a sagging cot in my wrinkled whites in a small dark room that was filled with snoring men.

2

I decided to be a doctor when I was twelve. I was very clear about it. When I think of that twelve-year-old and her decision, I seem to look through her eyes again while she is sitting high in an apple tree in the spring. I see a whole orchard. In climbing up, I have shaken the limbs and bruised the blossoms. The pollen has brushed all over me and covers me with gold. The owners of the orchard don't want me to climb their apple trees, understandably, so I've had to sneak. Now, when I get up here, I can see all the trees covering the hillsides like clouds, and they smell sweet while the limbs are dark and the blossoms are white and the petals are thinner than skin and curled at the edges and cool.

That orchard is all built over now, of course, even though it's been only twenty years since I climbed there. Things change fast, and I changed too. Nothing was ever that simple again, even my desire to be a doctor.

What happened in between then and now was just what happens to everybody. Many things you learn get layered over a promise like that, and you almost forget it.

Finally, right after college, I married a man who was going to become a doctor. (What you want at twenty-one is more prudent than the crazy dream of a kid.) I had majored in zoology, so when I graduated and got married, I got a job as a lab technician to put my husband through medical school. I liked being married. For one thing, it relaxed me. As a teen-ager I'd been very tense. Now even my looks seemed to improve. I have slightly auburn hair and hazel eyes, and I wear glasses or contact lenses. I always used to wish my eyes were brown or blue, and not an in-between, all-mixed-up color, and I didn't like how thin my nose was. But being married helped me ignore what I thought of as imperfections. I enjoyed the challenge of turning out delicious food on our budget, and I became a gourmet cook. My husband began to have a good reputation for entertaining.

Of course, the students and the professors he brought home to dinner talked about medical cases. I was fascinated. I kept asking them a lot of questions until my husband told me that it made him tense when I did that. None of the other wives asked questions; they were all off having their own conversations, and I was the only female hanging around the men.

"But I'm interested!" I protested.

"Well, be interested in a more subtle way," he told me.

That was hard. With my background I understood most of what they were talking about, and I couldn't ask just those lay questions like, "How do you feel about socialized medicine?" The deeper he got into medicine, the deeper I fell, too. I began to read from his texts and to eavesdrop on those conversations as if I had a secret vice.

Then one evening, at the home of one of my husband's professors, after dinner his wife took me aside and said, sadly, "My dear, you want to be a doctor yourself, don't you?"

I gazed at her in astonishment. Suddenly I felt open, full of fresh air, like a child again, and humbly grateful to her for permitting me a revelation, as though she were the queen. But I didn't reply. I think she went on to talk about herself, but I don't remember anything she said.

Then I became very anxious, and for months denied the whole episode to myself, until the strain was obvious even to my husband and I had to have it out with him. We had intended our marriage to be a

11

straightforward one in which each of us was free to do what he or she wanted and to be what he or she was. After a lot of discussion and argument it was decided that I could go to medical school, but that I would wait until he was finished and making money before I withdrew my financial support. I was pleased and thought we were being very logical and fair. Then he chose plastic surgery as his specialty, which meant an eight-year residency.

I could see that my desire might wear out before he was finished and I was terrified, both of his inexorability and of my own wild rebellion. I *had* to go ahead and apply.

With the help of recommendations from two of my college professors and my lab supervisor at the medical school, I got in. That was the end of our marriage. To become a doctor, I myself felt that I divorced myself from the human race, in a way. I was an outlaw, self-serving and aggressive. It never occurred to me then that I condemned myself unjustly for traits that were good in a man. When my husband and I broke up, I believed there were no hard feelings, and I shut out any pain. We both assumed I would go it alone.

Medical school was wonderful. Within the first two weeks I got my cadaver, and the minute I put my hands in that body, I knew this was where I should be. I felt like a kid again, with engrossing projects as exciting as building a complete village with blocks, or doing a chemistry experiment with beautiful, precise method. I went through medical school invigorated by what I was learning.

Because I was one of the few women in my class— 13 out of 130—it was sometimes implied that I was there as a favor to my ex-husband, even though medical schools make sure no such influence is brought to bear on an application. It was uncomfortable that I was now divorced, for it suggested that I had gotten in under false pretenses, using my husband until he was no longer necessary. But I was so busy and happy that I ignored the few innuendoes. I didn't want to believe anybody could be nasty, and I didn't want to be troubled by such fleeting misgivings.

It was when I went for my internship interviews that I began to notice how the male doctors reacted to my sex. Perhaps their attitude was stronger because the internship shows that you really mean business; until then, you can easily drop out at any time, and a few of the women who got into medical school did. For example, a friend of mine in college had gotten into the best medical school in the country. She had had all A's and was truly brilliant. But she got pregnant halfway through her first year and dropped out to get married, move away, and start a family. I know now that that kind of sabotage of herself must have come from what has been documented as the female "fear of success," but at the time it was taken as proof that women were not professionally serious or worth the investment. As a matter of fact, a larger percentage of men than women drop out of medical school.

I almost didn't get an internship at all. My applications were lost by the secretary of the medical school office. I found out about it only when one of my professors came up to me in the hall and said, "You know, it's after the deadline, and I thought you were going to apply for an internship at Grey's."

"I am. I sent it in."

"Well, we haven't gotten it. Better make out a new one. Send it return receipt requested this time, or take it over to Grey's in person. I'll try to reopen the admission procedure for you."

In order to reapply, I had to get another copy of my grades, and when I went to the office for that, the secretary found my original applications, to three different hospitals, filed with my student chart. I was shaking so hard when she handed them over that all I could say was "Thanks." She apologized for accidentally filing them, but I was remembering how she'd sent all my material to my home address instead of my student address so I got my notices later than everyone else, and I couldn't trust myself to say anything. I wasn't paranoid; I found out later that she

13

made such "mistakes" when dealing with any woman who came through the school.

When I came across town for my interviews, the sky was a blank, cold gray; an edgy wind was blowing, and dirty patches of icy snow remained in the corners of curbs and up against the buildings. I walked up the three broad front steps of Grey's and into the cavelike porch, chilled to the bone.

For a general, or rotating, internship, you have an interview with the head of each department you are going to work in. Although I was too old, I thought, to want a residency in Surgery—it would add another five years to my training—I knew I should have a Surgery rotation. I wanted a Medicine service, thinking I might go into private practice as an internist, and I would add Obstetrics, Gynecology, and Pediatrics as background for a general practice.

I was sitting out in the corridor, waiting for my interview with the head of Surgery, when it seemed to hit me all at once that I was doing something strange; I became very nervous. The head, Dr. Cohen, came to the door and invited me in. He was smiling.

"Come in, Mrs. Donnan!" That had not been my married name, and I was *Dr.* Donnan now, but he rushed on, almost boisterously. "Another woman to grace our halls, eh?" He laughed. "Well, whenever a woman comes along, I've always found her to be a conscientious student, very conscientious. Congratulations on getting this far!"

I smiled and nodded.

"You're a little late in applying, however . . ."

I had to say yes. I wasn't willing to offer the excuse.

"Well, well, well," he chuckled. "A little scatterbrained, eh?" He looked at a copy of my application. "A rotating internship is what you want? You're sure now?" He laughed again.

He laughed so often that I had a hysterical impulse to giggle whenever he chuckled, but fortunately, when he went on to talk about his surgical service, he became serious. "One of my surgical residents this year just happens to be a woman, you know. A very

14

careful mind, very painstaking—which is all to the good in Surgery, of course. I often ask her to sew up my patients. It takes her only half as long as these men who've never held a needle in their lives, and her stitches are works of art. I'm transferring her to my lab, just where we need that kind of precision."

I was intimidated, for transfer to the lab was tantamount to being kicked out of the program.

He was still talking. "We need more women in Surgery, actually; I wish more would apply. I want you to know, however, that I've found it is most difficult for women to do the rotation. It requires immense physical strength, of course, not to mention stamina." He sighed. "My wife, as a matter of fact, began her career as a pediatrician—hard work, that, you'd never guess it. She's working in my lab now, too; the hours are regular."

I nodded and expressed the opinion that that was certainly a consideration. I was dazed. I had never withstood such an onslaught of condescension before.

My Obstetrics and Gynecology interview had a different twist to it. The panel of three men seemed almost identical to me: they were all sandy-haired, rotund, and amiable-looking.

One said, "I remember that your husband interned at University several years ago, Mrs. Fairleigh."

"My name is Dr. Donnan now," I corrected him.

"Oh, ah. Yes. So, you changed your name. I remember your husband. Interesting record. What is he doing now?"

"He has finished up a residency in Plastic Surgery at Mencken," I said.

"Plastic Surgery!" one cried, and all three of them leaped upon the topic as if it were a godsend at a cocktail party. They spent fifteen minutes questioning me about my ex-husband's specialty and the techniques plastic surgeons were using nowadays and discussing the Elizabeth Taylor movie they'd seen.

These two interviews bewildered me with their

15

shallowness. They weren't quizzing me on my abilities or my plans.

At the end of this one, one of the doctors said, "By the way, speaking of husbands, do you think we ought to pay women as much as men?"

I smiled broadly and said, "No. I think you ought to pay them much more!"

An intern's pay was $800 a month. Only a few years before that, interns had earned $100 a month. I knew what they were asking, and at last I'd been able to speak up—on time.

Next I talked to a woman resident who was finishing up that year. She spent most of her time warning me about things, and she especially told me not to have a baby while I was working there, since that would put a burden on all the other interns and residents.

"I don't intend to," I said.

"That's what they all say," she retorted.

"But I'm not even married anymore!"

She went on to tell me about a woman several years earlier who, she said, had caused the hospital to be short one resident by leaving when her husband had to transfer.

She told me a long story, and as it unfolded I could see that what had happened was actually not the woman's fault. She had notified the hospital in December that she would be continuing elsewhere, and they had filled her place; then, in the middle of June, right before the medical year began, a man had decided that *he* wasn't coming after all. When people were moved about like dominoes to fill up that gap, the vacancy had ended up in what was originally the woman's specialty, so she was blamed for the shortage of one important staff member.

I was beginning to wonder whether this hospital in particular had been the right choice for me after all. By the time I got to my interview with my professor, Dr. Poirier, who was chief of Medicine, I felt knock-kneed and cross-eyed. However, he encouraged me.

"This is a wacky hospital, my dear," he said. "But

16

then, all hospitals have a neurotic spirit; otherwise, they wouldn't have enough energy and stubbornness to do the job. We get the best interns and residents, and the best work out of them. You'll find yourself increasingly loyal to the place. After a while you won't even notice its quirks. It's like a beloved old autocrat, full of wisdom—and orneriness. You'll forgive him everything."

I got my internship, probably thanks to him.

3

Grey's Hospital had been built and added on to at three different times, so it was an awkward combination of styles and an inconvenient combination of levels. It sat on the top of a small hill in what had become one of the slummier areas of the city. The central structure, the Thomas Harding Grey Building, was of massive gray stone, three stories high, with corridors running off on two opposite sides from the central area. In this building was Admissions and Records on the first floor, and on the top two floors, like the attic in *Jane Eyre,* the psychiatric section.

The Elsie McMahon Levering Memorial Building made a terrible contrast to the gray stone: of smooth red-orange brick, with a lot of green copper trim, it was connected to Grey on all three floors and the basement by long corridors that sloped gradually from the gray building down to the red one. Levering had the medical wards and Pediatrics. The rooms in Levering were high-ceilinged and lath-paneled, like old-fashioned summer cottages. They were always being painted summer-cottage colors, too, the favorites being pale green and pale aqua. These rooms had a kind of subtle echo since the surfaces were so hard and there was never enough fabric in them to dampen that echo. It made Pediatrics a Babel.

The last building, Kinderkopf, had been built after World War II flush up to the back of Grey. A ten-story high-rise, it had the emergency rooms, intensive care units, all Surgery, OB-GYN, all private Medicine, and all the labs and administration. Technical rooms like operating rooms and labs had been modernized once since the building had been built, and the top five floors had been air-conditioned. The building looked like a glass and concrete apartment house.

Each story in Kinderkopf was shorter than the tall ones of Grey; Kinderkopf had six floors where Grey would have had five; therefore it was necessary to have a few steps from Grey to Kinderkopf, as well as a short ramp, which patients in wheelchairs were not allowed to try by themselves.

The hospital was huge and slightly incoherent with all its accretions and connections. My professor had suggested that its spirit was eccentric as well, and I soon found internship threatening to drive me crazy too.

The last day of June was hot with bright sun and heavy with humidity. The staff meeting room where we got our assignments was in the basement of Kinderkopf, next to some kind of heating area—hot water, maybe—because the room temperature was boiling, and everybody's clothes were already limp.

I got there early and took a seat high up near the back, where I could see everyone who came in. Although I don't remember feeling so observant then, I can remember all the details of that first day. All internships throughout the country begin on July 1. On June 30 there is a meeting to introduce the new people to all the technical details of their services and their hospitals—they get assignments, schedules, clothing issues (white jackets and trousers for the men, white jackets and skirts for the women), and are given tours of the areas and introductions to key people such as lab supervisors. The staff meeting room was a large

18

auditorium on the basement level, sloping in rows up from a subbasement to a basement level with windows near the ceiling on two walls. All large meetings would be held here, including Complication Rounds, about every other week, when a difficult or interesting case would be presented and discussed in a particular specialty and every staff member in the hospital could come. This might be the only day of the year when the people there would be dressed in something other than whites, but the young men in street clothes were all somber-suited with white shirts. It was the teaching staff and residents in their white jackets who showed any gaudy colors—their shirts were bright, with pink the favorite. Doctors in white do that; their shirts and ties are the only things that express any personality.

The director of the hospital was a tall, gray-haired man who looked sixty but was really in his early fifties. Medical practice seems to age doctors faster than other people—probably during internship and residency, when they don't get enough sleep. He looked contented now, though, solid and competent. From my angle, his glasses glittered when he moved his head.

He began, "Gentlemen—and Lady," and bowed to me. Everyone turned to stare. I hadn't thought I would be the only woman! The fact was that there were others, an intern in Radiology, one in Anesthesiology, and two residents in Pediatrics, but I was the only intern who would be out on the floors. After the little flurry his gallantry made, we all listened to his introductions and explanations.

I had chosen the rotating internship because I didn't know yet which specialty I was most interested in. When I got my schedule I was relieved. I saw that they were being nice and had given me Medicine to start out on. I expected many of the cases on Medicine to be elective hospitalizations; the worst ones would go to Surgery. There wouldn't be so much life-or-death pressure, I thought, and there it would be easy to accustom myself to the hospital routine. It was a good idea, of course, to start out on the service where you could get chemotherapy, medications, and dosages established early, since that knowledge would be useful on all the other services. I was glad, too, that they hadn't given me the Emergency Room first thing. Of course, some intern has to start out there, but everybody agrees: "Don't have an accident on July 1."

My schedule on Medicine was, like everyone else's, every weekday from 8:00 A.M. to 5:00 P.M. or whenever I managed to finish up; every third night; and every third weekend, or 8:00 A.M. Saturday until 5:00 P.M. Monday. Medicine had the most rounds of any service. I called it a merry-go-round. First there were Work Rounds at 8:00 A.M., for catching up on patients and their treatment, then 9:00 A.M. Resident Rounds, specifically for the team to discuss a particular case. We would sit in the Doctors' Lounge and each of us on the team (three interns, one resident, a staff man, one nurse, and some medical students covering one section of the service—nine people in all) would examine the test results, x rays, and new data from the day before on an interesting or difficult case. Not every patient got that amount of discussion; some were pretty routine, and we had time for maybe two or three at most in the hour. Private doctors, who liked to admit to one particular section of the hospital all the time, might be in and out until 10:00 A.M., and you had to be available for instruction and consultation with them on an ad lib basis. Then, from 10:00 to 12:00, there were ward rounds, followed by all of us—including those not specifically responsible for ward patients— and led by the attending (the staff doctor, superior to the resident, supervising for a month). Each case had to be written up, of course, by the intern assigned to it and the result added to the patient's folder. Throughout the afternoon, then, I did the routine work: IV's and drawing blood and whatever else had to be done. The important task was to keep the patients' fluids adjusted and in balance. It wasn't all scutwork, for I had some responsibility for the conduct of the case, especially if it was a patient of a private doctor, who might come in at any time and who discussed the orders with me rather than with the resident. Also, I might be admitting new patients or preparing discharge papers for others. And at any time I might be interrupted by someone coming up from emergency, or even by a cardiac or respiratory arrest on the floor.

It wasn't as unusual as it sounds, since people are always dying in hospitals, but the very first night I was on duty there was a code call. A code call was an emergency—a cardiac or respiratory arrest. For that call I had to wear a special beeper in addition to my regular one. The regular beeper was flat, about 3½ inches square, and I had to buy a belt to attach it to, since the waistband of the skirt I had been issued wasn't strong enough to hold it. The code call beeper was 7 inches long, but narrower, maybe 2½ inches wide, and flat. It was black with red stripes, and I had to wear it on the other side in order to be balanced. With the two beepers attached to my belt, and holding tight to them as though they were guns that would fire if I jiggled them, I was off and dashing down the hall even before I learned from pushing the response button which room I had to head for.

The team consists of the intern, the resident, two anesthesiologists, and a nurse to record everything. They converge on the room with the crash cart, which holds everything you might need. You always follow a particular order. First the board goes under the patient's back so his body doesn't sink and bounce when you need to work on it. Then the order goes: (1) Airway (you ventilate by endotracheal tube and bag, or mouth-to-mouth resuscitation, to keep the oxygen going to the lungs and then to the brain); (2) Heart (you pound or thump the chest in order to get the heart beating; the rhythm is three or four thumps to each breath); (3) IV (you get this started in order to give medications, like bicarbonate and calcium to help regulate heartbeat and to draw blood to get a picture of what's happening); (4) EKG (for electrocardiogram, the German invention to monitor the heart); and (5) Shock—if you need it (you place two elec-

21

trode paddles on the chest at opposite sides of the heart to shock it into beating).

On this team I was responsible for the airway, and in order to get at the patient on the high hospital bed, I had to crawl onto the bed with him and, kneeling, ventilate him.

Breathless from running, I straddled the patient's head. My knees were separated in order to get his head back for the intubation of his trachea. As I worked swiftly and carefully to ventilate him, a question popped into my mind. If he woke up and opened his eyes and saw the first thing in his line of sight, my crotch, would he think he was in heaven, or in hell?

Well, he revived all right and opened his eyes, and I scrambled off the bed so fast I fell off it. Jerry Carter, my resident, picked me up off the floor, laughing. "God, Phyllis, you're the first *intern* I've known to fall out of a hospital bed!"

I laughed, too, and muttered something, thinking of what a sight I would have made if I'd fallen on the other side of the bed onto the crash cart. I could see myself skidding down the hall, tubes flying, bottles spilling, hypos shooting out everywhere. It was a good thing that by then the patient was out of danger.

From then on, I wore slacks when I was on code call. Since the hospital issued only skirts to women, I had to buy my own slacks, but it was worth it not to have my ass so cold or immodest while I was trying to save someone's life.

After about two weeks, during which all my patients were a blur, I began to feel that I was settling in. I had seen or done almost everything when I was a medical student on the floor at University Hospital, so after I had gotten familiar with the layout and staff people at Grey's I thought it would be more of the same, only now with increased responsibility. Emergencies were efficiently met. Admissions were routine. I was handling my responsibilities well. The men on the service were encouraging, and I was learning even more than I had thought possible, discussing alternative therapies with the attending and the visit (the expert from outside the hospital also available for a month at a time) as well as the private doctor for whose patients *I* did the primary care.

Now and then, a patient would take one look at me and say, "I don't want a woman for my doctor," and I would reply, "Fine. That's your privilege. I'll ask one of the men to take over your case." I thought nothing ruffled me. The male interns and residents accepted me, and I enjoyed the few off-hours I spent in the lounge with them watching baseball on TV.

I began to see a patient as a whole person. One old man came in with prostate cancer. These prostate cases come in because they can't urinate, or with pain from metastasis to bone sites. Different kinds of cancer spread to different places—some to organs, some locally, some to bones. His cancer had metastasized all over. The treatment is blood transfusions plus hormonal therapy, neither of which cures the cancer or even lengthens the patient's life, perhaps, but he feels better immediately, and might live several years in comfort.

His family was superb. They visited him all the time. When a situation or procedure was explained to them, they responded gratefully, accepted the treatment, and asked intelligent questions. They didn't want me to tell him the diagnosis. They said to me, "He's sixty-nine. He don't need to know he's got cancer. We just hope you can make him feel better." Everyone was pleased when he was well enough to go home. They couldn't thank me enough. I knew that with a loving, supportive family like that, he would have several enjoyable years ahead.

A young woman came in with lupus erythematosus, a multiorgan disease in which the immunologic system begins attacking the body's own tissues, especially the cellular DNA, creating as a result compounds that accumulate in the kidneys and blood vessels like sludge. It's called lupus because it causes big reddish rashes on the face that makes the patient look like a wolf.

This patient was in one of the crises of the long, up-and-down progress of this disease. She was thin and pale from anemia, but bloated because the damaged kidneys were retaining fluid. She was hallucinating from the brain damage.

She needed to be watched very carefully, and her body fluids had to be regulated with precision, keeping the electrolytes in balance. This was very important. If a patient was going to die, there was a kind of game—of keeping him in electrolyte balance—otherwise it would be felt that it was the intern who had killed him. Electrolytes are sodium, potassium, and chloride in the blood, normally balanced by the kidneys, which get rid of excess amounts. If the potassium level is either too high or too low, membrane instability in the heart and arrhythmias result, stopping the heart. The balancing of electrolytes was a fine and tedious procedure involving much drawing of blood and much intravenous additions of the deficient ions.

This patient was so wasted, however, that her veins were very fine and thin and very difficult to tap. But her mother had been a lab technician and often helped me draw blood. She remained at her daughter's bedside all the time, and finally the young woman came out of the crisis. She was now responding well to steroid therapy and was beginning to be built back up again, and I was pleased.

I lay on that lumpy mattress in the on-call room and saw the light growing stronger behind the shade and heard the morning sounds begin along the corridor outside. I found myself wondering how the lupus patient's mother must have felt. I'd been so efficient and cheerful, but I felt vulnerable now. Before I realized what was happening, tears dribbled down my face into my ears, cold and wet, so I heaved myself out of bed and went straight to the bathroom to wash up for the day.

4

Dr. Speir and I went in to see Mrs. Black on 8:00 A.M. rounds, but since she was his patient, I had very little to say to her. I stood by and admired his manner; it was pleasant and serious, and communicated a kind of confidence that her illness, though troublesome, was not deadly. She seemed to respond to his attitude. Of course, she herself was probably a socially accomplished woman, with her husband in politics and her experience in entertaining for him. They both conversed agreeably.

I couldn't get back to her until about 1:00. When I rapped on the door and stuck in my head she appeared to be sleeping, so I started to close the door again, conscious that I'd *wanted* to visit her and wondering what to do with myself for a half-hour.

"Who's there?" she called, raising herself on one elbow.

"It's only me, Mrs. Black. Sorry to disturb you. I can come back later."

She laughed, sitting up. "Come in. You look like a little girl needing to ask for lunch money too early in the morning, afraid to wake her mother."

I laughed, too, and went to the foot of her bed, holding my clipboard with her chart. "Did you really have a good night, Mrs. Black, as you told Dr. Speir? I see you took advantage of the sleeping pill. Dr. Speir didn't consider that significant."

She seemed rueful. "I'm afraid I often resort to sleeping pills, Dr. Donnan. It's not unusual for me. I suppose you're so overworked, you fall asleep right away." She smiled.

I agreed heartily, forgetting the bags under my eyes and my unusual sleepless night.

"I don't have the demands on my time that you have, of course," she went on. "Maybe if I worked I wouldn't have insomnia. I do catch up on my sleep with little catnaps during the day, so I ought to be content, but I dislike lying there awake when it's the time for sleeping. Do you know what I mean? I guess I haven't the patience—or else the ability to keep my mind occupied."

"Are you in any pain?" I supplied.

"No, that's all gone."

"Does the IV cause you any discomfort?"

"Oh no. You're very careful, Doctor."

"I try to be. Have you any nervousness concerning the needle itself?"

She laughed. "Your phrasing is charming. It's true that the idea of filling me up like a tank of gas is strange, but it's better than the idea of draining me, as an undertaker or a ghoul would do. Seriously, the needle doesn't bother me anymore. It's considerate of you to ask. In my experience, interns are often unskillful and callous."

I bowed slightly. "I apologize for my colleagues."

"Will you be able to come back at four?" she asked eagerly. "My daughter will be visiting me—oh." She stopped abruptly. "What is the age for visitors? She's only ten, you remember."

"She should be twelve."

"Ohhh." She was very disappointed. Tears may have sprung to her eyes, but I couldn't be sure. We both started talking again at the same time. I heard her say, "The last time . . ." while I said, "Tell me when to expect her, Mrs. Black, and I'll be sure she gets up to see you."

"Thank you. I want her to meet you. She'll be very impressed. But you must call me Stella, you know," she went on. "You've been calling me Mrs. Black all this time, and I asked you to call me by my name." We grinned at each other for a moment. Then she said briskly, "Come. I feel quite refreshed. Can you sit and talk for a while?"

I nodded.

"Just let me get out of bed and we can sit in the chairs like normal people, and I can get to know you."

I was flattered. "In fact," I said as I moved the footstool out for her, "how would you like some coffee or tea? I'll bet I can get some for us."

She stood on the stool and clapped her hands. "Excellent! We'll be very genteel, won't we? Who would have thought that a hospital offered such amenities as afternoon tea?"

After I got back with our cups, we had about a half-hour before I had a call from the lab. We sat, as she had said, like two people in a living room, while the sun came around to that side of the building and began to heat up the room. Mostly she asked questions about me. Her questions reminded me of the boldness of my ambitions because she took me so seriously. She was like an admired teacher from long ago reviving the dignity of my aspirations. I was moved, and embarrassed by being moved. As I left, I noticed how the sun struck her hair so that rich reddish highlights glinted in the dark of it; her light brown eyes glowed. I felt a moment of apprehension that I might grow to love this woman.

The lab that paged me was alarmed. The previous day a woman had come in on whom I had done a routine admission, taking a blood sample among other things. The call from the lab was frantic, saying that her blood sugar was down to 10. Now a normal blood sugar is 70 to 110; if it were 10, she would be dead. She had been admitted for two days of routine tests, which her doctor made a practice of ordering at certain intervals in a patient's life. She didn't like taking tests as an outpatient and was willing to pay for them herself, so she was here. This woman had not seemed at all ill the day before.

I asked the lab when the sample had arrived, since it had been posted—sent to the lab for analysis—the

27

previous afternoon. They answered that it had come in that afternoon. Obviously the messenger had had it in his pocket until then, or laid it down somewhere and no one had seen it, and overnight the red cells had simply eaten up almost all the sugar.

I looked into her room. Seeing that the woman looked to be in the peak of health, and was in fact lying there reading a murder mystery and eating chocolates like a normally foolish patient, I went in and, to her annoyance, drew another blood sample—no easy task, since she was a fat woman.

I called the supervisor of the lab and told him I would be bringing up a fresh sample for Mrs. McKinney because the first sample had been allowed to deteriorate before it had been analyzed.

"What!" he shouted. "Impossible!"

I tried to interrupt him, but he went on shouting into the phone about licensing and lab procedures, and though I said "Excuse me" several times, he didn't pause, so I finally hung up.

Immediately the phone rang, and when I picked it up he started in again, yelling, "You can't hang up on me! That's the kind of behavior on the floor—you little Hitlers coming up! My lab has been here longer than you ever will be and we have safety devices and checks against error, and our girls are the best technicians I can get . . ."

This time I had managed to talk while he was talking, and I said, loudly, "The way the lab operates is not my problem. A sample must be delivered on time. Promptness is extremely useful in avoiding errors," and I hung up and started off.

The phone did not ring again and I went up to the lab and delivered the sample. However, as I was boarding the elevator this man came running down the hall, called to me, and, to my amazement, jumped into the elevator with me just as the doors were closing.

He demanded that I not abuse his messengers. He demanded that I show proper respect for him. He demanded that I learn a little about hospital procedures, and more. His shoulders were working up and down.

His fists were clenched and driven down into the pockets of his lab coat. He was a thin man, and as he glared at me, ranting, his Adam's apple bobbed up and down his red-flushed throat. The elevator, loud with his scolding voice, continued to descend. Then it stopped automatically and the doors opened. People gaped at us. I quickly overrode the controls and shut the doors. Our noisy elevator went back up without collecting the passengers, whose startled eyes had just caught a glimpse of his swiftly traveling tirade.

Now I was laughing. That made it worse for him, and as I walked off the elevator at my floor he walked off with me and accused me of the worst thing he could think of: "You're no lady!"

I stopped dead, turned to him, and drawled, "You're right. I ain't no lady. I'm a workin' woman."

Hearing the commotion, my resident, Jerry Carter, came down the hall. I turned the lab supervisor over to him, and he agreed with me about the sample, and in fact told the man he'd better stop yelling at a doctor. My opponent turned on his heel, but before he went through the door to the stairway he said angrily, "Not only is she not a lady, she's not a doctor."

"No?" the resident said coolly.

"No! She's only an intern!" And the guy disappeared and the door whooshed behind him.

We stood there grinning at each other.

Soon after, I got a call to go down to Admitting for a new patient. One of the secretaries, a middle-aged woman, said, "Yes. Mr. Witowski is right over there." No one was sitting where she pointed. "Wait a minute. Where'd he go? His wife's gone too."

I shrugged. "Maybe she's helping him go to the john."

The secretary gave me an annoyed glance. "He's in for a medical workup before probable thoracic surgery, not urological problems. He doesn't need to use the toilet."

I shrugged. Thoracic surgery meant work on his lungs, either a total removal or a resection, cutting out a part of a lung. Having corrected me, she was peering out over the admitting lobby.

"Maybe he ran away," I said flippantly, while feeling sympathetic. At the moment I too would have liked to get out of a trap. I ignored a temporary but unmistakable feeling of dread in myself.

"Dr. Donnan," said the other secretary. "Five just called. They say Mr. Witowski is already up there."

"Huh!" I gathered up the material I needed and headed for the elevator.

The older woman called out to me, "If anyone can handle that one, it's you, Doctor," and although she was smiling, her voice was dripping with hostility.

I was glad when the elevator shut off the sight of her vindictive face. Maybe it was envy: when a secretary or nurse saw a woman doctor, she might feel that she'd made the wrong choice; she might have done better for herself, but she was stuck now. I told myself with my naive callousness that that was her problem, not mine.

When I got to the floor, I was told that Mr. Witowski had walked right up to the nurses' station. "I wish you'd been here," said the nurse, chuckling. "He came in like a visitor, you know, followed by his wife. He came up and leaned over the counter, and said, 'Say. Where'd ya put Witowski?' I told him 509 but he's not here yet. Dr. Donnan will be bringing him up, and it's a little early for him to be having visitors. 'Ha!' he said. 'I'm him. Where's this 509?' Well, he's in there now, Doctor, and he's going to be something."

I marched down the corridor to 509. Inside were four beds. Two patients were already there, and Mr. Witowski was rapidly moving back and forth between his open suitcase on the bed and a small dresser with all the drawers pulled out. His wife sat on the straight chair at the foot of the bed, watching anxiously. He was grumbling at her.

"Mr. Witowski," I rapped out at him. "Dr. Donnan."

He looked up and glowered. "So?"

"I'm your doctor."

"No you're not."

"I certainly am, sir."

"I got a doctor. Honneker's my doctor."

"He's the surgeon, Mr. Witowski. I'm your doctor here on Medicine."

"What do I need another doctor for? One's too many."

His wife spoke up, to my surprise, and said, "Is this because he's not on the surgery floor yet?"

"Yes, that's right, Mrs. Witowski. If he's going into surgery, we do a medical workup on him first. You have a heart murmur, Mr. Witowski, and that has to be checked out."

He grunted. "If I gotta have another doctor, I don't need some little baby girl for it. I can just as well ask my granddaughter."

"Oh," I said brightly, sitting down on his bed to preempt his attention. "You have a granddaughter? How old is she?"

"She's twenty, and old enough to know better, getting together with the lot of them to force me to come in here."

"How was that, Mr. Witowski? You look like you'd put up some fight."

"Damn right," he muttered, looking at me with less of a sour face.

"What made them think you ought to come in?"

"A coupla weeks ago I fell downstairs. Anybody woulda done it. It musta been sumpin' on the stairs. Damn carelessness."

"Did you break anything?"

"Hell no! Got up and walked away from it." He looked like he would strike a pose and pound his chest and yodel like Tarzan.

I smiled. "I bet it would take a lot to slow you down. How on earth did you ever come to enter the hospital, then?"

He let out a gusty sigh. He had finished unpacking and now snapped his suitcase shut. "Where's this go?"

"On the rack in the closet, Mr. Witowski."

I waited until he had put it away. "Did you have

31

any vomiting or dizziness afterward?" I asked. That would suggest concussion.

"Naw. Just that I couldn't sleep. Just that."

"Oh. How come? Any particular reason?"

"My chest hurt. Now, I've never had any trouble with my heart. My heart is just as sound as the next man's. This here murmur the doc heard don't mean a thing."

"You may be right," I said. "There are plenty of murmurs that mean very little. I have a murmur myself."

"That so?" He looked interested.

His wife interrupted. She seemed anxious. "It was his ribs, Doctor," she emphasized. "He might've cracked a couple."

"So that is why you got the x rays, then," I said.

"Well, hell, I didn't want it and I wished I didn't have it. I just as soon I *didn't* have it."

"They found a spot on your lungs," I said simply and calmly.

He peered at me. There was a long pause.

His wife put in, "He used to smoke two packs a day until he stopped."

"Tell me about your smoking, Mr. Witowski. How long had you been smoking when you stopped, and when did you stop?"

He seemed as hostile as ever again, but now that he had gotten into the history he was committed to it. "I did like we all did. We started when we was boys —sixteen, seventeen. I been smoking ever since. Nobody said it wasn't any good for you. All that come out only a few years ago. Then Maggie started naggin' at me, naggin' and naggin', so finally to shut her up, I quit." They threw a glance at one another that contradicted his belligerence.

"How long ago was that?"

"Six years."

"Was it difficult for you? Did you go ahead and do it cold turkey?"

"Well," he growled, "I won't deny it was tough. But

32

I made up my mind to do it, and I wasn't going back on it."

I had an idea of how hard it was from a friend of mine who stopped smoking. A man who could quit at the age of sixty after almost forty-five years of two packs a day had done a herculean feat, I knew, and I thought he deserved a lot of credit for it. "That's the kind of hard work people don't usually recognize. Well, if you can do that, you can do a lot of things."

"You're not just flattering me to get around me, are you? You never can trust a woman like that."

"That was an honest compliment," I replied. "I also do need your cooperation."

"Well, I'll tell ya then," he said grudgingly. The rest was a near-monologue, with little prods and questions from me now and then, while he paced back and forth on the other side of the bed from me. The two other men in the room listened as attentively as I did, which was easy since Witowski talked so loudly. "I been healthy all my life. Had a outdoor life, ya see. Carpenter. Got myself a partner, had our own business, worked on a lot of houses out in the south suburbs, all over there. Sometimes we had tough times, but we always turned out good work, work you can be proud of. See these hands?" He showed me gnarled and heavy-veined hands as handsome as a Michelangelo sculpture. They looked strong and capable. "These hands have done some of the best work around, you bet your life. Strong. They don't belong in no hospital. Nothin' to do in a hospital, get all itchy. When I'm home I can do carving, woodworking."

"You don't think you could do some of that during your stay here?"

"And get shavings and sawdust all in the bed?"

"You don't have to lie around in bed all the time," I told him.

"Ya don't? Huh." He paused, then said, "I'll believe it when I see it." He was glaring at the two bedridden men in the room, one with an IV going.

"I never wanted to come in here. I went to the other hospital and they tried to get—uh—aspirins from outa my lungs."

"Aspirates."

"Terrible!" he went on. "Sticks down yer throat and feels like they're stickin' into yer lungs and you can't breathe."

"They do try to reach your bronchial tubes," I told him. "They will use fiberoptic equipment. Fiber optics consists of flexible quartz that will carry light and pick up an image and transmit it around a corner or bend. We can see places we never could before. There's a sophisticated device attached to the fiberoptic scope that will take a sample. I know it's painful."

"Oh yeah? How come they call it discomfort and tell ya to be a big boy?" For a split second it looked like tears sprang to his eyes, and I saw that he had felt humiliated by his treatment at University Hospital. Then he picked up steam again. "All my troubles started with that damn x ray. I was retired and beginning to get a little culture in my life the way I had no time to before. Me and my wife discovered the Fine Arts and them galleries downtown. We go around eleven o'clock and spend an hour and then have us some lunch in a little restaurant or a sandwich picnic in the park. Now, I don't wanna spend all my time in a hospital just when I was startin' a whole new life. That family of mine, pushin' on me and pushin' on me, they don't understand what I want out of life now."

"Mr. Witowski, I will get you out of here as soon as I can. We'll check the heart murmur; the EKG will be painless. We'll x-ray you again. We'll try to get bronchial aspirates again, and that will be painful, so you can have a sedative before that, to help."

"Why all this testing anyway? Why don't they just go ahead and operate?"

"It's never a good idea to subject anyone to unnecessary surgery."

He grunted.

"I'd like to do the physical exam now," I said, pulling the curtain on the rod around his bed. "Mrs. Witowski, will you wait outside, please?"

"Wait a minute! Now wait a minute!" he protested.

"Sit here on the bed, sir," I said, laying down his chart, fixing my stethoscope in my ears and pretending not to hear him, so finally he climbed up and we proceeded with the exam. He was a normally healthy male of sixty-six, well nourished and well muscled. His heart murmur didn't sound serious to me—no rush of blood back through the valve—but it would be checked quite carefully. His lungs sounded clear. The exam proceeded normally until I discovered he had only one testicle.

"Well," I said, "so far it's all as expected, but it's unusual that you have one testicle."

"Whadda you mean? I got two down there."

"Sorry, you're wrong."

"No, *you're* wrong!" his voice bellowed, and then he lowered it so the other two men couldn't hear. "I got two."

"You have one. Look." I showed him the scrotal sac and told him to feel it. When I saw how red his face was I turned away, saying, "I'm sorry to embarrass you, but, you see, I *am* your doctor."

He must have felt it, because then he said, "Well, I got along okay with just one, didn't I, all these years?"

When I had finished, his wife came back in, and as I was leaving I heard him laugh and say to her, "Maggie, this cute young girl's been feelin' me up, and she says I got one nut. What do you thinka that?"

She blushed a bright red and whispered something to him.

"Just what I said!" he chuckled.

5

As I was walking down the hall, I heard a woman call out to me, "Nurse, help me, will you?" so of course I dashed right in.

She said, "I need a bedpan."

She was suffering from emphysema and couldn't get out of bed. I got her the bedpan and helped her sit up on it.

Patients often have to eliminate while a nurse is there to help them or hold them up, but the custom is that a *doctor* is not required to be present—in fact, a doctor should be absent from this procedure. So I raised the bars on the bed, and asked the patient if she could manage until the *nurse* could come.

"I'll send one in immediately," I assured her.

I left her looking bewildered and annoyed, sitting high on the pan in the middle of her crib.

Then I saw what time it was—4:20—and I realized that Mrs. Black's daughter must have been waiting for me to smuggle her onto the floor; she would be disappointed and nervous. I rushed up the stairs to Six. Arriving out of breath, I saw no youngster in the main waiting room. I looked frantically in the lounges and at the nurses' stations, but I couldn't find her. By the time I dashed into Mrs. Black's room to apologize, it was almost five o'clock.

"Oh, Mrs. Black . . ." I started, when I saw that a thin girl was sitting by her mother in one of the armchairs. "Oh," I said.

Stella Black smiled.

Then her daughter stood up for me! I felt as if she had made me old all of a sudden.

"Dr. Donnan, this is my daughter Miranda. Rags, this is my doctor."

"How do you do," said the girl, sticking out a tiny hand, and of course I shook it. I took a good look at her. She was very thin, I thought, tall and skinny as girls are before they start to fill out. She lacked her mother's dramatic coloring. Miranda was all beige; straight, light brown hair worn long and tucked behind her ears, a sallow complexion, pale eyebrows and lashes that seemed to flicker. I saw that she had her mother's eyes, though without their charm.

Miranda looked straight at me with never a smile. She said, "I just came on up. Mom didn't have a chance to tell me to wait for you."

"You didn't have any trouble?"

"No."

"Nobody stopped you?"

"I guess nobody saw me.'

Stella said, "Please, sit down, you two." We were still standing, talking at each other. Miranda let me take the easy chair, and she pulled up a straight one. Though she was a tall ten-year-old, her feet dangled from this chair, and suddenly she became a child again.

"I especially wanted Rags to meet you," Stella said, "because you're a woman doctor, so rare. Perhaps Rags will become a doctor some day."

"Dr. Ballantine at school, Mother," the girl reminded her.

"Oh, yes. I forgot."

"Well!" I said. "So you want to become a doctor."

The girl looked coolly at me. "I didn't say that."

Stella laughed, and the girl suddenly blushed. I may have blushed, too. Stella got up swiftly and went to her daughter, touching the back of her head with her palm in a caress. Then the woman turned to me and back to her daughter in a swirling motion, with her arms out to both of us, and said, "I hope you two will become very well acquainted," and she smiled.

Then we had to have a kind of a conversation. It didn't seem to work out all that well, but thinking

37

about it afterward, I realized that Miranda did seem to be thawing toward me some. Of course, her mother had to pay a lot of attention to her to keep her from being jealous of me, but Stella was such a skillful woman that the effort was scarcely noticeable.

I thought the nurse would surely kick Miranda out when she brought in the supper tray, but she didn't. Stella prepared to give her daughter some of her meal. My parting reminder was that Stella ought to keep her appetite up and not get into the habit of not eating enough. Losing too much weight is a problem common to cancer patients. Not only do they tend to lose their appetite, but the cancer itself metabolizes more rapidly than the normal tissues and can use up the food energy. Meeting Stella's daughter seemed to irritate me, and I was just as glad to get to the cafeteria for some supper myself.

Later that evening I got called down to the ER for another patient, Tom Foley. A big man, he was coming in for a workup on a urinary tract infection and probable diabetes, which he had finally stopped ignoring. I could see at a glance that he was going to be troublesome, for the minute he saw me he said, "Oh, God, no. That's the last thing I need!"

"Mr. Foley," I said peremptorily.

He was looking away, his face red. As I organized his chart and the papers on my clipboard, he seemed to be fussing at something, and when I looked up he was straightening up his tie that had been loosened when I first came in.

"What are you doing?" I said sharply.

"I'm getting the hell out of here," he said gruffly.

"Oh, no, you're not," I said, just as hard.

"Oh, yes. I'm not having a woman."

"You bet you're not," I joked. "I'm the doctor on your case, not your date.'

"Get me a man," he demanded.

"Nope," I said. I wasn't going to let it happen again. This patient wasn't dying, and he could afford to stifle his prejudice for once. "Why did you come in so late, Mr. Foley?"

"I work, you know," he sneered.

"I was referring not only to the late hour of the day, but also to the advanced nature of your illness."

"I don't have any illness."

"Why are you here, then?" I challenged.

"You tell me!" he challenged back.

"Easy," I said, running my pencil down his chart. "We already have your basic blood and urine. Your blood count shows you have an infection. Your urine shows you have an infection. Your temperature has shot up to 103. Your blood has a very high sugar level. After a lot of pain in one eye, you have gone blind in it. And, I bet you it hurts when you pee." I sat back and waited.

He said nothing, glaring at me.

"I'll tell you what's wrong with you," I continued. "You have diabetes. You have let it go so long that you're blind in one eye. You have lost a lot of weight and strength. You are in a significant amount of pain, especially when you urinate. You are now subject to any number of infections. Isn't that so, Mr. Foley?"

Still he said nothing. I was looking hard at him still, noting the tensed face, the thin wasted muscles on his big frame, and a tiny tremor in his fingers. Wait a minute, I said to myself, something is bugging you too much about this patient. Cool it. But my bullying seemed to have worked. At last he said something: "Yeah."

I went through the whole interview then, dragging the information out of him at every step. He wouldn't volunteer a thing. I was irritated with him from beginning to end, but I managed to control it, hoping to win his cooperation. The physical exam revealed nothing grossly unusual. He was thin, and when I hit him in the kidney he couldn't hide his reaction: there was cva tenderness; that is, in the costal-vertebral angle in the middle back, where spine and ribs connect. There were changes in his left eye secondary to glaucoma, which had already caused blindness in the right.

39

By this time we had a routine analysis of his blood, and when I saw what it told us I almost let out a yelp. At some time in the past he had acquired syphilis.

I said, "I see that you contracted some venereal disease in the past."

He said irritably. "That was years ago. I don't have it anymore. It was treated and it went away. What is this, a third degree?"

I ignored that. "What was the treatment?"

"Uh . . . pertussin—somethin' like that," he mumbled.

I was appalled. I had said "venereal disease," not "syphilis." Now he was telling me he'd had gonorrhea in addition to syphilis (gonorrhea does not show up on blood tests as a rule), and not only that, he'd been treated in a very outdated way. "Not permanganate!" I cried.

"Yeah, that's it, permanganate."

"All right," I went on. "That might be what is at the root of your urinary infection. Permanganate washes as well as the gonorrhea itself can cause strictures in the urethra."

"Huh, that so?" That was all he would say.

I proceeded, "All right, then, now what about the syphilis?"

"Are you kidding? You're talking about the VD I had."

"That's right. Syphilis."

"I never had it."

"You did."

"I never!"

"Your blood shows—"

He interrupted angrily. "Listen. That's none of your fuck—That's none of your business." I sat there coolly, unmoved. "It's none of your business!" he insisted.

"Every part of your medical history is significant," I informed him.

"I didn't have it, I tell you! This is my private affair."

40

We glared at each other. I was going to continue arguing with him when the light dawned. He hadn't had it, he was telling me. He was telling me *he* hadn't had it. The only other way, then, was that he had gotten it *in utero*—congenital syphilis.

"Your mother had it," I told him quietly.

It was as if I had slapped him in the face. He said, "It's not what you think! My mother was a respectable woman. *She* . . . But I'm not about to discuss these matters with a woman."

"So. Her husband gave it to her," I went on.

He clammed up entirely. I didn't need to know the family story that resulted from the fact, but I did need to know the medical story. These questions were part of the routine. I had asked them before, but he had not told me the true answers. I asked him why not.

"Listen. These things are my private business. It happened a long time ago. I was treated. I was treated successfully. Everything went away." He had been speaking in a measured, slow, patient voice. Then he speeded up. "It really bugs me you can't let these things lie. All that is finished and done with. And here you come along, spying, spying around—this clue here, that clue there!

"It's all finished, I tell you. Why can't I be left in peace!"

The poor guy. I could begin to understand how imprisoned he felt. His own blood was betraying his secrets. However, it was my job to make sure everything was taken care of. I had to go through the whole questionnaire all over again, which took time I could not really afford. Then, when that was taken care of and no new information was forthcoming, I wheeled him over to x-ray, for the routine chest films. On the way, I managed to worm out of him some more details about his present condition, such as the pain in his back where I had pressed hard for tenderness, the stickiness of his urine, his actual weight loss of fifty pounds, the dates of losing the sight in his eye, and the fact that for the glaucoma attacks he'd found that putting a hot compress on his eye helped. Perhaps he

41

told me more because I was wheeling him and he didn't have to look at me. Still, he spoke reluctantly and surlily. When I saw from the scars on his films that he had had tuberculosis at one time, too, I did let out a groan. Another thing he had concealed.

Fuming, I wheeled him up to his room. I got his IVs started: antibiotics for the infection and large amounts of fluid plus insulin to get his blood sugar under control. I told him he was going to have to learn to give himself insulin, and that a nurse would teach him how to inject himself and a dietitian would tell him about his new diet. It was hard enough to get normal people to stick a needle into themselves; this man was going to be impossible: he took no responsibility for his health whatsoever. By the time I got the IV started and left him it was 10:30, and we were both exhausted.

But I would still have to tackle him again the next day.

6

The next day was one of the worst I'd ever had, definitely the worst since I'd begun.

When I went in to Mr. Witowski's room he was arguing with Berman, one of the other men. "You just make her lay off!" Mr. Witowski was saying.

"Listen," the man said. "She's my wife. She has a right."

"She has no right," said Witowski, "to stink up a hospital room. Hospital room! Don't she know what a stench she makes?"

"You're not talking about my wife like that!"

"Ha! Whattaya gonna do about it? I can just see

42

you leapin' outa the bed and jumpin' over here to beat my brains out, draggin' yer pissbag with ya. Captain Marvel, huh?"

I called out, "What is this?"

The two men fizzled out and were silent. After a moment of surly quiet the third man, the onlooker, explained: "This man here wants this man here to tell his wife to stop smoking while she's visiting."

"Hm," I grunted. "That was informative. Thanks. Does it bother *you,* sir?" I asked my informant.

"Well . . . Say, I don't want to make any trouble."

"All right, then." I turned to Mr. Berman. "Actually, does your wife's cigarette smoke bother *you?*"

"Listen," he said, "you get used to it. You got to get used to things."

"You are actually bedridden, aren't you?" I asked him.

"I cannot leave the bed," he corroborated.

I had a dilemma. The man whose wife smoked could not get up and leave the room and visit with her in the lounge; Mr. Witowski, who objected to her smoking (passionately, because of his own smoking history, no doubt) and with whom I sympathized, *could* walk around to escape; and the third, who I hoped would cast the deciding vote, sat on the fence.

I said, "None of you smokes. Any time now a patient might be put into that fourth bed who has to have oxygen. I'm sorry, Mr. Berman, but I believe your wife could manage to use the lounge when she wishes to smoke." Having to arbitrate a patient dispute made me nervous.

"Uh, do you see what I mean?" I said.

"I do," said Mr. Berman with dignity, "and I fully understand. My wife isn't gonna like it, though," he added.

After I had settled the argument his way Mr. Witowski seemed mollified, but his experiences that morning put him back into his old irascible temper. Even with a sedative, they couldn't get any aspirates from him. When I returned to the Respiratory Physiology Lab to pick him up, he was lying on a cart off by himself in the holding room, moaning.

To save taking Mr. Witowski up to his room and back down again, I had a phone conference with the resident, and we decided we'd have to do a needle biopsy. When I explained to my patient that we were going to have to poke a needle through his torso into the area that showed on the x ray, he almost blew up.

"Goddammit!" he yelled. "Needles in yer arm, needles in yer ass, now needles in yer back!"

"I know," I said, "I really know. It took me the longest time to get up enough courage to stick a patient. Here," I went on, "I want you to walk instead of getting wheeled. You're too big a man for me to push around." I laughed.

He grinned a little, sitting up and swinging his legs over the side. Then he said, "Hell, I ain't got no shoes. I got this little gown and it's all open up the back, and cold. Look, Doc, I'm not in here for my ass, it's for my chest. Why don't you let me wear my pajamas? And my slippers?"

I felt like letting out a big exasperated sigh but I didn't. It was against the rules. It would be inconvenient, but I wondered. "You brought that stuff to the hospital, huh?" I said.

"It's all in that little closet." He looked as hopeful and confident as a little boy knowing his mommy would fetch his teddy bear for him.

So I did. Ordinarily a messenger would have gotten these things, but somehow I found myself going up to his room to fetch his pajamas, robe, and slippers and bringing them down to him. Then he insisted on being shown to a room where he could change privately. At last we were ready to walk back to Radiology for fluoroscopy. The radiologist took out a huge needle and, after consulting the x ray and preparing the skin with Novocain, plunged it seven inches deep right into Mr. Witowski's muscular back.

The old guy nearly passed out. I found myself teetering.

But I pulled myself together. I saw when the plunger

was being pulled back, the needle withdrawn, and the slides being made, that what we had gotten was some necrotic tissue—not the white and pink of healthy lung tissue, but greenish-black stuff, like a pencil lead. Then the slides were sent to Cytology and Pathology. Mr. Witowski staggered out of the room muttering and clutching his chest. "Take me back!" he yelled at me. "Take me back to my room!" And he seemed to whirl us up the elevator and down the hall to his room, where he tremblingly collapsed on the bed, his clothing in disarray.

"These so-called 'procedures' . . ." he panted, "these 'procedures' stink. Torture! Torture chambers you got here. Stab a man in the back, stick a tube in him, and suck out his substance! Vampires!"

"Mr. Witowski," I said, "you're going to make yourself sick with all this fuss. It's over now, and we got what we wanted. You can relax now. Listen to yourself. You're wheezing."

"Just leave me alone," he said. "Just get out of here. I don't want to see you no more."

"Certainly," I said with poise, and departed.

This was not particularly good preparation for my next patient, Mr. Foley. In fact, I had been a little shocked by Mr. Witowski, believing I had done such a good job in winning his confidence the day before. Now I was going to have to work on a man who already hated my guts—and, if the truth were known, the feeling was reciprocal.

A doctor is not supposed to have such strong reactions to a patient, I told myself sternly, and here you are, just opening yourself up to any number of irrelevant emotions. Pull yourself together! Tighten up! Stop and think! Be efficient, calm. Don't lose your intelligence, common sense, distance! Distance! Distance! I kept saying to myself as my rubber-soled shoes went squeaking down the corridor, taking me closer and closer to the room that held Mr. Foley. I ignored everything in my path until I felt I must be cross-eyed

45

from concentration. But it worked. By the time I arrived at his door I was cool and collected.

Then I had to go back to the nurses' station to get his chart.

When I finally made it into his room, however, all thoughts of *my* problems were whipped away by what I saw of my patient.

He was lying flat on his bed on top of the covers, wincing and slowly moving his head back and forth with his hands cupped over his eyes. A nurse had just turned back toward me from the intercom.

"Oh, Doctor," she said, "I was just calling for you."

"What is it?" I demanded.

"He just came back from Ophthalmology, and he complains about his eye."

I asked him what had happened. I got his hands down from his eyes, but he kept the lids clamped tight.

"You're trying to blind me for sure!" he accused bitterly.

Finally I got him to open the lids one after another, and I saw right away what had happened. I had ordered an ophthalmology report, and they had put drops in his eyes to dilate the pupils. It had been exactly the wrong thing to do since it antagonized the glaucoma that had blinded his right eye in the first place. His pain must have been excruciating.

I quickly wheeled him back to Ophthalmology, where they used different drops to close the pupils down again. I breathed a sigh of relief. When I did the rest of the routine checks on him, he was curt and grim.

At 1:30 I was able to have some lunch, and right afterward I got a call about someone coming in in kidney crisis. I dashed down to the ER, where they'd already drawn the woman's blood. As I examined her and took some history from her, I could see that she was worsening. Her respirations were shallow, her blood count dangerously high. There were a lot of rales (crackling noises) in the lungs and decreased breath sounds. I called the Intensive Care Unit immediately to ask for a bed. They assigned me the last one they had and I put her on a cart and took her up.

This woman was quickly going under. I had brought her there with not a moment to spare. We hooked her up to the monitors and the intravenous and began giving her antibiotics. She was in too weak a condition for dialysis just yet. In dialysis, a patient's blood is continuously shunted through a machine where it circulates through coils in a bath of electrolytes and nutrients and then goes back into the body; the machine does the work of the kidneys in removing wastes from the blood. I had to bring her around and build her up. But try as I might, she kept failing. The IV medication made no difference to her condition; infection was rapidly taking her over.

The intensive care staff hovered over her all through the afternoon, reporting to me, and once or twice I came down to check on everything.

In the late afternoon, I got a call to come deal with Mr. Foley. What now, I wondered.

At the threshold I stopped short. He was struggling to zip up his fly while he looked like he was going to keel over.

"What the hell do you think you're doing?" I barked at him.

Startled, he looked up. "You tell me," he snarled back. He quickly put on his jacket and grabbed his suitcase.

"You are not leaving," I informed him.

"Wrong again, Toots."

"When have I been wrong about you, Mr. Foley?" I demanded.

"Get outta my way!"

I closed the door and planted myself before it. He would have to move me to get at the handle. "Come on, now . . ." I began.

"Listen," he said, "I've had enough. The incompetence, from the beginning, that I have had to suffer . . . !"

"You're not very flattering."

47

"I *am* referring to you, Toots."

"Listen, Buster," I said. "You are the one to blame. You held off coming in until there was no doubt of the diagnosis. A first-year medical student could've diagnosed you. An informed layman could have diagnosed you! Let alone you yourself. You let yourself go until you were all messed up . . ."

"Not half so bad as what they make you here, though!"

"That is a lie."

"Listen, sister, you and your pals and supporters have given me a sore eye and a sore pecker, and I'm not going to hang around waiting for any more women to get their hands on me and do more damage!"

"What do you mean . . . ?" I had ordered him to be taken to Urology to have his urethral stricture taken care of. Suddenly I understood. Which was it, I wondered with awe, a probe or a dilator up his penis? I could imagine. And on top of having your eyes almost dropping out from pain . . .

"I can understand . . ." I began.

"None of your switching tactics, kiddo. I'm getting out of here while the getting's good. You're never going to see me again."

"Listen, Mr. Foley," I said, being reasonable. "The bad stuff's over. From now on, it's all uphill. You need us. Your blood sugar was easily brought under control by the second day and your fever came down and you were taken off the IV . . ."

He interrupted with a yell. "Get away from that door! I never hit a woman before," he warned me, "but I'm gonna do it if you don't get out of my way!" I was pressed to the door, and someone, hearing the shouts and trying to barge in, was pushing the door in the other direction, against me. Suddenly I stepped aside, and an orderly and a nurse almost fell into the room.

Seeing these two new adversaries, Mr. Foley yelled in self-defense, "I am leaving!" He was so upset that tears squeezed out of the corners of his eyes.

"If you leave, it'll be against medical advice!" I

threatened him, as if that were the worst thing in the world for him. It was for me, of course. He laughed, and lunged at the door.

I trailed him down the hall, arguing with him, pleading with him, trying everything I knew to keep him there, but to no avail. So I ripped a form off for him and flung it down on the desk. "All right then," I said, "you leave here and it's your own responsibility!"

"That's fine with me! That's *great* with me!" He signed it without even reading it.

He strode deep into the elevator, turned briskly around to face forward, and plunked down his suitcase. He folded his arms across his chest and grinned at me, triumph lighting up his tiny-pupiled eyes as the doors closed on him, leaving me there dumbfounded.

With a kind of anguish, I realized that I had started to sympathize with him and it was too late.

Then, when I went along to check Mr. Witowski, the nurse in charge intercepted me with the information that he had signed himself out and left an hour ago.

"What? What is this?" I squawked.

"I'm sorry, Doctor," she said. It sounded insincere. "I tried to get you, but you were in the ICU at the time and Dr. Honneker happened to be on the floor."

I would have to seek out Dr. Honneker and have a discussion—which would possibly be uncomfortable—about why Mr. Witowski had flown the coop.

As I stood there a moment trying to take it all in, the nurse finally said, "Mr. Witowski left you a note."

"Why didn't you say so in the first place?" I asked irritably, but she didn't reply. She merely handed me the note.

It read: "I'm going to call you Monday morning and find out what's the story on my chest. I'm going home. I got lots to take care of. Witowski (Pete)."

Two patients gone on me. I felt awful.

7

The next day, when I was starting Stella's IV, I noticed that her spirits had drooped, so I tried to cheer her up by making small talk. I didn't succeed, however, in getting her back to her usual gracious behavior. She began to be surly. I had decided I might just as well leave when I noticed that she was clenching her fists while the IV was going.

"Don't do that," I said. "It interferes."

She exploded. "Interferes?"

I straightened her hands out for her. "Please," I said.

As I let go of her hands she cried out, "Why? Why me?"

"What do you mean, Stella?"

"Why me, I tell you! Is it to make me pay for what I've had? Is it to punish me? What is it for?" She appealed to me.

I had seen this kind of emotionalism before, even while I was a medical student. I had often wondered how I would handle it if it were my patient. I knew there were various things you could do to ward off a patient's attack. Sometimes you could soothe them, sometimes you could joke them out of it, sometimes you had to slap them, so to speak, to make them shape up. I didn't know exactly which would work with a woman like Stella, and I knew I hadn't done too well with Mr. Foley or Mr. Witowski, so, hesitantly, I started to pat her hand, and said, "There, there."

She pulled her hand away from me with a jerk (fortunately it wasn't the one with the IV in it). "Get your hands off me!" she said with disgust.

I jerked my own hand back. "Now, Stella . . ." I began.

" 'Now, Stella,' " she mimicked me, screwing her face up. "What the hell do you think you're doing, patting my hand!"

I was appalled at the transformation in her. She was actually ugly. I said, "This isn't like you, Mrs. Black."

"What the hell do *you* know?" she charged. "How do you know what's like me?"

"I realize I'm just an intern—" I tried again.

She interrupted me. "Oh shut up! Just shut up!" Tears were streaming down her face. She reached up with her free hand and tried to rub them away, but succeeded only in smearing her face with mucus and tears, like a little kid.

I grabbed some tissues for her, asking, "What is it? What's the matter? Are you in pain?"

"Pain!" she almost yelped. "Yes, I'm in pain!"

"I'll get you something for it," I offered, and started away.

But she cried out, "Listen to me! Don't you go doping me up, patting my hand, filling me up with salt water! I expect you, *you* of all people, to listen to me!"

She continued, "*I* have listened to *you*, kid, and now I expect the favor to be returned."

The stuffing seemed to go out of me. She made our relationship an arithmetical exchange. But I recognized the logic and justice of her claim, so I was determined to stand there quietly and let her have her say.

She paused, calmer. Then she looked at me. "I can't do it, can I? Now that I have you waiting, I can't say it."

"Say what?" I encouraged her.

"I seem to have spent my whole life learning to be kind to people, truly kind, trying not to hurt them, trying to help them rest easy and be comfortable in my presence and trust me completely to understand and

51

accept them, and to fear nothing from me, and now I can't stay angry."

"But that's an admirable life, isn't it?"

She made a little grimace. "A saint's. It costs something. It costs a kind of truth."

"Truth," I repeated. "Don't you think there's a kind of fad for honesty nowadays, which is really just a license for cruelty?"

I could see a light in her eyes as she began to respond to the discussion, but then it went out. After a short pause she said, "Doctor, the maggots laugh at me for indulging in an intellectual discussion."

"What maggots?"

"The ones that are feeding on me."

I was horrified at the morbid imagery. "Come now," I said. "Don't let your imagination run away with you."

With her previous intensity she cried, "I hate it, I hate it! You turn me over and you'll find them there, eating, eating me up! It's not fair! I tell you, it's not fair!"

"Wait a minute, wait a minute!" I felt as though I were calling to her, as though she had moved dangerously far away. "You're just depressed. Of course, I can understand that, it's the hospital and having your movements restricted and all, and the chemotherapy taking so long to have an effect.

"But believe me," I continued, "you're going to get well! Why, we're giving you the best of care. Dr. Speir is the best doctor in the state for your kind of condition. *He* doesn't sound depressed and hopeless like you, now does he?"

She gave me a suspicious look.

I persisted. "Does he?"

She had to laugh a little. "Of course he doesn't."

I echoed her heartily. "Of course he doesn't. Now look here, young lady, I don't want you spoiling my rotation by going off the deep end like this. Just think how discouraging that would be, when what I truly believe is that my working on you is going to have successful results."

"Yes, I see," she murmured, looking chastened.

"That's better," I encouraged her. "You are going to get well, you know," I added after a moment. "You really are. We plan to discharge you in just another few days, don't we?"

I offered the proof in a hearty voice, but I myself was dissatisfied. Maybe I had protested long enough to hear myself speaking a part that didn't fit and that I didn't like. It wasn't clear why I suspected I had failed somehow. I did believe what I was saying—I had to, or how could I keep on working like this?

I was interrupted by my beeper. They called me back to the Intensive Care Unit, where my kidney patient was undergoing respiratory failure as her lungs clogged up from her infection.

We kept her lungs open with chest tubes and positive pressure ventilation. The tubes are put through the chest wall and keep the lungs open by suction. The oxygen supplied through a tube down the throat has to be carefully regulated, and the blood oxygen level tested every hour. We continued feeding her antibiotics through the IV and kept her fluids and electrolytes carefully adjusted. It's amazing how much physical labor is demanded in such a fight; perhaps it's partly because of the terrible tension.

It was one of those crises you see all the time with kidney patients, and she had been in the hospital dozens of times like this, though this latest time was apparently the worst so far. Her family was in and out of the waiting room and took turns for the five minutes they were allowed in the ICU itself. One sister in particular was very well informed from so many previous experiences, and she kept calling in and insisting on speaking to me to get the latest blood values and such.

But this patient was failing. Although she was only forty-five, she was so debilitated from kidney disease that even with the weapons we gave her in the form of antibiotics she couldn't fight off the massive infection that was taking over her whole body. I worked off and on all night long, carefully monitoring her, adjusting the IVs with every change in the indicators, manipulating the respirator and testing her blood frequently. When she went into acute distress, the oxygen tension—the amount of oxygen in her blood—had to be tested and corrected every fifteen minutes as her lungs lost their ability to absorb oxygen.

That little room became as familiar to me as my own apartment. It had no outside window, but one whole wall was glass, which could be seen from the central desk. Attached to the wall, with hoses and wires coming from them, were a number of machines, chrome-edged and enameled different colors—pale aqua, red, and gray. Some of them were hooked up to the patient so that she looked like a corpse being drained rather than nourished by an infernal machine. The light in the room was bright and glaring. Every machine seemed to make a different noise—a *click*, a *whoosh*, a little *blip*, a bubble—all in different rhythms, until I felt hypnotized.

Then at last the heart monitor stopped its beating signal and produced one unending tone, and though the other machines continued their pace, I had to pronounce her dead.

I called Jerry Carter. He gave me the task of informing the family since I had been the last physician assigned to the case. Wearily I made my way to the waiting room where I realized, before I even saw the family, that the sun was streaming in and it was full day. Saturday—my weekend off had already begun.

I glanced down at the chart I held to find the names of the relatives. She had been a divorcée; only a sister and several cousins survived her, and I picked a name at random. "Mrs. Herzog, I'm sorry to inform you that Mrs. Macklin's heart finally gave out, at seven-fifty, just a little over half an hour ago. We did everything we could, but the infection was just too strong for us . . ."

There was a moment of stunned silence. I saw the blood drain from one woman's face and she looked faint. Then the four people all started to speak at once.

54

From a distance I heard bits and pieces of what they were saying, angry, bitter, and hostile.

"A half-hour ago! Why weren't we informed?"

"What's going on here? She was ambulatory and coherent when we brought her in . . ."

"Who are you? Why did they assign an intern . . . ?"

"Demand an investigation! We'll have an autopsy . . . !"

"Are you actually a licensed doctor? Licensed to practice?"

"You should have taken her straight to the Intensive Care Unit. I saw you sitting there with her when she should have been receiving medical care!"

I couldn't see who was saying what, but I heard each piece of recrimination that they hurled at me, and I protected myself by murmuring that I was sorry, backing away and excusing myself. I left them, still complaining to one another, and staggered off down the corridor a safe distance to where I could finally break down and cry.

It was a little side office that I stepped into, and I thought there was no one around to see me early on a Saturday morning, but almost as soon as I entered an elderly doctor followed me in.

"What is it, Doctor?" he asked me, as I gulped and tride to hide my tears. It was impossible since my face and nose flush and my eyes get pink. On me, crying is ugly and unconcealable.

In a low voice, to keep it from breaking, I told him what had happened.

He sat on the edge of the desk, looked at me, and sighed. "Let me tell you about that family," he offered. "Mrs. Macklin has been a victim of kidney disease for fifteen years now. She's an old familiar at the hospital. I won't pretend that her death won't break up the staff, since they'd all grown so fond of her. I guess they're proud of having kept her going for so long. It'll be hard to let that effort go, too. But she could have been saved at almost any point along the way if her sister had allowed us to take one of her kidneys for her. She was the only person immunologically matched to her sister's skin and blood types. A cadaver donor was much more difficult."

"Not the woman who kept calling and checking on her?"

"Probably. She refused." He paused. "What's happening now was almost predictable, given such a situation, don't you think?"

I said, "I guess so," but actually it was incredible to me that anyone could refuse a life-saving donation like that to her own sister. The family was taking out on me the blame that they should have laid on the sister. It helped me a little to know why they'd unfairly accused me of incompetence, but I realized the chilling fact that I'd lost a patient. It wasn't a game or a TV show or following a set of instructions anymore. I was responsible. The time had come when *I* was responsible.

Even though I was not on duty, I went to Stella's room before I left for the weekend.

"Good morning!" I said, as cheerily as I could manage, as I walked into her room.

"Good morning," she responded. "You look awful."

I laughed. "Well, I've just been up all night, is all."

"No wonder!" she exclaimed appreciatively. "Well, sit down a second and take a breather."

I accepted her invitation. I said, "How are you feeling today? It's a beautiful sunny day, I see. The clouds are all swept away." Indeed, it was like coming out into the fresh air to be there in her room, just taking it easy. I was glad I'd decided to drop in. She was looking at me with what I thought was perceptive concern, however, so I said, "Don't worry, I'll be all right. It's a bright spot in the day just to come see you."

"What do you mean?" she said quietly.

Then I realized I should be talking about her, not me. "Oh, well, you're doing so well, you see. We're building you up just beautifully, don't you think?"

She was silent.

"I believe you've gained a couple of pounds since

56

the beginning of the week, when you first came in, and there's more color in your face."

"Do you think so?" she said, low, searching my face with her eyes.

"I do," I answered sincerely, with a rush of hysterical confidence.

Then she smiled. It was as if she'd relaxed, trusting me as her doctor to see that she got well.

"You'd better get some rest," she said, "before you fall over."

"Yes!" I chirped. I'd become punchy. "You're right, you're absolutely right! It's my weekend off, in fact. Did you know that? Well, I'd better be getting along. You'll be fine," I said, patting her hand. "I'll see you first thing Monday morning."

And with an energetic step, I put a kind of confusion behind me and headed for my apartment and sleep.

8

I slept around the clock twice. When I woke up, it was past ten on Sunday morning and a fine day again. I got up and padded around my little apartment, turning on the morning symphony and making myself a piece of French toast. I had planned to take it completely easy, but by noon, I was very restless, and I knew I would never be able to stick close to home or stay alone all day, and I also knew that the tensions of the week could be discharged in only one way.

I called my friend Hasselblad. We had a very warm relationship. We'd been medical students together at University. He seemed to be one of the minority who was not too defensive about a woman classmate, and we often studied together for exams. We also slept together once in a while—when the need arose. Neither of us wanted this to develop into anything serious, and we had therefore a relaxed, helpful arrangement.

He was interning at University Hospital and fortunately was off today, just like me. He had planned to go sailing with Lewis, with whom he shared a boat, and was glad to take me along.

The afternoon was terrific. The very sky seemed to fill the sail and press itself against our faces. The work of sailing—balancing the boat, rigging the spinnaker, taking it down—was physically satisfying and seemed to take some of the kinks out of me, so that by the end of the afternoon I lay back in the cockpit and felt the pleasure of the calmer sail home and appreciated the vigor of two handsome men's bodies.

I thanked Lewis sincerely, and turned to check with Dick Hasselblad on what we were going to do now. But there was some mix-up, and Lewis reminded Dick that he was supposed to go to a professor's cocktail party at seven o'clock.

He decided to bring me to that, too, as if he didn't want to interrupt what we had going, and I was willing. He waited for me at my apartment while I changed quickly, then took me to his apartment to wait for him to change. But neither of us could hold off any longer, so we had sex, even though it might make us a little late. It was good, like taking a long, cool drink of water after tennis or something, and we were soon on our way to the party.

By the time we got there, most of the people seemed to have arrived. The host was a famous OB-GYN at the university, and everyone who came was from the medical school, it seemed. Dick and I got split up right away, so I wandered around from group to group to see if I recognized anybody.

I saw one of the surgical professors, Dr. Mansfield, who was having what I thought was an intimate tête-à-tête with another doctor's voluptuous blond wife, but he hailed me. "Well, Phyllis! You still around?"

I smiled politely. "Looks like it," I said.

He continued to talk to me, so I went over to him. He didn't introduce me to the other woman, but instead

58

pursued an energetic conversation with me; she just stood there with a rather blank look in her eyes until, about halfway through our encounter, she wandered away.

He said, "You married again?"

"Nope."

"Huh! How do you manage, then? Or shouldn't I ask?" He rather leered at me.

"As a matter of fact, my intern's salary is sufficient."

"You're interning!" he exclaimed, as if it were the most surprising thing I could reveal. "Where the hell are you interning?"

"Grey's." I was going to leave it at that, make it a bland piece of information, and escape, leaving him to his blonde. But something made me add, "But you knew that last year, Doctor."

He laughed. "Oh. Oh, yes. It must have slipped my memory. You won't mind me saying this," he said, smiling confidentially, "but I never expected you to go on."

"Oh?" I challenged him. "Why?"

He pretended to be a little embarrassed. "Well, I knew your former husband, you know. He interned under me. Fine chap. I couldn't help but sense when there were difficulties at home, you know."

"Are you claiming that I had a bad effect on his work?"

"Come now, Phyllis. You know how delicate surgery is."

I cleared my throat. "You seem to be making a different point than the one you started out with," I said, smiling.

"What?"

"You *were* saying that you didn't think *I* would continue in medicine. We weren't talking about Bill. But are you actually saying that I don't deserve to continue, because Bill suffered some?"

"Oh, no! Of course not."

I simply raised my eyebrows.

He took the initiative again. "I'm just saying how

59

emotional you were. It's somewhat ominous for a physician, don't you agree?"

I thought how slimy he was, and caught myself pulling back in disgust. At the same time, though, I accepted the legitimacy of his standards of rationalism and efficiency, if not the accuracy of his interpretation of my past. But somehow I was uneasy; his words troubled me, and I couldn't say why.

"How many women are graduating this year?" I shot at him.

"Well, you can't tell at this early date how many will make it."

"Of course you can. It's their last year."

"Oh, I don't know how many. I don't keep track of that kind of thing. Not many, of course."

"You ought to be recruiting more."

"To be frank with you, Phyllis, women in the school are a nuisance and a bother."

"Oh? How do you mean?"

"They require special . . . arrangements."

I burst out laughing. "You mean they want a women's john? A place to sleep in privacy?"

He glared at me as if I had used dirty words.

I went on. *"I'm* still using the doctors' john and *my* on-call room isn't segregated."

He shook his head and smiled wearily. "Well, they're not all like you, Phyllis." He walked away finally.

I saw a woman watching me. She stepped over and introduced herself. "I couldn't help overhearing some of your conversation with Dr. Mansfield. Is it true that you're going to become a doctor?"

I was too tired to tell her that I already was a doctor. I merely nodded.

"And what are you going to go into?"

"I don't know yet."

She smiled. "I expect most of you go into Pediatrics, so natural. But I must confide in you, if I were really ill, I wouldn't go to a woman. Isn't it awful of me? But that's just the way it is, I'm afraid. A woman could not inspire me with the same *confidence,* you know?"

60

"Have you ever been to a woman doctor?"

"Oh no! That's what I'm telling you!"

"Then how can you really judge?" I asked.

"Oh, I see I have offended you. Please forgive me. Of course you must do what is best for you, and who am I, a stranger, to intrude? Excuse me, I see my husband is beckoning me."

I looked, too, and saw no one beckoning her, but she went to the group surrounding the host, put her arm into the arm of one of the men, and he made room for her in the circle.

I sighed, and went to freshen my drink.

Then I realized that I was in no mood to continue defending my presence in the medical profession, so I went over to Dick and said that I would like to go. I was glad that I didn't have to intern at University. Apparently sex bias was rampant there. I wondered if they had a "quota." I certainly pitied those women.

When we got back to his apartment we wasted no time, and undressed and got into bed. He was as eager as I, and since we were familiar with one another's bodies and knew what gave each other pleasure, we were soon well on the way. We were always active together, and relatively fast. Dick liked me to stroke behind his ears and down his neck. It delighted him for me to fondle his testicles, and I liked the sensation of a full hand when I tenderly lifted his scrotum.

Soon he entered me, and we were moving together in the light and then the deep rhythm of intercourse that led quickly to my coming in big roller-coaster sensations again and then again. He kept moving right through them and hanging on and hanging on until he came, too.

Sex with Dick was easy and fast, and I liked his simplicity.

Afterward, as we were lying together under the covers, I asked, "Are there any woman interns at University, Dick?"

He murmured and rolled over to look at me. He smiled sleepily. "Why? Are you jealous?"

I gave him a playful punch on the shoulder. "Of course not, you clown."

He grabbed my wrists. "What do you mean, of course not?"

"I was just kidding!"

After a long moment of silence, in which he seemed to be drifting off to sleep, I repeated, "Well? How many woman interns are there?"

He groaned. Then he made an effort to open his eyes. He failed. With his eyes closed, he muttered, "I think there's one, yeah, there's one woman."

"Huh!" My mind was working at full speed, going over all the people I had seen at the party. None of the women in my class were there. I wondered where this woman had come from. "Where did she take her degree?"

"What?"

"Where did she go to medical school?"

"Who?"

"That woman."

"What woman?"

"Dick! The woman you told me about, the one that's interning."

He really groaned this time. "Phyllis, for crying out loud! Can't you let a man sleep?"

"Listen, buddy," I replied. "You just got a good screw off me. The least you can do is have a conversation with me when I ask you to."

That roused him and made him a little angry. "What is this? What's the matter with you? You're going to make me sorry I answered the phone this morning."

I whapped him with my pillow.

He grabbed me. "Don't you ever do that," he warned. "What the hell is bugging you? You've been jittery ever since the party."

"That's it!" I cried. "That party! You wouldn't believe it. Listen, I had to get out of there. The atmosphere was dripping with hostility."

"Oh, come off it, Phyllis. What are you talking about?"

"You know Mansfield." Dick nodded. "Well, he

sucked me into the most incredible conversation. Did you know he's down on women?"

"Jeepers." Dick's reaction was laconic.

Undeterred, I went on. "He's all upset because woman doctors want a john for themselves!"

"Phyllis," Dick explained, "you overreact to these things. Of course a hospital administrator is going to be concerned when there's a demand for a major expense."

"Major expense!"

He looked at me coldly. "You don't think putting a whole new restroom in on each floor, trying to minimize the impact on the existing plumbing, dealing with the remodeling required and the disruption in patient care on the floors—you don't think that is a major concern?"

At last I felt like crying—either that or screaming. There was an infant inside my chest, with its mouth wide open and wet with dismay. I did realize how logical Dick's point of view was. Of course, how could a woman ask a hospital to spend a million dollars just for her? Just for bathrooms? I had a terrible compulsion to be rational. But the child inside me was convinced of injustice somewhere—somewhere. I had to leave.

I got up and started gathering my clothes together.

"Hey, Phyllis," Dick started to cajole me.

I started to say "I'm sorry, but I'm leaving," but I stopped myself. I just said, "I've got to leave, Hasselblad."

"Just because I could understand the point of view . . ."

"We're on two different wavelengths, friend."

"We did all right before." He leered in an exaggerated way, referring to our always satisfying performance in bed.

"That was before."

"Hey! Am I going to see you again?"

I was heading out the door. "Who knows?" I said.

9

I could hardly sleep after I left Hasselblad. I had enough on my hands just coping with patient care, just trying to reconcile myself to something like Mrs. Macklin's death. I didn't need any extra worries to contend with, like figuring out arguments for a women's bathroom. I'd never had any trouble sleeping before, but now all sorts of crazy thoughts were raining on me. I knew I shouldn't worry. I decided that I'd go to the hospital shrink the next day and get his evaluation and maybe a prescription for some tranquilizers. I was really looking forward to getting back on the job the next day. In contrast to the outside world, the hospital seemed a calm, efficient haven.

It was not to be. During rounds Jerry Carter, always a friend to me, made a point of challenging me publicly on the two patients who had signed out AMA—against medical advice. He especially emphasized the loud arguments I'd had with Mr. Foley, arguments that had shocked and disturbed the other patients. Apparently a couple of nurses had complained.

I tried to defend myself, though my heart was in my throat. "This patient was entirely recalcitrant," I argued.

"You are going to have to learn how to handle a recalcitrant patient, Phyllis. And you are not going to be able to dump your patients onto the resident or anyone else, as you have in the past."

"But those are people who objected to having a woman doctor!" I protested.

"And apparently they have reason," he observed.

"Reason?" I squeaked.

"All right, look," he relented. "This is an issue that will come up again and again, I'm afraid. For you it will probably take the form of an objection to a woman as the doctor on the case. Now you others, don't think you're getting off scot-free. As I said, this issue will come up again and again—how you deal with a patient's reluctance to be handled by you. Maybe they'll take a dislike to the way you wear your hair, your bedside manner, the particular procedure you've ordered. But every single one of you is going to have this problem at some time or another."

"How do you deal with it, sir?" said one of the interns, a real ass-licker.

"You simply have to be firm and gentle. But never —let me repeat, never—give in to a patient's request to have a different doctor. It is you who has been placed in charge of the case, and it is you who must retain the authority."

At the end of rounds, I made sure I talked to Jerry alone. This thing could not be left dangling.

I began directly. "I've been getting a lot of flak recently about being a woman doctor. I want to face this head-on, and I think you're one person who'll be honest with me. What's going on?"

"Phyllis," he said, "the way you handled Mr. Foley is a prime example of the difficulty a woman experiences being a doctor."

In a small voice, I asked, "What do you mean?"

"You're too emotional. Women are just excessive in that way. It may be the hardest thing you'll have to learn—to tone yourself down, get yourself under control." He smiled gently. "Patients expect a kindly, authoritative father-figure. That gives you an idea of the enormousness of the task, Phyllis. You have to learn to be a *father*-figure."

He left me to mull over his words in a kind of stupor.

It was while I was sitting there deactivated that I got a phone call. It was Mr. Witowski, asking about the results of his test. I told him I'd call him back. As I went to the Records Room to get his chart and the results

65

of the biopsy, I pictured the gallant old gent's dark, seamed face, and the light in his blue eyes as he spoke of his work and his new life.

When I saw the diagnosis I wiped all the sentimentality out of my mind. I dialed his number.

"Dr. Donnan," I announced myself briefly.

"Well, Doc? What's the story? Do I have cancer?"

"Mr. Witowski, you have cancer."

There was a pause; then he said, in the same tone, "All right. What should I do now?"

I told him he should call his surgeon and make an appointment.

"Thanks," he said. He hung up.

I could see him standing there, his craftsman's hand just leaving the phone, turning to tell his wife.

I went up to Stella's room to deal with her IV. Dr. Speir and I had discussed modifying the dosage in preparation for her leaving the hospital later in the week, since she seemed to have been built up a lot by our therapy. This would be the first time for the modifications. I stopped for a moment outside her door, checking over my notes to make sure I had it right.

As I stood there reviewing the orders, I didn't quite realize that I was hearing a man's voice, but when I looked up I knew I had overheard part of a conversation in Stella's room.

"Come on, Mom, get off my back."

I couldn't hear her reply.

"I suppose you'd like me to wear a double-breasted charcoal suit, white button-down oxford-cloth shirt, and a tie."

There was a murmur, and then he laughed sarcastically.

I walked in and found a young man of about twenty with a straggly reddish beard and frizzed-out hair, wearing a ragged shirt and jeans. He had sandals on, and his feet were dirty. I was shocked, and I must admit amused, to see that Stella had a hippie son. I should have guessed it, though. What were the chances? Upper-middle-class parents, wealthy, cultured, liberal, with good taste and good manners. How else could a son rebel, except to become ragged, sloppy, and crude. His face was ostentatiously bewildered and his voice was hard. I glanced at Stella. She looked despairing. At least he had the grace not to continue the argument in front of me.

"You're Jeffrey Black," I said. "I'm Dr. Donnan."
In a lounging way he merely nodded his head.

"I'm going to start your mother's IV. Will you leave the room until I call you back?"

His face went pale. So, there was something he didn't like about needles. I thought it might be a good lesson for him, then, to return to the room while the IV was going. I told him I'd call him right back in.

"No," he said quickly. "No, I gotta be going. See you, Mom." And he waved his hand and started out.

"Jeff!" she cried out. "Are you going so soon?"

He shrugged.

"Will you give me a kiss?" she asked.

"What?" he said. "And make Freud turn in his grave? Not on your neurosis!" He left quickly.

Stella and I didn't talk for a while. I inserted the needle and got the IV going. Stella was fighting for control, and when I finally looked at her face I saw her eyes were red from unshed tears. I sat down and looked at her chart for something to do while I waited for her to recover.

Finally she said, "Tell me about your day, Doctor."

"Are you sure you don't want to talk about yourself?"

"Yes, I'm sure."

"Well," I said, "I have an interesting patient. The case is really engrossing—not because of the medical details; it's a straightforward case with a straightforward therapy. It's the patient herself. She's a magnificent woman—yes, what anyone would call a magnificent woman. I guess because she's beautiful she doesn't realize what else she's got going for her. But she's very intelligent, and she reacts with precision, and she has courage. That last is the most important basic ingredient in her personality.

"You know, what happens to her seems to happen to everybody else at some time or another. I've never met a person who didn't have some kind of suffering in his or her life—never. But whenever it happens to a person for the first time, you tend to think you're unique, maybe because pain isolates you. Some people give in to it. But this woman keeps working, keeps learning, keeps growing. That's what I call courage."

I had said all this with my eyes on the meaningless sheets of paper again. At last I looked up, and I saw Stella's lids lowered, and tears falling.

"Is that what you think?" she asked.

"That's what I think about you."

"Thank you." Then she twisted her fingers together and said she would like to be alone.

As I left her room, I realized that I'd spoken emotionally. It alarmed me that Stella evoked such responses in me, like my desire to punish her son for hurting her, and overt praise. I had become intimate with her, that was the problem, and I'd have to pull back.

I'd made an appointment with the staff psychiatrist, who was able to fit me in at 6:00 P.M. The reason for the late hour, he told me, was that his schedule had filled up right at the beginning of the year, back in July.

I expressed surprise.

He smiled and said, "Listen, anybody who goes into medicine is crazy anyway. What's *your* problem?"

I explained my blowup with Foley, my relationship with Witowski, my response to Stella Black, and my distress at losing Mrs. Macklin. Then I reported what my resident had said about being too emotional, and my run-ins at the cocktail party. The psychiatrist listened to all of it with only a few questions here and there. I talked for a long time. It helped me to see all these recent events as part of the larger issues of responding and responsibility.

I had come to a musing stop when he said, "Well,

superficially these are the same issues that come up with every medical man. We could deal with them superficially, and you would be able to function rather efficiently. However, it's clear there are deeper-seated problems here, such as your attraction to a mother-figure and your repudiation of men. I understand you're divorced, are you not? Your very choice of this profession argues a profound dysfunction, an inability to accept mature womanliness."

I interrupted him. "For your information," I said, "I'm very good at sex."

"That may be; however . . ."

I pursued it: "I come to orgasm quite readily." I paused. "I'm multiorgasmic, at that."

He was silenced for a moment.

Although his eyes still looked bewildered, he was just opening his mouth again to say something when I said, "Your analysis seems to me to be somewhat old-fashioned. What you have in mind for me is a radical adaptation to a model of womanhood—wife and mother—that may have been convenient for everybody in the nineteenth century, but it is out-moded—dys-functional, to use your word—in an overpopulated era in which we're beginning to discover that resources are limited, and we don't need more babies.

"Now, I would be happy to manage a 'superficial' adaptation to the problems of medicine as you first suggested, but I would hesitate to try to accomplish it with *you*, Doctor, when your basic premises stink."

By this time my hands were shaking, and my voice was shaking, with anger—not the anger I felt at Foley, which was straight and strong, however ill ad-vised it might have been; this anger was scared and felt bad, and I knew I could be ground down into a frightened person. What I needed intact was my strength.

Without another word I got up and left.

As I closed the door I saw him smile, as though all his ideas had been proven correct.

A memory flashed through my mind. Last year I'd overheard a doctor complaining to another doctor about his wife: "She's only mono-orgasmic!" Now why did that come up, I wondered, as I sped down the corridor. Oh yes, "mature womanliness" and "dysfunction."

What's good about medicine is that there's always something to do so you don't have to think about your problems; what's bad about medicine is that there's always something to do so that you don't have time to think about your problems enough.

I got another patient that evening, a young woman, well dressed and apparently self-assured, who had just graduated from high school. Natalie Hoskins had been living with her grandparents in order to finish school in the States before she joined her family in Europe. She'd been having a lot of abdominal pain and nausea recently.

I learned a lot about her personality in the interview. She was intelligent, articulate, and completely forthright, eager to make whatever effort she could in order to find out her trouble and get it dealt with. I also realized that she was scared to death.

"Don't worry," I reassured her. "I'll do everything I can. This is an excellent hospital, and we'll surely find out what's wrong. I'll go with you to each of your tests, and explain them all to you."

"Thanks," she said. "I'll count on that."

When I examined her, I found a mass deep on the side of her abdomen—that is, I felt a lump, something defined or firm, instead of the usual compressible guts and organs—and her pelvic exam showed her ovaries to be enlarged. It was ominous.

The next day I took her everywhere. I couldn't stay with her throughout every procedure, since some of them were quite lengthy (such as the barium swallow and barium enema, with a whole series of upper and lower GI, or gastrointestinal, x rays), but I did manage to be with her throughout the endoscopy.

She didn't want to have it done. Like Mr. Witowski, she was terrified of having something stuck down her throat. She was afraid she wouldn't be able to breathe. I showed her with a sketch how it worked. The gastroscope, a slim tube, is passed behind the trachea and into the esophagus. She'd be breathing around it. It might make her gag a little, but the air passageway would not be obstructed.

A first-year resident in internal medicine was doing the endoscopy, being instructed by the attending, so it took longer than usual. Lying flat with her head over the edge of the table to straighten the length of the esophagus was uncomfortable for her, and Natalie clutched my hand tight in her own throughout the procedure. Through the tube we could survey the entire interior of her stomach. We saw a mass protruding on a stalk, and took a sample from it.

When we finally removed the tube she burst into tears.

"What is it?" I said, and—quite naturally, it seemed—took her into my arms, where she sobbed as if her heart would break.

The other people in the room tactfully seemed to ignore the outburst and began straightening up. It was time for another patient, and Natalie seemed to need only a short cry, so I helped her off the table and we walked out. Then I saw that people were giving me strange looks—at least, the nurse was frankly curious.

Oh brother, I thought, I can't do anything right. I wondered what they thought.

I helped Natalie into bed, told her roommates she might need a little nap, and left her. I took a moment to analyze what had happened. She was naive—emotional and open. Could they have thought I was attracted to her? But I was unremittingly heterosexual. There was nothing out of the ordinary in what I'd felt. She'd been anxious, even terrified; she'd needed a shoulder to cry on and I had been there. It was that simple.

I had a curious insight that there might be times when a patient needed an emotional response from a doctor. The fact that it was so simple and so primitive a need might make it threatening. Maybe it was a powerful need. Instinctively I had been able to respond, and now I was glad. I felt strong.

At that time, of course, I didn't know what responding would cost me.

10

We learned that Natalie's stomach mass was cancerous, probably a lymphoma. Since I had also found enlarged ovaries, her private doctor and I called in a gynecologist as well as a general surgeon, and they agreed to open her up. The operation was scheduled for the next day.

It was the gynecologist Dr. Danes and I who spoke to her mother. After I had introduced them I stayed silent. I had never had any contact with him before, though I knew his reputation (in more ways than one), and I was curious to see how he would handle this delicate business. He was gentle, treated her like an intelligent human being, and gave her no cause for alarm whatsoever. He did not tell her the results of the endoscopy; he told her that exploratory surgery was necessary to find the mass and remove it for microscopic analysis. She was left with the impression that what they wanted was the stomach mass, not to see what was happening in the abdomen or the reproductive system. She continued to ask him questions that showed both her anxiety and her intelligence, but he skillfully managed to avoid the implication of cancer, and even went so far as to tell her that the incidence of cancer in eighteen-year-olds was so minimal as to be microscopic, which was true. I was almost reassured myself.

It would be soon enough to tell them the truth after the operation.

Dr. Danes and I walked back down the hall, discussing the case. He was going to be off after he finished rounds, so I was eager to get as much information as I could before he left. He would be doing the operation, and I asked to scrub with him.

We came to the Surgeons' Lounge, and he said he would have to change.

I said I would wait for him, and then walk him down to the entrance, since there were aspects of the case that I still wanted to clear up with him.

"Oh, no," he said, "come on in."

I thought he was just going to change his jacket so, absorbed in what we had been talking about, I followed him into the locker area. We kept on talking.

After a moment I realized that he was going to strip! He had his trousers down already and was stepping out of them.

In a rush I remembered that he, like a few others in the hospital, was reputed to have seduced every willing woman there. I had never seen a pass made this way before and I didn't know what to do. As he took everything off, down to his skin, and began dressing again, I continued talking about the case like a robot: the reading I'd done on viral research, the etiology of stomach cancer, new therapies in treatment, my hope for my own research next year—anything and everything I could think of. Finally he finished dressing and we emerged and continued down the hall, both of us talking as before.

As I was heading away from the elevator after Dr. Danes had boarded it and was trying to catch my breath, the floor nurse stopped me with the news that something had come for me.

There on the desk was a large bouquet of magnificent yellow-to-red tea roses. Apprehensively I opened the envelope and took out the card. It read: "To the only doctor who would level with me. Pete Witowski."

Trembling, I sat down. I gazed at the roses, seeing with clarity the intricate curve of each petal, the sub-

73

tle and various changing of color, and the gathering of petals into each blossom.

I got to meet Mr. Black that evening. I knew he had been expected back on Thursday, but he had actually not arrived until Saturday. Stella had been disappointed that she hadn't been able to introduce him to me. She had told me a little about him, and it was clear that she had devoted her life to him. I was curious to meet him, and I felt a little nervous, too.

He was an extremely attractive, distinguished-looking man. When I walked in, he was standing by the window talking to Stella, gesturing widely so that his tall figure in the dark suit looked dramatic and commanding. When I heard his voice, I could immediately believe that he was a successful politician. I'd never heard—and of course never noticed that I'd missed—a perfect voice. It made you immediately revise your impressions of every man you'd met before. What a power! Of course you abandoned that irrational response very quickly, but it must have been a great advantage.

He was telling her something technical and political, and she was lying in her bed almost bathed in his glow. She looked like a little girl being given a gift her father had bought her on a trip.

When she introduced us, he came up to me and took my hand in a courtly kind of grasp, firm and motionless. He complimented me on my treatment of his wife and invited me to sit down. Then he asked me how she was responding to treatment, and for a few minutes he and I discussed her case as though she were someone from whom we had no need to hide any information.

Soon Stella interrupted us to introduce another topic of conversation so that we could get to know one another better, and we had an enjoyable discussion about recent advances in genetic research and their social implications. Mr. Black was an extremely well informed man. I asked him how he could manage it when he had such a busy profession.

74

With a wry smile he said, "Actually, Doctor, I must confess my political secret." He hesitated dramatically, as if rueful. "It's my wife. She's my research bureau. Truly, she teaches me everything. Not only can I delegate such-and-such research to her, but I can trust her to keep abreast of current developments, read controversial or innovative articles, and report their gist to me, including any significant details.

"Now you see what I mean when I say an intelligent wife is of inestimable value to me!" He gazed affectionately at Stella.

It was then that he managed to communicate subtly to me that he wanted to be alone with his wife; I admired his tact. I could begin to appreciate what having such a husband would mean to Stella. I hoped he and I could get together again so that I could enlist his considerable aid in fighting her incipient depression.

Natalie Hoskins's operation was scheduled for 9:00 the next morning. I went in to see her at 7:00 when she was just waking up—though I wonder how much sleep she actually got—and about to receive her shots for the operation. I had received permission to miss rounds and scrub on the case.

She seemed frail that morning. Her dark skin looked ashen, and I examined her carefully just to make sure she was all right. I asked her if she'd eaten anything, and she smiled wanly and said she wouldn't have been able to keep it down if she had. She was in good enough shape; she was apparently only terrified. I reassured her as warmly as I could that I would be with her in the operating room all the time, and that nothing dangerous would happen.

Dr. Danes and I scrubbed together. Dr. Cohen, the general surgeon, scrubbed at another sink. I kept looking at Dr. Danes out of the corner of my eye to evaluate his performance of the day before, but he made no mention of it whatsoever, and I could do nothing but puzzle over it still. Now I realized what I had not appreciated the afternoon before, that he had a magnificent body, and I wondered if I'd missed my chance.

Soon enough, however, it was all business, and we were in the operating room, Natalie was prepared on the table, and he was making the first incision.

The first incision is always a strange, almost black-magical moment, when the thin, shining scalpel draws a line of red across the abdomen. From that artful moment on the patient becomes more body than anything else, and therefore less than human in a sense. That first line of blood is always awe-inspiring to me, for it transforms a person and marks our entrance into a different world.

The whole abdomen was explored, and a tumor was found in her colon; that segment was removed by Dr. Cohen. There were large tumors in her ovaries. Of course the obvious thing was to remove both ovaries, but as I stood by Dr. Danes's side and gazed at the ovaries and saw him excise one and move his bloody, gloved hands over to remove the other, I stopped him.

"Wait!" I whispered.

Everyone looked at me in alarm. "What is it?" he asked. "Are you going to faint?"

"No, no," I replied, in a stronger voice. "Get . . . get a diagnosis on this one before you take out the other, will you?" My eyes and voice pleaded with him to leave this young woman at least one ovary.

But the one he had taken out proved to have cancer similar to the lymphoma found in the bowel. The pathologist made the definitive diagnosis very quickly, for there was no doubt at all. So the other ovary had to be removed as well.

Dr. Danes kept looking up at me with concern, but I managed to hold back my tears. I didn't want to distract anyone from the operation, which was lengthy and fatiguing. Nor did I want to appear "too emotional."

When we were finished, Danes and I and the nurses discarded our gowns and masks. Danes asked me why I had been so upset.

"I hated the idea of a young woman losing both of her ovaries." It had been the first time I had seen someone castrated.

76

"She'll probably die anyway," he replied gently, "before she has a chance to have any babies."

I didn't answer. I made arrangements for him to talk to Natalie's mother and for all three of us doctors to meet in Natalie's room tomorrow to explain the rest of the therapy. Then I excused myself. Right then I wanted to check on how she was doing in the recovery room, and to tell the nurse there to call me the minute she saw my patient becoming alert and able to react intelligently. Natalie had of course been awake to a degree before she left the operating room. Every patient must be able to pull the tube from his windpipe and answer, however groggily, to his name.

Then I went to check on Stella. I seemed to fly down the hall as though my legs weren't there. That's what standing next to an operating table in the same place for two or three hours can do to you.

When I came into her room I saw she was napping, but since she was a light sleeper I knew she would wake up anyway, and I didn't try to creep back out of her room. I was right. She roused herself immediately.

One of the unusual things about a hospital, I realized, was that you see people in bed all the time, undressed or in nightclothes; you handle their bodies, you touch their genitals, you see them and talk to them at their most vulnerable, unclothed . . . It was a thought that I didn't finish, for at that moment Stella was talking.

She greeted me and we passed the time of day. She inquired about my duties that day and why I was later than usual. I almost began to tell her about the castration—in the most general terms, of course—when I realized I shouldn't, so I contented myself with saying merely that I had stood in on an extensive operation and that I was tired.

She began quizzing me in the greatest detail about my duties, my schedule, and my responsibilities as a doctor.

"Why all this curiosity?" I asked her, smiling.

"I want to find out what Rags will be going into."

77

"Oh, you mean *if* she decides to become a doctor."
She laughed softly. "Yes, of course, 'if.' "

"Medicine will probably be quite different by then," I said perversely.

"Oh," she said, and her smile faded. I was glad when she changed the subject and we began talking about present-day adolescents. As Mr. Black had said, she was very well informed on current trends, so we had a satisfying, abstract conversation until I had to leave.

"You'll be going home by the end of the week, Stella," I said to her as I got ready to go.

"Yes, I know," she said in a colorless voice.

I didn't know what to reply to her lack of enthusiasm, so I excused myself and left, feeling disappointed.

11

I had the rest of the day to catch up on the patients that I hadn't seen first thing because I was in the operating room, and it took me the rest of the day to check them all out. In the middle of it, around noon, I got the call from Recovery that Natalie was being taken to her own room, so I went down to meet her.

Her mother was waiting for her. I knew when I saw Mrs. Hoskins that Dr. Danes and Dr. Cohen had spoken to her, for the woman was red-eyed from weeping. I realized that Danes had not told me exactly what he would be telling Natalie's mother, and that I would have to keep my mouth shut until I consulted with him again.

I could say to both mother and daughter that Natalie had come through the operation with flying colors.

She'd responded very well to the anesthesia, and it had in turn worn off quite naturally. There was no change in her pulse or blood pressure. I helped to make Natalie more comfortable until I realized that her mother wanted to be left alone with her beloved daughter, so I departed gracefully.

It took me the rest of the afternoon to check out all my other patients, and by 6:30 I was exhausted. Unfortunately it was my night on, so instead of having supper I sacked out, because I knew I would be bothered from 7:30 until 10:30 with bedtime instructions and permissions for pills. I fell asleep as fast as I could —which was instantly—fully dressed and with my shoes on, on a narrow cart in the dark end of a corridor. I'd attached my beepers to the IV pole at my head and I slept without moving until one of them went off.

When it did, and I scrambled awake, I didn't realize exactly where I was. I swung my legs over as if I were on my bottom cot and stumbled to the floor— the way you do when you expect a top step that isn't there.

It was a call from Dr. Danes. That seemed unnecessary, because we were going to get together tomorrow at 10:00 A.M. anyway to discuss the case with Natalie, but he wanted to make sure I would be there and we talked for a moment about her. Then he got down to the real business and asked me if I would be interested in a date.

Finally completely awake, I responded, "Of course."

We made a date for the following Saturday night. I turned away with a smile of pleasure on my face and saw one of the night nurses looking at me malevolently. Well, I figured, maybe she's gone out with him. I didn't know what I was supposed to do about it.

The next morning I met both Dr. Danes and Mrs. Hoskins outside Natalie's room. (Her own doctor couldn't make it.) We all said hello pleasantly enough, though Mrs. Hoskins looked tense. Then we trooped into the room.

Natalie Hoskins was looking immensely better this morning in spite of her nasogastric tube, an IV, a Foley catheter, and the plastic bag that collects the urine. Apparently the effect of her anesthesia had completely worn off, though she was still on painkillers. She was having a conversation with her roommates, and I was pleased to see that there was a cheerful, confident note in her voice. When she saw us, she made a comic face and said, "Uh-oh."

Danes gave her a very brief examination and checked the dressing to make sure it was still dry. Then he shook Natalie's hand.

She looked surprised, but shook hands back.

"I want to congratulate you," he said. "You survived the operation!"

Mrs. Hoskins looked shocked, but Natalie laughed immediately.

"Well, Natalie," he continued, "I think you should be able to understand what we have in store for you. What we found is that you have a kind of lymphoma, which we got out, and you'll be in for a procedure of chemotherapy now. I spoke to your mother about it yesterday and the day before, and maybe she mentioned it to you. Now it's your turn to hear it from us.

"After you've recovered completely from the operation, which I have no doubt you'll do very soon, we'll send you home. In about two weeks, your other doctor wants to see you in his office and he'll order a series of intravenous injections. I talked to him, and he is going to supervise this. He and I will discuss whether you'll come back into the hospital for the injections, or whether we can do it on an outpatient basis.

"It'll be tedious, I warn you, but it won't be painful. There are some possible side effects that I also must warn you about. You might get a bit nauseous, or have diarrhea, or suffer some hair loss, but . . ."

I believed his persuasive words, too, although I knew the side effects could be awful, such as horrible vomiting. She'd been watching him and nodding attentively, but when she took in the last detail—the loss of her hair—she burst into tears. I moved toward her, but her mother took her in her arms. Danes seemed to pull back a little and was silent. I made a mental note to advise her to buy a wig before she lost her hair.

Natalie quickly got control of herself, but she was still tearful when she asked, "Why?"

"Well now," he explained, "the medication must be pretty powerful to go on in and clean everything up, don't you think? Natalie, I know how it must seem to a girl who's as lovely as you are, but I can assure you it's temporary, and soon you'll be well again. Isn't that worth it?"

She didn't answer, but just gazed at him.

"Well, isn't it?" he prodded her gently, until she nodded yes. Then he laughed and said, "Shall I give you a lollipop or a balloon for being such a good girl?"

She responded to his teasing, and said shyly, "A balloon, please."

And he promised to bring her one the next time he came.

I was in a semiprivate room talking with a patient when someone I knew was admitted. Gloria Vassilly, the wife of a radiology resident, was Ted Gilman's patient.

I couldn't believe how bad she looked. She was about five feet six or seven, but she seemed to weigh 90 pounds now. Her feet and hands were huge; there was hardly any flesh on her bones. Her dull, stringy hair looked as if it might be coming out, and her skull was so knobby that the hair couldn't lie along it smoothly. Even her eyelids were thin and wasted. She looked as though she'd just gotten out of a concentration camp, except that she was elegantly dressed.

I spoke to her, and she recognized me eagerly. Her voice had always been pleasant, but now, though she was ingratiating, there was an ugly tightness to it. While we talked small talk, catching up on mutual friends, part of me sat back and observed her medically while another part kept remembering just one picture of her from the past, singing beautifully at a friend's wedding.

After five minutes of talk she said, "So you're really becoming a doctor after all. I thought better of you, Phyllis."

"Why, what do you mean?" I asked.

She leaned closer to me. Her eyes twinkled, a macabre effect in her bony face. "I really know from watching my husband what getting to be a doctor is like, you know," she confided. "Oh, Phyllis, you're just getting started, but don't you know yet how it just eats you up? He hardly ever pays any attention to anything else anymore." She went on to describe in detail his reading habits—which I had to admit to myself were close to what mine had to be to keep up with what I had to know—especially reading at meals, and she laughed unconvincingly about his falling asleep the minute he came home.

When there was a pause, I excused myself and left gladly.

I found Ted Gilman later in the day and asked him about his new patient. He looked unhappy.

"Phyllis, this one's a doozer. She's classic anorexia nervosa, and nobody's been able to crack her. It looks like we're going to have to tie her down to get the IV into her, and not only that, to keep it there."

"What does her husband say?" Anorexia nervosa is a condition in which a patient can't eat, or eats but vomits for so long that the weight loss is too great. It appears usually—though not always—in women, and typically in a teenager on a diet who can't stop, getting trapped into a horror of being fat. It's a ferocious illness.

Ted looked unhappier than ever. "He's just not talking, Phyl. I was told he's keeping out of the way so as not to prejudice her case."

"Hm." We looked at one another, speculating silently about the radiologist's motives. His wife was obviously very sick indeed, not only in physical danger from her weight loss, but also emotionally to be able to do such a thing to herself.

82

It made me feel uneasy to have this case around, but that was nothing compared to what Ted went through. It was a case he was working his heart out for, and his patient was seemingly cooperative but actually quite the opposite. Though he had a quiet restraint that made him act chivalrously, I bet he felt like hauling off and socking her once or twice.

For example, Ted couldn't find her when he wanted to talk to her or do a procedure on her. She was all over the place with amazing energy, up and down the halls, introducing herself to patients and offering to do errands for them, taking messages to the nurses that one patient hadn't had a bowel movement yet, another needed a codeine pill, a third wanted a bedpan, a fourth hadn't had her enema.

The first job was to rehydrate her by vein. She couldn't be nourished except by her own eating, but it was doubtful that she was taking in what actually disappeared from her tray. After the initial gain of five pounds of water weight, she didn't gain any more.

Whenever I happened to be in the room with her, because of my patient, I could tell with more and more certainty that, whatever was going to work with her—if anything—it was not going to be courtesy. She spent the whole time I was there telling me about how good the hospital was, how good the nursing was, but implying misgivings about the personalities of everyone she had any contact with, and especially the competence of each doctor, except me of course. She sat bolt upright and bony in the middle of her white bed and talked incessantly in her dry, hard voice.

My own patient begged me to change her room, and I could understand her distress with such a talkative, nervous roommate. But I couldn't do anything about it. Fortunately Gloria was as often out of her room as in.

On her sixth day, I was walking by that end of the floor when I heard the sounds of vomiting in the women's bathroom. The cubicles cannot be locked (so you can aid a patient in distress), and I dashed in.

Gloria was on her knees in front of the toilet bowl,

her arms, scarred from the IV needle, embracing the cold porcelain. I almost knocked her over when I threw open the door, but that was fortunate, since it prevented her from quickly flushing down the evidence: swirling in the water and quickly thinning out were brownish juices and a few lumps of undigested food. She had been forcing herself to vomit.

I had the impulse to grab her by her wasted shoulders, pull her back, and shake her, but I caught myself and touched her gently instead. Even so, she squawked, a hoarse scraping sound like the last of her retching, and she looked up at me from her position before the toilet bowl, her eyes wide in their sockets.

Then she got control of herself, rose to her elongated height and retired to some pencil-thin privacy inside her body. Without saying a word she turned, sidled out between me and the opened metal door, and walked away, crossing her arms on her chest like folded, plucked chicken wings. She was barefoot, and I saw that the skin on her heels was beginning to get shiny and transparent, just as it must be on her hips, buttocks, and shoulders or at any bony protuberance, though she was still in good enough condition not to get bedsores.

I told Ted Gilman what had happened; he replied that the nurses knew she was taking every opportunity she could to vomit what she ate. She'd already lost two pounds of her new gain. He said he was getting a psychiatric consult on her and we eyed one another with hope.

Stella had improved, as we had expected her to, and was going home. I managed, I thought, to smooth out my relationship with her to a calm rationality and respect.

"Well," I said, as I disconnected her bottles, "I guess that ought to hold you."

She smiled wanly. "Yes," she said in a low voice, "I feel like a car that's been gassed up. I'm in for a long trip across the desert, aren't I?"

"What do you mean?" I joshed her. "What desert?"

She flushed with embarrassment. "Oh, of course I didn't mean anything . . ."

"I should hope not!" I encouraged her. "Why, with your husband on his way and everything, you should be glad to be going home."

Suddenly she sat down. "Oh, I am!" she assured me earnestly. "It's just that I'll miss the hospital. Listen," she said. "Sit down with me one last time."

I obeyed.

She continued, seriously. "I shall miss the hospital. Yes. It seems perverse, I know. But the scale—you see, the scale is different here. It's manageable. I have a bathroom, I have my room—a place to entertain, so to speak, a place to be private. My meals are fixed for me.

"Like a hotel," I added.

"Yes, but not like a hotel. In a hotel you're a stranger and everybody's distracted. But here, I have people coming in not only to visit me, but also to care for me." She paused for a long time. "That's what's so hard to give up—like an addiction, I guess —being taken care of."

I was silent. I was conscious of agreeing, and thinking that such an addiction does disable you. You get so you can't depend on yourself anymore. But out of respect for her feelings I didn't say anything critical. I knew that she would bear up and take on her old responsibilities. Why not let her indulge in a little self-pity?

"Well . . ." She turned to me. "Have I forgotten anything? Do you have any more instructions for me?"

I looked at her for a moment, wondering whether Dr. Speir had given her the same speech Dennis Danes had given Natalie, and reluctant to try it myself.

"What is it?" With her usual sensitivity she saw that something had dawned on me.

I wanted to be as gentle as I could. "You . . . Stella, you . . . I haven't made sure that you understand all the possible effects of your chemotherapy."

She suddenly looked bright, like a hostess meeting an uninvited guest at a cocktail party, or a doyenne confronting a workman. "Of course." She got up and went to her suitcases, opened one, and checked her bedside table in a new flurry of activity.

I kept watching her.

At last she said, still haughty, "Among other things, they said I might lose all my hair. Do they mean *all* my hair?"

Without waiting for my nod, she caroled, "I'll be like a newborn babe again!"

At that moment her husband knocked at the door.

He tried to have a conversation with me, but Stella was in such a hurry to leave that she briskly ordered him about, getting him loaded up with some of her luggage. She had a considerable amount for a hospital stay of only two weeks. He did manage to say a quick good-bye to me, but Stella got out of there without once more meeting my eyes.

I usually walk people to the elevator, but this time I didn't have the energy. I was relieved that she was gone.

Elegant in her colorful summer dress and white sandal pumps, she seemed the Stella I had first met, the beautiful, graceful lady. But she had changed, she had lost the serenity I had first appreciated in her; and though I hoped she would be able to repair it, I felt sorrow that she had let something so precious slip from her grasp. As I stood alone in her empty room, I knew that the real Stella Black had departed some time before, without my knowing it.

Soon I felt entirely different. Maybe I shook myself, or closed off a certain weakness in myself, but *I* was *my* old self again—in one sense at least. I took a glance at the past two weeks and suddenly laughed. The scenes of Foley backing me to the door; the crazy Macklin family turning on me and all yelling at once; Mansfield, who in fact was shorter than I was, buttonholing me at the party; that poor bewildered psychiatrist; and, most of all, me talking a mile a minute while Danes undressed completely in front of me and then dressed himself again. I could see it all for what it was—a particularly hectic, demanding period in an absurd, crazy life. That was all it was. So, I asked myself, what else is new?

12

My date with Dr. Dennis Danes was very interesting. The first thing I said to him was: "Do you deign, Dr. Danes?" His retort was: "I trust you to make no wisecracks about my name"; then he took my arm and led me to his car.

I had had no intention of making any wisecracks about his name, but from then on I couldn't think of anything else. As we drove along the river with the top down, I found myself gazing sightlessly at the dark water and thinking up all the puns I could, especially "Dennis deigns" and "Dense Dane" and variations thereof; my mind went on and on in an irrepressible orgy of unspoken puns, and I began to giggle.

So, to get my mind off puns, I broke into song. That's a laugh in itself, since I can hardly carry a tune, but it broke the ice, gave *him* something to make a few wisecracks about, and let me forget my puns. The only problem was that, after that, my mind kept repeating the asinine tune I had dredged up until at last I got so interested in Dennis Danes himself that I could forget everything else.

We spent one of the pleasantest evenings I'd had in a long time, and never spoke about medicine at all. This was striking, since medical people can never get together without talking shop. But with Dennis, all our conversations were what I'd call normal, and definitely nonmedical: some back-and-forth about background, political opinions and such, and a lot of joking.

He didn't take me home. Without asking, he drove straight to his place, giving me only a smile when I protested.

He came around the car and opened the door on my side, reached down his hand, and said, "Come." He pulled me up from the low sports car with one effortless movement.

He was straightforward but thorough. He took my wrap, got me seated in a wide, deep sofa, and went about his apartment arranging the lighting, the music, and producing a bottle of well-chilled champagne. When he popped the cork, he gave me a knowing smile. When we had each drunk a glass of the wine he began to make love, first murmuring and kissing my face and throat, then moving his hands down to unbutton and reach under my blouse.

"Wait," I said, "let's get undressed."

"No, no," he chided gently, "just let me take care of everything. You'll see, it'll be nice and subtle."

Sliding more deeply into the pillows, sinking beneath his hands, I responded to his expert lovemaking. I tried once to give him some of the excitement he was giving me, but he stopped me, again quietly, and told me just to relax and let him show me. He slipped his hand under my bra, straining it, and lifting it off my breasts, he ran his thumb around my nipple, sweetly, under the cloth of my blouse.

Neither of us completely undressed; he kept on a sleeveless undershirt and I still had my blouse and my bra wadded under my arms like bindings. Now I understood the kind of special excitement he had in mind, something surreptitious implied, by our not fully undressing. He caressed every part of my body and then deep between my legs; smoothly, strongly, insistently, until I came with a powerful build-up and a shuddering release, and before the last contractions had died away he laid his body on top of mine and inserted his penis into my widened, moist vagina.

His eyes, half-closed, watched mine not inches away,

and when he judged it right he began to move himself in me. He took my hands and placed them on his naked hips and showed me how he wanted me to move him, to stroke him and lift him, and then he slowly pulled his shirt up until his bare chest pressed against my breasts. He fitted his hands against the swells of my breasts on each side, and then, after a while, he lifted himself off me, pulling us apart from where our sweat had glued us together, and covered my breasts with each hand, pulling himself in and out of me vigorously, smoothly, deeply, so effectively that he seemed to be skimming my clitoris with his penis and driving into my vagina until I couldn't stand it any longer, and I came again in one grasping gulp, dragged away from him, and began to come again, and at last he came with me, with a thrust so deep as to pin me down, and then he jerked partly away and then disappeared into me completely, throbbing and diminishing until he settled his body heavily onto mine.

I let my breath out in amazement as I slowly subsided. Drowsily I was aware that he had been right, it was "nice and subtle," though powerful. We both fell asleep until the weight of his body became so heavy that I awoke. I murmured for him to move. "No, wait," he said, and he reached onto the floor or the end table or something for a box of tissues, some of which he used to prevent any spilling onto the sofa when he uncorked me.

We lay languorously until the pile of records was finished and the tone arm lifted into silence; then he sighed and got up and went to the shower. I was going to join him there, but he made it clear he didn't want me to. He took a quick shower, and dressed while I was taking mine.

He drove me home, and, as I was leaving the car, I said to him, "You know, we never once talked medicine!"

"Ah, Phyllis," he said caressingly, "I don't think of you as a doctor."

I knew I'd like to do this again. He was very good, and I said so.

"You're so direct," he murmured. "Goodnight, my dear." He drove off.

We did do it again, often.

I thought I'd found the perfect lover. The only drawback in our affair was the need for secrecy. The staple of hospital gossip was the sex life of anyone who had a sex life; Dennis himself had first become known to me by his reputation and the gossip about him. But what our tight little society could accept in him I felt would not be tolerated in me. For me to acknowledge my sexuality directly might jeopardize my professional standing and seriousness. Many patients didn't want their doctors to have a sex life at all; they needed an unthreatening, comforting priest-father. In addition, some people unconsciously felt that no woman should have a sexual identity if she were to be any kind of professional at all.

I was very careful never to appear interested in Dennis in any way, even when he was the topic of conversation, so it was a shock when I heard someone say, as I walked past a Nurses' Lounge, "I haven't seen your Dennis at any parties recently." A cord holding my limbs together seemed to break and disable my legs in midstride, while a freeze clamped down over my mind and I turned around, ready to deny any connection at all between me and Dr. Dennis Danes.

It was two nurses going into the lounge who were talking to one another, and they weren't looking at me at all. Of course, one of them had dated him—maybe not so long ago. Who hadn't? I wondered.

He and I agreed on a strange method to prevent anyone's seeing him come or go around my apartment. I lived in a block of four-story row houses. I knew that the downstairs hall five houses down from mine went all the way back to the fire escape. Dennis and I would park around the corner, slip into that house, and take the fire escape to the roof. Then we would clamber across the uneven flat roofs of the intervening houses to the fire escape on my building, sneak down it past garbage or cats, and enter through my back window.

When I first suggested this route to him he was intrigued by the piquancy. When it began to get cold, icy, and snowy, he might be less pleased with our star trek. We'd figure something out when the time came.

He was a good lover, and I loved sex. For me, it was the natural expression of an attraction to someone who could give me, and to whom I could give, pleasure. Though at first I tried to be more active, Dennis always guided what we did in bed, and I soon accepted his initiative, for he had more sexual energy and was master of more techniques than I had ever before experienced, and he was full of delights for me. With a little guilt that I wasn't thinking up or giving him as much, it seemed, as he was giving me, I surrendered much of the control to him.

A Mrs. Jefferson became my patient. Thirty now, she had been a diabetic for years. She came in because her diabetes was out of control—blood sugar high, sugar in her urine, and diarrhea. I had admitted her, done all the tests, and was checking her history with her to make sure everything had been covered when she admitted that she'd missed her last four periods.

The pelvic exam corroborated her pregnancy. She would have to be transferred to the antenatal section of Obstetrics. There is a medical feeling—which I now think is a kind of prejudice—against a diabetic pregnancy. It is considered hard on both the fetus and the mother.

After making the arrangements, I went back to her room to take her to OB. It happened to be afternoon visiting hours when I walked in, and I was surprised to see her sitting on the edge of her bed, her hospital gown so loose as to expose her buttocks and genitals as she swung one leg back and forth. There were a couple of visitors in the room, one a middle-aged man who was clearly embarrassed and studiously avoided looking at her; she paid no attention to anyone, but chewed gum and read a magazine.

I had been told that diabetics come to think far less modestly about their bodies than other people do; I believe it's because they're so vulnerable that they pretend their bodies are unimportant and casually manipulable. I came in briskly and pulled the curtain between her and the rest of the room so we could talk and the others could be spared, so to speak. She spoke to me, however, in a loud, lecturing tone, as though to keep everyone within earshot informed.

As soon as we began talking, she produced the charts that she had kept on all her body functions, urine sugars and acetones and how often she had urinated each day. While we were sitting there talking, the nurse brought her syringe in for her; suddenly, without a word, she gave herself an insulin shot in the thigh. It must have been her regular time, but she made no reference to it at all. It was brutally abrupt.

Then I said, "You must have been warned not to get pregnant, weren't you, since you're a brittle diabetic?" "Brittle" means that the diabetes goes out of control easily and frequently. She could have too much sugar and become acidotic and go into coma, or too little sugar, giving her an insulin reaction that leads to shock.

"Oh, yes," she said airily.

"Well," I said, "you *are* pregnant."

"I know, I know."

Thinking of Mr. Foley and all the information he had hidden, I asked, "Why didn't you mention it to your doctor?"

She looked at me with a confidential air and said, simply, "I was told not to get pregnant. Well, I wanted to get pregnant. I did. Now I don't want any hassle about it. We'll just treat it as a fact of life, okay?" And she laughed. "It's too late now."

That, of course, was true. I smiled and gazed at her speculatively. She looked older than thirty, actually. There was a lot of gray in her dark brown hair, and around her eyes were dark shadows and fine lines, magnified by her glasses. She was never completely still. If she wasn't swinging a leg or moving a foot back and forth, she was touching her face or pushing her hair off her forehead or clasping her hands behind her head. She made a lot of nervous movements, and she projected a powerful will. It was my guess that if any diabetic could pull off a difficult pregnancy, she would. She *would* cooperate.

I told Mrs. Jefferson I was taking her up to the antenatal floor and that she'd have to be followed by her internist, an obstetrician, and an ophthalmologist.

She hopped down off the bed with a gleam in her eye. "That's all I wanted to know," she announced, as if pleased at my acceptance of her pregnancy. "Let's go."

Her regimen was quickly established over on OB and she soon went home. It was one of the most determined pregnancies I'd ever seen. I saw her again when I was on OB and she came in with vomiting. She delivered prematurely and the baby had difficulties at first.

I hadn't realized that Mr. Foley was not unique in withholding information from his doctor. I could understand Mrs. Jefferson's reasons, but I hadn't been able to penetrate Mr. Foley's. I sighed to myself. Mr. Foley had become very important to me because I had failed with him, and because his case was one extreme of the whole issue of a patient's self-revelation. I also worried, once a case had been so explicitly antagonized by my being a woman, that most male patients would not accept my authority, and I wondered whether I had the knack of coping with them. When I remembered Pete Witowski, I was only somewhat reassured.

With pleasure, Ted told me a few days afterward how Gloria Vassilly's psychiatric consult had reacted. Apparently Gloria had first laughed hysterically when the doctor came into the office and announced who he was, but after fifteen minutes of incoherent and misleading chatter she had calmed down and cooperated.

She was as objective about herself and her condition as anyone observing her would have been, though without analyzing why she was doing what she was. She told him all her convictions and dreams about food and eating and fasting, and she described all her tricks to avoid being suffocated by either her food or her flesh. When he asked how she would handle her case if she were the doctor, a flicker of emotion appeared on her face, and she herself was struck, and said, "Aha!" But after that enigmatic exclamation, she'd giggled and teased and then clammed up.

The psychiatrist, after some pondering and some discussion with everyone, including her husband, suggested a bargain to her. Every half-pound she gained would yield her some privilege, like a certain number of trips up and down the corridor. Otherwise she'd have to stay in her room. He made no comment whatsoever about *how* she would gain the weight, whether by eating more, by accepting a hyperalimentation intravenous (that is, feeding more nourishing fluids by the subclavian vein), or by failing to vomit. It was just a naked bargain.

After apparently judicious thought, she accepted.

I was transferred out of Private Medicine onto the wards before Gloria's case was finished, but I saw Ted Gilman often and I asked about her; I also went to see her a couple of times in the evening when I had a moment.

She made a slow and cranky recovery, with many setbacks and ugly episodes. She made Ted into a nervous wreck. After a few visits I had to stay away from her. She flattered me and complained about her own doctors, including Ted and especially her husband, in an insidious manner. She'd never again discuss with her psychiatrist anything about her emotions or motives, but she reported the caloric content of each food she ate, described each little expedition she took down the hall, and analyzed the case of each patient she'd become acquainted with. But she dealt with the psychiatrist quite well as long as their relationship remained on an immediate and quasi-legal level. She even suggested a new privilege to aim for, that of using the piano in the basement lounge.

Dr. Danes and Natalie's internist had allowed me to manage her case for the rest of the time she was in the hospital. It went along very straightforwardly and nothing unexpected happened. Natalie had lots of visitors—kids from her high school class—and I had to make sure she tried to keep it down since she was rooming with three other women, one of them pretty irritable from abdominal surgery. But Natalie was as cheerful and pleasant as she could be, showing off her bandage and describing the scar underneath as if it had been as minor as an appendectomy. I watched over her for a day or two, but she had withdrawn from me and didn't seem to need the support she had previously asked for.

I noticed that whenever she thought no one was paying any attention, she gazed at herself in the mirror and brushed her hair or styled it. Finally I made a point of discussing Natalie's emotional state with her mother.

"Mrs. Hoskins," I opened the talk, "what is your understanding of Natalie's case?"

Her eyes filled with tears. "What do you mean?"

"Do you know what's wrong with her?"

Her voice was low but firm when she answered. "I understand that she has a kind of cancer and that, though the doctor got all of it that he could find during the operation, she might get worse."

"I see." I perceived that Dennis had told Mrs. Hoskins part of the truth, hopefully, rather than as bleakly as he had spoken to me. "How much does Natalie know?" I asked. "Is she being heroic, with all her cheerfulness?"

"No," her mother said, trying not to break down. "She really doesn't want to know.

"And I don't blame her!" the woman continued. "She's the brightest, the best girl a mother could want. It's not fair for this to happen to her! It's not fair, I tell you!"

She accused me, and I stood there transfixed by an echo. That had been Stella's plea, too, that unreasonable protest.

Heavy with something dragging at me I said to her, "I know. I know it's not fair."

Natalie went home soon after, cheerful as always. It was Mrs. Hoskins who looked haunted. I believe that after several months they went to Europe where Natalie led a gay, idle life. Three years later, she's back, I understand, in the hospital with a recurrence. Her lymphoma is a chronic cancer and needs to be constantly "managed." She will always live under the threat of death.

PART II

September

Ward Medicine

13

I was glad I had been assigned to one of the men's wards. Unconsciously hoping to defend myself, I thought a men's ward could give me a respite from the kind of emotional invasions of my psyche that I'd suffered on Private Medicine. The wards seemed to me, in my ignorance, to be set up to minimize demands on your sympathy and to maximize efficiency. For one thing, a team consisted of fewer people than on Private Medicine—one medical student, one intern, and one resident here, in contrast to two or three medical students, three interns, and one or two residents there. A team handled twenty-five patients on each ward: ten active, as we called those getting primary care, and fifteen inactive, that is, those needing nothing but scutwork, but a lot of it; while a team on Private Medicine would handle fifteen active patients at a time. We would have no time for nonsense, I thought.

Our hours were longer, too; first, because we were up earlier having work rounds at 6:30 to be ready for the chief of service making rounds at 7:30, and second, because many admissions took place at 2:00 A.M. and were very time-consuming. Sleep became even more precious than before, and I began to feel like a soldier, always being awakened in the middle of the night and required to wake up immediately alert. Soldiers are also not supposed to feel very many emotions.

The intern who was turning his job over to me walked me speedily through the ward the day before I started. In a brisk voice, he explained that I'd have all public assistance, or charity, patients—people with no financial resources, no insurance, no welfare. Alcoholics, senile men, drug addicts, malingerers, and "dumps." "Dumps" were people disabled by age, disease, or injury, whose families could not or would not care for them anymore and who had nowhere else to go but the wards. As an example he pointed out one comatose old man, Al Whittaker, and we paused at his silent bed.

"The old guy isn't going to survive," he said. "They brought him in five days ago—stroke. Diabetic, ancient—as you can see. Comatose since he came in." He walked on.

The old man, Alfred Whittaker, was such a still, small figure that his chest hardly stirred the blankets as he breathed. The only movement around him was the flow of liquids through his tubes; a nasogastric tube from his nose to his stomach to remove fluid so that he wouldn't vomit and get it in his lungs; an urethral tube, or Foley catheter, into his bladder and a urine bag collecting his urine; and fluids to keep him hydrated, by intravenous. Periodically he was receiving low-bulk proteinaceous food through the nasal tube. He was pushing the limit on the rule of thumb that says the more tubes, the worse the patient. He was diapered but had no bowel movements because he wasn't eating. I saw from the outline of his frail body that he had only one leg. His chart said the other leg had been removed when it had gotten gangrenous from statis ulcers, ulcerations due to venous insufficiency, and vascular disease from his diabetes. His face was finely wrinkled, and his flesh was flabby in his coma, but his color was good.

The other intern had walked on, but I stood at the foot of the bed for a moment, gazing at the still form.

My first night on, I was called down to the Emergency Room to admit an old man who was a "dump." I had been told that unless a ward admission was a real emergency, the first thing you did was to go to the Records Room, try to find the person's record to see if he had been admitted to another team in the hospital, and then try to get him admitted to that team so he wouldn't be dumped on our service. I was allowed *not* to find any charts that showed he had been admitted to our service, which would make us responsible for him. One of the reasons the service didn't want "dumps" was that their problems had very little educational value to justify the drudgery. Also, it occurred to me as I neared Emergency Admitting, if you could get him admitted elsewhere, you could go back to bed.

I saw with dismay that this man looked like the worst we could get. He was ninety years old at least and he stank. His pants were wet and reeking of dirt and urine, and he had defecated and managed to smear the shit around on his lower body. His wizened little frame was tight and shaking, and his features were screwed up shut. He was cursing nonstop in a thin but hard, loud voice. There were a couple of people standing near him who were probably members of his family, and I felt a twinge of sympathy for them. He looked impossible to handle.

I had to make them wait there twenty minutes while I looked for his record, but in the end I admitted him. The man who had helped bring him in stood in the corridor watching me wheel the old guy away. When I turned the corner, I could see that he was still there.

It was 2:30 in the morning, and in the relative quiet of the hospital I was pushing along a tiny but mean old man who never paused in his loud cursing. He was a bundle of sticks, and as I pushed him up the steep, short ramp into Grey to get to Levering, where the wards were, his body pressed back in the wheelchair toward me so that his fetor was overwhelming.

The male nurse I got to help me looked disgusted for a moment, but whether that was from having to do the job at this hour or from the job itself wasn't clear. The job itself was not unusual. First we had to wash him off. We had to hold him down. Every once in a while he'd jerk or swing an arm, and I got one wallop. Finally we got him cleaned off, and none too gently, at that. His skin was very irritated, with sores,

101

so he must have been incontinent for some time now. In effect, he had diaper rash.

Then I drew some blood cultures, got the lab studies, and, again with the strong aid of the male nurse, did a spinal tap to make sure his fever and secondary dehydration were not due to meningitis. By this time he had calmed down. Then I got fluid, salt water, started on him intravenously. In such an extreme case you have to let it come very slowly—his body and blood are just like dried soup, and adding water too fast is dangerous. We put the urine condom and a big diaper on him.

I didn't get back to bed until 4:00, and I had to be up and alert again for rounds at 6:30, to present his case to my resident so he could present it to the chief at 7:30.

Mr. Smith was actually looking much better in the morning. He was sleeping and snoring. The IV was still in him, and the rate was still appropriately slow.

The next day the man who'd brought Mr. Smith in surprised me by coming to visit. I had been walking through the ward, and was startled to see a figure sitting by Mr. Smith's bedside. Usually people leave the old ones and never return. But this man came back. You could tell, now that the old man's face had filled out a little and you could see his normal features, that they were probably father and son. The man in the next bed was talking to him but he wasn't listening. His eyes wandered over his father's form and followed the tubing up to the IV bottle. The son was about fifty. His clothes were mended, not always neatly, and mismatched, but they were clean.

Smith's son nodded to me as I paused by the bed and we talked. I found out that the old man's eldest daughter, a woman of sixty-nine, had devoted her life to caring for her father, but at last she couldn't carry him up and down stairs, she couldn't keep him clean, and he wouldn't eat for her anymore. Still, she'd refused to give him up, until at last her brother had almost literally taken the old man from her arms to bring him in. Smith's last dehydration had destroyed

102

his mental functioning. His curses the other night had been the last coherent speech his brain would be able to manage.

As I spent more time on the ward, I came to realize that the old taking care of the old was common. Once I saw a case of a retarded man of sixty whose eighty-year-old mother had unwillingly had to give him up. Our "dumps" were not all scandalous abandonments by young, healthy offspring. I started to ask Mr. Smith whether he'd like to see the social worker when he again startled me by softly whispering "Sssh!" with his whole hand—a laborer's hand—perpendicular to his protruding lips.

I was silent, puzzled.

His eyes looked at his father and then returned to me. "He did it again," he told me quietly, and then I could hear a dripping as the old man's yellow urine drained across his rubberized undersheet and dribbled to the floor beneath the bed. His condom must have fallen off.

I called one of the aides, who came matter-of-factly and, with his son's help, moved Smith back and forth in order to change his sheet. She reattached the condom. The whole event had deeply shocked and embarrassed his son.

I didn't see the son again for another two days. By that time Mr. Smith was able to sit propped up, and with some teaching by the aide he began to use his fingers to put food into his mouth. He got it all over his face. His son came back at the same time as before, late afternoon, and he appeared again suddenly, sitting by his father's bed. The old man didn't recognize him.

He continued to visit his father every few days, in spite of the old man's unresponsiveness. He helped us with his father, who could never do more than feed himself with his fingers and grunt when he was about to defecate. Then his diaper would have to be changed. Whenever he spoke, which was seldom, his few words were slurred and confused.

I asked the son about the old man's situation, since

103

with his minimal improvement it would be better for us if he could be moved elsewhere and free a bed. But the son's wife couldn't care for him. She worked as a domestic and wasn't home during the day. The grandchildren apparently couldn't do it. The man's eldest daughter was now too old herself and his other children were dead. In addition, the son was out of a job, and had been for some time. They hadn't gotten Mr. Smith on welfare because the family had been taking care of him. Finally I asked, "How can you keep coming when he doesn't really recognize you?"

He just sat there, looking at me, and smiled gently. Then he reached over and touched his father's arm.

Old Smith remained on the ward for my entire stay, and I have no doubt he's still there. Some of these cases are with us for years.

The ward service got many alcoholics. Most often they'd be brought in by the police, from jail or the street, where they'd been without liquor for a few hours and were going into withdrawal. Both men and women, they'd be very agitated, crying loudly or whimpering, trembling, lashing out with jerky movements of their limbs, vomiting or shitting or pissing on themselves. They'd appear usually in the middle of the night, and they disturbed the rest of the ward. Those in the worst shape would cry out against the bugs—the black beetles and cockroaches that they saw streaming down the walls and crawling all over their bodies. In terror, one man hopped down off a stretcher and opened his pants to look at his belly. He wailed and scooped at his body, again and again, apparently to dislodge the bugs he felt and saw on himself.

We had to tie these patients down to get them sedated with huge doses of paraldehyde or Librium, quantities that would have knocked other people out. A real alcohol addict can die from withdrawal itself if not treated properly with huge quantities of sedatives.

The alcoholics had to be rehydrated, and since they

were so undernourished, they needed vitamins through the IV. Some of the patients looked like prunes.

Of my whole month on Ward Medicine, probably half my time was spent on these alcoholics, all of whose conditions were alike. They began to gain some personality and individuality only when they sobered up and calmed down. Unfortunately, once they began to recover, fill out some with new water weight, and get some food into themselves, they'd sign out and go off to do some more drinking, only to come back in again in the same awful shape as before. While I was there, I admitted four men twice and another man three times. I myself didn't see the others again, but most of them were repeaters and familiar to the nurses, aides, and orderlies.

On rounds one day, as we walked past the bed of an alcoholic I had admitted the night before—on an IV, restrained in his bed, trembling, muttering, and salivating uncontrollably in withdrawal—I said to the staff doctor, "May I ask a question, sir?"

He turned to look over his shoulder at me. "Well, yes, of course, Miss Donnan."

Suddenly appalled by his substitution of "Miss" for "Doctor," I stopped walking, thus requiring him and the others who accompanied him to stop too. I went on with my question. "Is there going to be a seminar on alcoholism?"

"Hm. Now what would you have in such a seminar?"

"Well, the effects of alcohol on the body are so widespread—and profound—heart, liver, blood, the brain. And the malnutrition. Once you get an alcoholic dried out—and drying out itself is a fascinating topic—the chemical changes in the brain or the blood, and the management of the drugs you're using—everything—and the other medical problems these patients have after you've cleaned them out . . . It's a complicated story, surely," I finished.

He smiled. "Your enthusiasm does you credit, my dear. We're all familiar with these complications secondary to alcohol. I'm afraid it's just a familiar story, that's all. It happens all the time. We devote our seminars, as you know, to the unusual and difficult medical situation." He paused a moment. "Though perhaps you yourself might work something up that might supply some information we don't already know. It might be a very good project for you."

I looked him straight in the eye. I knew what he was doing; he was putting me down by minimizing the seriousness of this medical issue, and by trying to push me into a project that would amuse him and win me no credit.

"Thank you, Doctor," I said briskly. "I'll keep that in mind."

Acknowledging by the look in his eye that he too was aware of the undercurrent in our interchange, he let it pass.

I could see that many of our ward patients were "dumped" by more than one person. I remembered the intern I had replaced, who had left with hardly a backward glance. He seemed to leave no gap behind. No one ever mentioned him again—not the nurses, the patients, the resident, or the attending. I hadn't even noticed him around the hospital before I'd met him. Now that I knew him I saw him now and then, but without interest. While he wasn't impressive, he wasn't a troublemaker, either. He was capable, colorless, and safe. I found that I had no desire whatsoever to be like him.

I missed having a resident like Jerry Carter. My resident on the ward, Fred Manton, was not a man who made many friends, it seemed. He was a good administrator and kept the service well organized, but he seemed to be more interested in efficiency than anything else. With all the noise and activity on the wards, perhaps it was just as well.

14

Most of our patients were senile, like Mr. Smith, or abandoned, like Mr. Whittaker, or derelicts, alcoholics, addicts, or crazies. I'd thought the ward would be grim. But there was a striking quality of health and calm here; I think its source was the nursing staff. It was while I was examining my tenth alcoholic in three days that I saw that strength in action.

My patient was a skinny man named James Bradley, who looked sixty-five but insisted he was forty. From other physical evidence I guessed fifty-five would be closer to the mark, and in fact his driver's license said he was fifty-three. He wasn't a bum; he was one of the millions who are alcoholics and still maintain a superficially normal life, though he was beginning to have trouble holding down his job. Now his medical insurance had run out. He had long ago been divorced and was estranged from his children. He'd been in an accident and had been brought in for observation and drying out. He hadn't hurt anyone, just totaled his car.

After examining many alcoholics, I'd learned a trick to find out just how far gone a patient was. I held my hand up in the empty air, thumb and forefinger tipped together, and asked what color the string was. Often a patient would tell me a color, and even tie the string in a knot for me.

When I did it to him, Mr. Bradley gave me a startled look from his rheumy eyes. "There isn't any string there! Boy, *you* oughta be in bed, not me!"

"Okay, that's right, Mr. Bradley. You passed. There's a lot of alcohol in your bloodstream, though, and you're in a bad nutritional state, so we're going to give you fluid and sugar water via intravenous to hydrate you."

"Oh, no! Oh, no!" he said, scrunching back on the bed and drawing his legs up, hiding his arms between them and his scrawny chest.

"Well," I said reasonably, "that's really the only way we can build you up fast enough."

"Oh, no! Oh, no!" he kept jabbering, and I realized from his stare that he no longer heard me.

The impressive thing was that the ward nurse, who had been nearby but not so close that she could hear our words, sensed that something had gone wrong. She quietly appeared at Mr. Bradley's bedside opposite me. She took in his fear at a glance, then looked at me and tipped up her chin in a silent question; taking my silence as yes, she turned to him with complete attention.

She stood with her hands clasped at her waist, where he could see them, and spoke seriously. "Mr. Bradley. It looks like something has upset you. Can you tell me why?"

He was silent, trembling, but he was now gazing at her without the previous vacancy in his eyes.

She persisted, still upright and never making a move to touch him. "Mr. Bradley, can you understand what bothers you? If you can, can you tell me?"

He choked. "IV," he whispered.

"Ah." She nodded. "I understand. Have you ever had an IV before?"

He nodded yes.

"Was it unpleasant?"

Suddenly he nearly shrieked. "They did it when I wasn't looking! I woke up and there it was! Damn thing hurt so much I might've got gangrene."

"Did you take it out yourself then?"

"What? I'd bleed to death!"

"Listen to me now," she said. "I want to give you the information we all have had to learn." Then she went into one of the clearest, most complete descriptions of how an intravenous works—what veins you go for and why, the safety precautions and ability to

108

change location if there's discomfort for the patient. She must have noticed that he got pale a few times as she spoke, but she just continued, and by the time she had finished he was looking better. Finally, when she saw that he wasn't entirely convinced, she volunteered to have me stick her first if he would promise to do it after her.

I guess that challenged his honor or sportsmanship or masculinity, because he agreed. I was reluctant to stick her, because by now I was in awe of her. Then she took my arm for a moment, under the pretext of helping me with the paraphernalia, and pressed it briefly, and I became as cool as ever in the small transaction we were sharing.

When I put in the IV, I've never done it better. It was as smooth as anything.

Mr. Bradley looked faint, so the nurse told him to put his head between his knees because that happened to most people at first. Then she told him the story of watching her first operation and how 7 out of 17 nurses fainted, first one and then another around the glassed-in viewing theater, and how 12 out of 24 medical students did! I appreciated her saying this, though it was probably an exaggeration.

She said he didn't have to watch, that we'd go for the easiest one in the lower arm, and he had good veins; and with her talking and his cooperating, we got him attached to the IV in no time, reassured, sobering up, and dignified.

When I mentioned to her that I'd seen a lot of fear of the needle, she just grinned and told me most people were like that, at least at first.

Her name was Kathleen O'Connor. She wasn't the only impressive nurse on that service; all of the nurses seemed strong. However different their personal styles, they all seemed to take a pride in their work that in turn made the patients feel they must be worth it. The personalities and presence of nurses were felt in ways I'd never perceived on the private medical service. I didn't know what was missing until it was supplied by good nursing care—and also the nurses' support for *me*. I also discovered that the nurses knew more of what was happening to a patient and how best to deal with it than anybody else.

Kathleen was the first woman friend I'd found since medical school. When I looked back on it, I found it strange that I should have spent so much of my life without close women friends. Through college, working, and medical school I'd had women acquaintances, but my important relationships were with men: dating, marriage, supporting my husband's career, and then, after my divorce, trying to get through medical school where all the professors were men and 90 per cent of my classmates were men, and dating again. I didn't talk to women at parties, and other women weren't interested in talking to me, either, until the women's movement, which seemed to introduce us to one another again.

Working so closely with the nurses, and admiring how they handled their patients and themselves, I was able to relax on the ward service even though it was a grinding job. The nurses' station became a second home to me. There was a small, ill-furnished lounge behind it where doctors' rounds would sometimes be held, and the closet held a hot plate, an old toaster, tea, coffee, peanut butter, jelly, bread, and crackers. We used the juice refrigerator for our own juice, milk, and 7-Up. I would take a morning, an afternoon, and, if I were on, a late evening break there that would last as long as I could prolong it before some patient difficulty took me away again.

Kathleen O'Connor and I kidded each other a lot —that appealed to me. She was a woman in her forties, with reddish-gray hair that was frizzy the way hair gets when it turns gray. She wore it in a kind of thirties bob, not very becoming since she was a tall rectangular woman with an equally rectangular face. She must have come from *Anglo*-Irish peasant stock. The people of Irish descent whom I knew were small-featured with rounded facial outlines. I asked her about it, and she replied with a big laugh. "Ah," she said, putting on a beautiful but almost unintelligible

110

brogue, "the way of the tyrant, no one else speaks of that blood among us, but the devil himself knows the evil we endured." Beneath her grin and ribaldry her voice was low and liquid, like a stone beneath cold water.

"Kathleen," I said, "are you telling me some British infantryman raped a great-grandmother of yours?"

"Doctor," she mimicked me, still in brogue, "are *you* askin' me such a question? I didn't take you for a dummox.

"Sure," she went on, "it must have happened many times, don't you think? And maybe once or twice there was love in it."

She had a charm with words and was very well informed about Irish history. When I asked her if she'd learned it in school, she laughed. There'd been a young Sister who told her pupils tales from the old mythology once a week at sewing time, speaking softly as though the tales were contraband. Kathleen's father and her father's friend Tip propounded to one another strategies in the crises of the Irish past, getting drunker as they progressed in their debates. Her grandmother described *her* grandmother's life on a little farm in the west of Ireland, short reproving tales to show them how much they had to be grateful for —though Kathleen had always thought the life must have been grand, except for the starving—and when they lay together in bed at night, Kathleen and her sister made up stories of themselves as maiden schoolteachers living together in a stone house with a view of the sea, beautiful, sparkling, and green and caressing and treacherous.

Kathleen's family was broken up now, the grandmother dead long ago from a large tumor swelling her belly like a pregnancy, the father dead from drink, the mother dead from exhaustion. The eight children were scattered over the country and hardly heard from one another now. She could tell me what each one had been doing a year ago for sure, but nothing more recent. When I asked her whether that bothered her, she shrugged and said, "Oh, you know how it is."

One day I was sitting with Kathleen, Harriet Jackson, and two other nurses, drinking coffee in the lounge, and Kathleen asked me, "How did you get to be a doctor?"

I was about to blurt out airily that it was the most natural thing in the world, given my training and stubbornness, when second thoughts made me nearly inhale the hot drink. I saved myself from drowning by gulping down a large mouthful, burning my mouth, and making myself choke and cough.

They all burst out laughing, and Kathleen quickly came over and started thumping me on the back while I, bent over, hacked any droplets out of my larynx. By the time my throat had calmed down and my airways felt clear, my face had become beet red, no doubt, and tears were squeezing out of my eyes.

"Hey, you didn't have to hit so hard!" I protested to Kathleen. "Anybody got a Kleenex? I gotta blow my nose."

Harriet handed me a small, hospital-sized tissue box. "You don't even have any tissues," she mocked me. "You can't do anything without us."

I smiled. "Damn right!" I said, and blew my nose with a honk. "Every morning when I come in, I check to make sure Evelyn is in a passably good mood so she won't bite my head off"—Evelyn was the mildest-mannered, shyest-appearing nurse on the floor—"find out whether Ruth has gone to bed with Hank yet and embarrassed the whole ward"—Hank was an orderly in the ER who had a crush on Ruth and tried to hang around, speechlessly gazing at her, whenever he brought a case up to us. The nurses now were giggling and laughing and beginning to move around to rinse out their mugs and get back to work. "I see how many drug addicts Harriet has scheduled for me to IV," I continued, and Harriet smiled because she was the best vein-threader in the hospital and often had to do the difficult ones, like the addicts who'd used up all their good veins. "I'm at your mercy," I concluded to them. "But you better watch out; I'm going to learn everything you know among you,

112

and then I'll be Superdoc, and you'll have to try to get on the good side of me." I went on down the hall and we split up, going to our next duties, all in good humor.

I depended on these women, I trusted them to be responsible and effective, and I respected them. And they had asked me how come I, who was a woman like them, was in the superior, privileged position of a doctor while they were just nurses. When Kathleen had asked that question, the four of them, sitting casually on a torn vinyl sofa or typing chairs and holding heavy dimestore mugs of hot coffee, had turned their faces to me and waited, their eyes expressionless.

I thought I had become very close to Kathleen. She was the one, really, who gave me my first information on hospital gossip—rivalries, affairs, medical mischances, mistakes, and saves. We discussed men sometimes, and it helped to talk with her about my divorce, though I thought I put that all behind me five years ago; and we talked about sex. We laughed a lot and joked. But she never broke through the doctor/nurse barrier to ask me to her house for dinner or anything. I invited her a couple of times, but she made up obvious false excuses. And if I was leaving the hospital at the same time she was and her husband was picking her up, she didn't introduce me to him.

That separation from Kathleen outside the hospital was prophetic of what would happen to all my relationships.

Down the hall from our men's ward was a women's ward. About 3:30 each afternoon there was a flurry of activity in our ward. After half an hour, the ambulatory patients would get their fellows' wheelchairs out and push them into the TV lounge, a former porch attached to the end of the ward. The ones left in bed felt abandoned. One man called out unintelligible encouragement, while others made equally incomprehensible bitter complaints.

Then almost the whole women's ward came stately through the men's ward. In the lead were always two

113

women, both very upright though neither was more than five feet tall, dressed neatly in their hospital bathrobes and carrying large navy blue purses. Behind them came a phalanx of female ward patients, some in wheelchairs like their male counterparts, some pushing the wheelchairs. Alll had neat gray or gray-blue hair. A few chatted and giggled in small discreet voices as if they were heading for a reception.

It was a pleasure to watch them go by, walking as though on promenade on Sunday afternoon: some in bathrobes, some with coats on, but all with a kind of sweet pleasure or shy anticipation on their faces, heading through the hushed men's ward for the sunporch and an hour of television and male companionship before dinner.

On some days we could not allow them to pass through because a patient was receiving a certain kind of procedure, like the insertion of a Foley catheter. In that case. the ladies might crowd up to the doors and one of us would have to shoo them away; they'd scatter like birds.

About a week after I'd been on Ward Medicine, I got a vague call to stop in Room 532, a presurgery room, before I left for the night. It was not a staff call. When I did manage to get there at about 7:30, I saw with pleasure that sitting upright in bed with the air of a monarch was Mr. Witowski!

"Hey, Mr. Witowski!" I said, walking over to him eagerly, "why'd you run out on me?"

He laughed. "Dr. Donnan, believe me, it's a pleasure to see your young and beautiful face again."

We laughed at his compliment. I asked him what he was doing back in the hospital. I'd thought I'd never see him again.

Seriously he said, "Well, you told me what I have, and Honneker says I got to get cut, so of course I'm here."

"But—you signed yourself out before."

"Didn't I tell you I had things to do?" He paused for my reply.

114

"Yes, you did, but . . ."

"Well, now I done 'em. I'm ready now for what has to be done." He looked at me as if he were saying the most reasonable thing in the world.

"What were the things you had to do?" I asked with sincere curiosity. When he hesitated, I quickly told him he didn't have to tell me if he didn't want to; I didn't want to pry.

But he did tell me. Quietly, he listed the things he had arranged in the interval. He'd made a will, which he had never done. He'd put his bank accounts, his house, and his car into his wife's name. He'd made his children the beneficiaries of his insurance. He'd sold the last interest in his firm and put the proceeds into a trust for his grandchildren. He'd left written instructions for his wife about his wishes for a funeral and burial. He'd discussed all of their finances with her as he'd never done before, taught her what he could, and made sure she met the lawyer he had just retained.

"But Mr. Witowski!" I protested. "You're not going to die!"

"Come, come," he replied. "Looks like I can teach you something, Doc."

"What?"

"Listen," he explained. "I'll tell you like you were my granddaughter herself. You tell me I got cancer. This is a bad disease, right? Let me tell you, I feel better to fight it if I got everything arranged so it don't hurt my wife and family if I lose the fight. I'm a sixty-seven-year-old man. I go into the operating room for this doctor to open up my chest. Who knows what all he will find? Who knows if he finds all of it? Who knows if I will live through the goddamn operation? You want me to go into all these risks without arranging my affairs? I been a happy man all my life. I lived like I would never die. Well, I was ignorant, it's never too late to learn. You don't make an estimate on finishing a house without giving some leeway for bad weather, shortages, labor problems. So, the same with this; I'm not going into this without giving some leeway. That's all it is. Now, sis, don't you go thinking I've gone crazy."

I had to laugh at the tone he took with me. He was even patting his stomach as if he might just like to be patting my hand.

"Well," I said, "you're all right."

We talked some more. His operation was scheduled for the next morning. He was as calm about it now as he had been troubled about the tests before. I was amazed at the transformation. I filed it away to be understood later. In spite of his explanation of something that seemed self-evident to him, I didn't understand it then, but I had the feeling that eventually I would.

He came through the operation quite well, in spite of his heart murmur, which had turned out not to be innocent, but due to a valve affected by rheumatic disease, probably from a strep throat as a child. I visited him several times when I could take a few minutes at my lunch break or after hours or while I was on in the evening. The surgeon thought he had gotten all of the cancer because it had been contained in one lobe and had not spread to any draining lymph nodes and he had a hopeful prognosis.

Mr. Witowski was as cheerful a man as you'd ever hope to see, and once or twice when I walked into his room I surprised him and his wife huddling together, lost in low-voiced conversation, enthusiastically comparing travel folders of Europe. They said they were bound and determined to visit Venice before it sank out of sight.

I should have known, when I'd received his roses, that Mr. Witowski would be all right. But he reminded me of my awkwardnesses on Private Medicine.

I'd be walking down a long featureless corridor going for somebody's records, or I'd be pushing a patient's wheelchair past holding rooms and cubicles on the lab floor, or I'd be rolling a vein under my thumb to check its resiliency, and I'd see a scene from the days on Private Medicine, which seemed so long ago, and marvel at my brash callowness.

116

I was more introspective than before, in flashes. I spent a lot of time just walking down long halls; in the past I'd have been going over the routine, the procedures, the diagnostic possibilities. Now I'd learned enough that I didn't need to be compulsively repetitive to make sure I made no medical mistakes. Often I looked back over the patients I'd been in charge of. I could say that I'd made no awful mistakes, except for Foley. He had not been heard from since.

In fact, I was remembering Foley as I sat companionably drinking coffee with Kathleen and Harriet one late afternoon during visiting hours.

"What's the matter?" asked Harriet. "You're breathing like a stuck pig."

"Oh, Christ," I said, embarrassed.

"Hey," said Kathleen softly, leaning to look at me. "What is it, Phyl?"

I looked at them and wondered whether I could discuss a case with them that I'd failed on.

"Oh, it's just a case I was remembering."

"You look like it must have been tough," said Kathleen sympathetically.

"Well—yeah, I guess it was."

"Where was it?" asked Harriet. "Here?"

"Here in the hospital, yes, but not on the ward."

They didn't press me. And then because they were quiet, I simply took the initiative and presented the case, just as I'd have done on rounds, straightforwardly and unemotionally.

The two nurses listened attentively to my presentation and then sat for a moment in silence.

"You know," began Harriet hesitantly, "he reminds me of that guy we had last year, do you remember, Kath?"

"What was his name?" Kathleen mused. "He came in every now and then, you see. He had an irregular heartbeat that would terrify some green Emergency Room resident and convince him he needed to be admitted right away and get a cardiac workup. The man went back and forth between us and University. They were always glad to send his record over to us—

117

Hallett, that was his name!" she recalled triumphantly.

"That's right," said Harriet. "And when he came here the last time, he'd just been over at University. Secondary syphilis—they'd started him on penicillin there." Secondary meant he'd had it for at least a year.

Kathleen and Harriet identified him to one another with the same command of medical facts that I'd come to expect of them as well as of myself.

"Boy, what a nuisance!" Kathleen went on. "Everybody cringed when he came on the ward."

"Why?" I asked.

"He had a really loud voice," Kathleen said, "and nothing suited him. He'd lie there, you see, and complain." She began a masterful imitation of a hard, querulous old voice: " 'Nobody can tell me what's wrong with this heart of mine, nobody. I been to twenty hospitals. I been to hospitals in Houston, St. Louis, Chicago, Baltimore. I been all over. Nobody can find out the story on my heart. None! Believe me, I been to the best, and they are all mystified.' "

We were laughing. "God, was he boring," Harriet said.

"Yes, but do you remember how he'd give a little imitation of his heart?" Kathleen grinned. "He'd say, 'You listen to it here, and it goes de-*bee*-bip, and you listen over here, and it sounds like bum-de-dum-de-dum. If you stick around long enough, you can hear *pum-pum-pum*-peepee-*pum!*'"

"We couldn't get him to shut up," Harriet laughed. "As soon as he could, the resident got rid of him. He said Mr. Hallett should never have been admitted in the first place."

The two women were playing a joke back and forth between them now. Kathleen said, "He got rid of him, all right!"

Harriet said, "Mr. Hallett proved he should have been admitted, after all!"

"Why?" I said, ready for the punch line.

Kathleen explained, "It was some poor student nurse, her first day on the ward. She had to give him

118

his penicillin shot before we discharged him. He was standing by his bed getting dressed, saying, 'There. I told you so. I knew they wouldn't be able to figure it out.' He bent over for her, she injected him in the hip, and just as she was taking the needle out he grabbed his chest, choked out, 'What the hell—' and fell over on the bed."

"Arrested," supplied Harriet, meaning that his heart had stopped.

"So the proof of needing to be admitted is dying." Kathleen laughed ruefully.

They told me he couldn't be resuscitated; they couldn't get air into his lungs. Probably a penicillin reaction, though it couldn't be proved by the autopsy. "Poor bastard," said Kathleen. "The doctors are still mystified!"

"What do you guess happened to my diabetic? Any idea?" I asked.

Kathleen answered without thinking twice. "He went to University Hospital."

"You know that for a fact?" I asked, relief showing in my voice.

"Nope. But I know the type. He'll tell them over at University what lousy care he got here, and they'll take him in and fix him up a little better than you had a chance to, and he'll sign himself out of there and complain about the treatment he got there, too. You'll learn not to listen to patient's complaints about another doctor. You can fall for it at first," she warned.

Kathleen had helped to lessen my guilt, but not to get rid of it. Maybe it was good for a doctor to have a tiny hook in his or her arrogance, the reminder that she really hadn't handled a patient well at all.

When I was checking Mr. Whittaker's tubes the following day I detected a difference in his breathing. There was a rasp in his throat and some movement. He was trying to swallow. Excited by this sign of his reactions returning, I called the nurses to come and see.

Then I charged the two men on either side of him

to keep an eye on him and call someone if they saw any change. The patients on the ward were usually quite reliable observers.

It was the man in the next bed who told the night nurse that he had heard the old man moaning and making gurgling sounds, and she came over with her flashlight, checked him, and when she saw that he was almost awake, got him to understand that he had a nasal tube in him, not to panic, that he could swallow, and that she'd sit by him while he had his wits about him. She pulled the curtains around his bed and turned on his lamp so he could see her if he opened his eyes, and then she sat with him with her hand over his so he could feel it until he seemed to sleep.

When I came on at 6:30 the next morning it was the first thing the nurse told me, and it became the focus of rounds. The attending took the occasion to give a long lecture on the tenacity of life, required me to present any readings from Mr. Whittaker's chart that would have predicted his regaining consciousness, and went on to inspire us with several stories of miraculous remissions and revivings that had occurred in his experience.

We were all quite high that morning. As soon as I could escape from rounds and other duties I went to Mr. Whittaker's bed, prepared to stay there for hours waiting for him to wake up. When I got there he was already wide awake, staring up at the ceiling with a bewildered look on his face.

"Mr. Whittaker!" I cried, perhaps startling him a little.

He tried to turn his head, but the tube prevented it.

"Ah," I said, "it's good to have you back."

"You're probably distressed about the nasogastric tube. I'll take care of that right now." Propping him up a little straighter, I carefully removed the tape and the long tube and quickly disposed of them. I cleaned his face. I held the glass of water and a straw for him to drink no more than a sip at first to moisten his mouth and throat.

His eyes closed with a flutter of the lids, and he let out a long, feeble sigh.

"I'm very pleased," I said to him quietly, "that you're recovering. You're probably tired; get some rest now. Everybody will be happy to help you whenever you need anything."

He was already asleep, and I stood looking down at his body as small as a boy's, feeling a kind of tender delight that he was safe.

15

The prison ward was on the same floor as my open ward, but at the end of the building, behind three locked and barred doors. One of my occasional duties was to draw bloods there.

Most of these men were or had been drug addicts, and had used up all their veins. The only place that I could try was the vein deep in a man's groin. There were no curtains to pull around the beds in the prison ward, so the procedure took place in full, but distant, view of everyone in the ward. It looked like a man dropping his pants whereupon I did something to his genitals.

The first time I came on the prison ward, I was greeted with a roar of ahs and tart whistles. When they saw what I was doing, the tumult increased, with wisecracks and hoots.

I felt hot. The man I was working on lay there with a grin on his face, now and then uttering a hammy sigh as if I were really doing a good job on him. For a procedure that took about two minutes from start to finish, they got an awful lot of mileage out of it.

I tried to calm them down by telling them exactly what I was doing, but they pretended not to believe me. So the next time I had to do it I had my own trick ready.

Peering at the man's penis, I said, "Well, well, well. Huh!"—as though I'd seen something interesting.

The man was instantly concerned. "What is it?" he said. He didn't assume I was admiring his endowment; in this setting, at least, the first reaction was anxiety.

"Oh . . . Well, I don't know what it is," I'd reply in a judicious but slightly puzzled tone.

"Where? Let me see."

"I don't think you can see it from your angle." There was a heavy, suspenseful pause; then, when he started to ask something, I said, "I think I'll just make a note of it."

"What does it look like?" By this time he was really tense—not to mention that his penis was as limp and small as a worm.

"Hmmm. Kind of pinkish-bluish-yellowish. I'll tell your resident about it," I went on, suddenly brisk, "and he'll follow it up—if he thinks it's serious."

"Okay. I'd sure appreciate it."

I was able to pull this on four men because the minute I started, he'd want to keep the conversation quiet and private. At last, however, when there was no promised follow-up and no one could feel anything on himself, they caught on. They didn't bother me so much after that, though, maybe because they didn't agree on how to react to my trick. Some were amused and admired me, some were resentful, some were just embarrassed and wanted to avoid me.

I sometimes had to draw bloods in the police and firemen's ward upstairs. I never had any problem there, both because curtains could give me privacy, and because these men were not on drugs, so they had good veins in their arms. These men were more often in for alcohol-related problems.

In the meantime, my affair with Dennis Danes was going smoothly.

Unfortunately the hospital was full of gossip about anybody's affairs, and I had to listen in silence whenever Dennis was mentioned, which seemed excessively often.

Once, at afternoon break, Kathleen remarked, "I saw Dr. Danes the other day, jogging along the path beside the river."

"Oh?" said I.

"That man," she continued, "takes care of his body as though he were a racehorse."

"What does he do?" I was elaborately casual and uninterested.

She began to tell me about the care he took with his diet and the exercises he religiously performed—even doing isometrics in the operating room and wearing isotoner driving gloves. I let her go on and on, fascinated with new evidence of my lover's physical mastery.

"You sound a little critical of him," I observed.

"Oh—" She stopped. "I guess I am. I'm suspicious of a man who pays so much attention to himself."

"Oh, come on, Kathleen," I teased her. "You're attracted to him yourself."

"Now don't you be saying such things," she replied in some confusion, laughing. "I'm an old married woman . . ."

"So what?"

She spoke almost at the same moment. "But that don't prevent a girl from havin' ideas, now does it?" she joked.

After a moment of laughter she went on. "You know, he spent his residency here, and he was the bane of the nurses' existence."

"He was after them all the time?"

"No, not so much. He was still married then, before he came to be known as the Screw King, and didn't move around so fast. No, what he did that drove the student nurses out of their minds was to sun-bathe on the roof outside the residents' rooms.

123

It's right across the alley from the nurses' dormitory, you know."

"Yes?"

"Well, he was always doin' his sun-bathing in the nude, you see, and he put one of those molded paper surgical masks over his genitals, you know, and there he lay, stretched out with that big handsome body of his, and a big blue codpiece on him that made you think he was as big as all that underneath."

I laughed. I could appreciate the turn-on. Of course he did it on purpose. I had a new concept: a cunt-teaser.

"Did any of the nurses ever stand at her window and strip, just to see if he'd raise the boom in salute?"

"Phyllis!" Kathleen mock-reproved me. "We were all modest girls then. Not an impure thought ever crossed our minds!"

"Kathleen," I informed her, "you must have been born on the Blarney Stone."

"Ah," she said, "and hard it was on me puir mither."

When I teased Dennis later about his nickname, the Screw King, all he did was to raise his eyebrows. "It's a royal title, don't you think?" he smirked.

Mr. Whittaker had been recovering steadily. Paralyzed on the left side, he was still confined to bed and would never leave it, even out of the hospital. He became something like the ward mascot, which pleased him very much. Ambulatory patients would clasp the toes or foot of his good leg for luck as they went by, whether on their way for tests or just getting through another day. I asked who'd started that, and Whittaker himself answered that it had been one of the junkies who came in for two days and then disappeared off the ward. He'd been an eighteen-year-old kid, pimply and nervous.

"He'll be back," the old man said. "Mark my words, he'll be back."

"You're a wise man, Mr. Whittaker," I commented. He laughed, the cackle of an old man. "You can

124

call me Al," he permitted me. "All the other docs do."

It was true, both children and old people were invariably called by their first names. Most women patients, as well, were called by their first names. It was the rare doctor or nurse who used the formal name for such patients, and it seemed that the patients thought you were cold or timid if you didn't address them familiarly. I felt most comfortable calling a patient the respectful name, letting him know by my *manner* that I was deeply concerned for his health. I made a game of remembering each patient I'd had back through medical school, what I'd called him, and what it meant. Most recently, I'd used the first name usually for someone I didn't respect. Mr. Witowski was Mister, but I'd call Mr. Foley "Foley" because we were fighting. I wondered whether other doctors used names similarly.

Al Whittaker had the curiosity of a child about what was going on around him. He never volunteered anything about his former life, and he never had any visitors. He didn't talk a great deal, but he sometimes reported on a particular procedure that merited his observation, like drawing blood and how that went, a barium swallow and fluoroscope series someone had had done, physical therapy on the ward, how somebody took care of his false teeth.

Some of his descriptions would have everyone laughing, such as the one from his own experience about the proctoscopic and sigmoidoscopic exam—that is, the examination of the rectum and lower bowel— and the compromising position the table cranks you into. "Just a step on the lever," he said, like a demonstrator, "and the machinery whirs, and then all of a sudden you feel yourself bending, bending until your ass is higher than your nose, you feel the guts sag inside you, the proctologist cranks open your ass with a little metal instrument as cold as the devil's dick, and then he goes into that there windy cavern with a long, thin flashlight, looking for gold." He cackled. The scatological humor on the ward was both boyish and

125

ribald, and the men laughed uproariously at Al's graphic description of "the spelunking expedition *you* might go on but were mercifully spared since the good Lord hadn't made it possible for a man to see up his own ass."

His stories would exhaust as well as please him, and Al would fall asleep as the laughter died down. He took catnaps throughout the day.

My increasing confidence was compromised by the tension many of us were feeling as we waited to hear whether our applications for residencies next year had been acted on. I think it's unfortunate that a doctor has to decide on a program so early. We haven't even begun our internship when we have to apply for a residency in a specialty. Many of us have already decided on the complete program while we're still in medical school. I was more fortunate than many of my colleagues in not having anyone financially or emotionally dependent on me, so I could afford to postpone my decision for another year.

I was told that Grey's would have asked me to be a medical resident if I had wanted to, which pleased me very much.

I was intrigued by the research being done in one particular lab, and had applied to work there. Located in another city in a complex of good hospitals, it was doing very interesting work on immunological problems related to cancer. My own lab experience as well as my medical background had trained me well for this research. I wouldn't find out until December whether its grant had been funded.

I suddenly realized with a chill that many of my patients had had cancer.

Harriet seemed disappointed that I hadn't chosen a residency at Grey's. She and Kathleen had been impassioned critics of all the other hospitals we were applying to. They were formidable partisans of Grey's, and it amused me to hear them describe how badly one hospital's OR service was run, what a disruptive effect on morale all the sexual promiscuity at another was having, and how stupidly the architect had planned another's storage space. When they challenged me, not without irony, to stay on at Grey's where everything was perfect, I laughed with them. I could only explain that I hadn't made up my mind yet; besides, I'd already spent the last ten years of my life in that town, and it was time to move.

One night the Emergency Room called me to admit a man named Frank Murphy. He stood tall before me and confidently stated: "I'm admitted because I have SBE and I need antibiotic therapy."

I stared at him. "How do you know?" I asked. SBE means subacute bacterial endocarditis, an inflammation of the lining of the heart.

"Well," he explained, "whenever I have this fever, that's what it means. I been to the clinic and they drew blood and they said I got to come in."

"How'd you get it?" I inquired, going along with his nonchalance.

"I been on dope off and on ten years," he explained airily. Then he looked earnestly at me and frowned. "But I'm off now, I swear to God!"

The heart damage he'd received from contaminated heroin was a development common to drug addiction. After nine years almost all addicts will manifest this disease. He seemed knowledgeable and cooperative. My examination supported his diagnosis, which he'd probably gotten from some other doctor, of course. I found small spots on the retinas of his eyes, splinter hemorrhages in his fingernails, and a heart murmur not noted in previous exams. He seemed familiar with the hospital and its procedures. I admitted him, and he walked quietly beside me down the long corridor to the ward.

The lights were bright in the examining room, but it was dark on the wards in the middle of the night. One of the night nurses and I got the new patient to bed next to a man snoring gently and irregularly.

"What about the IV, Doc? I'll cooperate with you. I

still got a couple good veins left," he admitted disarmingly.

"Ssssh," I hushed him. "I'll start your IV after I've decided what the best antibiotic is."

He looked disappointed, though I couldn't be sure in the faint illumination of his overhead night light.

"Just take it easy," I said.

"Okay," he said grumpily.

It took me about fifteen minutes to get to the point of starting the IV. Mr. Murphy visibly relaxed, turned over as though he wasn't bothered by the tube, and went to sleep.

When we stopped by his bed during morning rounds, he gave a friendly smile to the resident and in turn looked at me in a way that implied sympathy. Fred Manton and I agreed to make Mr. Murphy's intravenous an intercath, a plastic sheath over the needle. He was going to need a lot of medication and every three or four days we'd have to change the vein. As we passed his bed I glanced back at him and he winked.

After rounds, I noted that he was sweating and trembling and that he'd made several trips to the toilet already that morning, pushing his IV pole along with him. "You're just coming out of it," I accused him sharply.

He agreed with me immediately, smiling sheepishly. "Can't put anything over on you, can I?"

His cooperative manner encouraged me. If he'd brought any dope with him, he could have managed to slip something into the line before this. He would have used my needle and line for his fix.

"Now listen," I told him. "You are not going to use this intravenous."

"What? What do you mean?" he asked innocently.

"You know what I mean?" I said. "What are you on now?"

"I'm not on anything," he whined.

"What did you have before you came in last night?"

He appeared to give up. "Oh, all right. Can't fool you, can I? I had five bags."

"That's all?" What was on the market at that time

was diluted, so five small glassine bags wouldn't hold much. (One of the dangers of addiction is the variation in concentration of the drugs available. Whenever the quality "improved" we'd get several deaths from overdoses.)

He said, "You know," shrugging his shoulders. "I just had to give me something to make it easier, you know?"

"Now you listen here," I warned him. "You're not using this hospital for a pit stop. If I catch you using my line for anything, I'll kick you out."

"Awwww," he pouted, putting on another act with mischievous eyes.

"Listen," I told him, "I mean it. I'll let you smoke grass, if you've got to have something. But I will not let you mainline here. Got it?"

He sighed. "Okay, Godmother."

I was going to have to check his urine every day to see if he was getting anything. At that time, taken in by his frankness and cooperation, I thought all that I'd heard against addicts was doctors' prejudice. I hoped that by being firm with him I could help Frank Murphy. When I explained it all earnestly to Kathleen, she said only that I'd learn for myself.

16

Before I left that afternoon, I noticed that Frank Murphy wasn't in his bed. Kathleen told me he'd just walked off down the corridor five minutes before, pretending not to hear her when she called out to him. As I stood there discussing him he reappeared. When he saw me, he gave me a jaunty smile and continued back to his bed.

I followed him. "I'm going to check your urine, you know," I warned him.

He opened his eyes big and wide. "Of course," he said, suspiciously cheerful.

I left orders for a male nurse to watch him whenever he urinated and collect samples. The next morning they showed no sign of drugs. His jauntiness, I guessed, was just natural. Why he'd depend on drugs if his nature was cheerful, I couldn't tell.

It was Kathleen, wise in the ways of the ward men, who watched him closely. The next day she spied him substituting another man's urine bag for his own. The analysis of his *own* urine showed a healthy concentration of methadone.

Kathleen, Fred Manton, and I had a conference with Mr. Murphy. He wouldn't tell us where he'd found the methadone, but it was likely he'd gotten it in the hospital. We asked him where the rest of the drug was hidden.

He spread his hands and shrugged. "What?" he asked innocently.

"You probably have enough to last you a couple of days," said Dr. Manton. "Where is it?"

"You cats are crazy."

"Come on," I said, "don't jive us."

"Why, Momma, I ain't jivin' you."

To intimidate him, we got two policemen to come and search him. They found a packet of marijuana taped under his bed, but that was all. They asked if we wanted them to bust him, but we said no. He needed the antibiotic therapy for his SBE, and I had after all given him permission to smoke pot. When we threatened him with the prison ward, he seemed to shape up for a while.

I was especially annoyed because he had managed to manipulate me. I saw that drug addicts could be very ingratiating, especially at first, but they were sneaky. I'd been warned about their using our IVs to shoot themselves up, and I'd seen Mr. Murphy do the urine-bag switch. I was told that another trick was when they taped an extra bag of urine to their backs

130

with a tube down to their penis; they could urinate into the pan right in front of you and you'd swear it was coming from their penis at that very minute, when it was actually stored-up normal urine. They'd wander out of the hospital, too, saying they had to collect a welfare check and then come back high.

Frank Murphy had a mood swing that was as untrustworthy as his patient behavior. He'd chat to the man in the bed next to him, having very serious discussions about life and life-styles. He recommended drugs to everyone; he had a treasury of information and described the specific effects of each drug and how they varied. He told the next man that he really ought to try it—he could use the IV—and a high would do him a world of good.

Then, that very evening, he might do something like rip the tape off and pull the needle out of his arm. The hammer I used to test reflexes disappeared. I'm certain he stole it for no reason at all since it was worth maybe four dollars, though he swore he didn't. He'd get mad at the food if it wasn't something he liked or if it wasn't cooked to his satisfaction. Once he complained about somebody's snoring and woke everybody up in the middle of the night yelling at the poor man; the nurse discovered that he'd disconnected himself again.

It was very irritating when he got his IV out because he didn't have many good veins left, so it was hard to get the needle back in. After five days, even his periods of friendly behavior failed to soften my attitude toward him; when he wandered over to the nurses' station at 2:30 A.M., while I was writing up another middle-of-the-night admission, and wanted to talk with me, however soft and serious he seemed to be, I told him to get the hell back to bed. The middle of the night was no time for conversation. I was working.

He swaggered back into the dim ward. "Okay, okay, Momma," he said. "No hassle."

There was another way in which Mr. Murphy was obnoxious on the ward. He had very noisy visitors. The nurses and sometimes the doctor would often have to tell them to keep it down. They might be quiet again for a couple of minutes, but then they'd break out again into laughter and loud talk.

We tried to limit the number of visitors to one per patient, but Mr. Murphy's visitors always managed to slip in somehow.

One evening in particular I noticed that he had four visitors around his bed, so I called out that three of them would have to go.

"Hey, no, Missus! Hey, just two? Huh?" they replied, turning to look at me and moving about the bed.

A half-hour later there were no visitors at his bed; he was lying back on his pillows with his eyes closed and a smile on his face.

When he hadn't moved, hadn't complained, hadn't burst out into some erratic behavior or talk by lights-out, the nurse went over and found he was dead.

Apparently Frank Murphy had died from an overdose, given him by his friends. We had to bring the police in before we could move him, and the ward was awake, in the darkness, with curiosity and excitement. We made a cubicle around his bed to shut out prying eyes, but every man on that ward, flat on his back or sitting up, was straining to hear what was being said. It might have been an accident, but it could have been murder.

No one regretted his death, not even the other two junkies who were crashing here rather than in the drug clinic because of their medical problems. Even when he is suffering the most, an addict's arrogance blinds him to the relevance of another addict's disaster to his own life.

It took only about fifteen minutes for the police to be satisfied with evidence and photographs, the flash from which must have flickered dimly all through the ward. Then we quickly put Mr. Murphy on a cart, and an orderly wheeled him down to the morgue for the autopsy.

There was enough heroin in his blood to kill him, that was sure, and the next thing was to track down and question the men who'd been visiting him at 7:00 that evening.

It all had the air of a TV show. Yet the ward was too shabby for TV, too odorous. When Frank died, he had urinated. That small stink was part of the constant background odor of feces in the ward. Shit, vomit, urine—there was always something imprinting the air. Nor did the patients have the faces you'd see on television. The most important difference between actors and real people is teeth. It isn't just that actors' teeth tend to be straight, it's that actors tend to *have* teeth. Teeth fill out the flesh in your face. When the face gets old and sags it will reveal any gaps underneath. The body of someone lacking teeth will not be well enough nourished and therefore will be weak. These people looked limp. Only the neatness and cleanliness of the ward and the ubiquitous presence of good nurses and staff people were similar to TV. But we all looked compulsive, worried, and overworked.

The comparison occurred to me because the outside world was going to hold a trial on the death of Frank Murphy. We talked about the trial as if it were something we might see on the tube. I, Fred Manton, and several of the nurses were going to have to testify. The patients who were to give depositions were the most excited of all. The trial was set so far in the future that the district attorney came down right after the arrest of two men to tape the patients' evidence for fear they would forget it or die before the indictment.

It was like Christmas and *Perry Mason* and a seventh-grade Boy Scout bull session all rolled into one. Everybody was quietly sitting bolt upright in bed, gleaming with a special morning scrub, when the district attorney and some other man walked into the ward. A sigh—of relief or anticipation—was heard. The patients leaned over toward one another to whisper and murmur conspiratorially. When the officials walked to the beds of the two deponents, the patients beamed and opened their eyes wide with pleasure.

133

The introductions went smoothly, the two patients seemed to calm down, and the DA's assistant got the tape recorder set up. Then the DA started the questioning, supposedly first of one man, then of the other.

It was incredible to see and hear the engine of the ward slowly crank itself up, catch, and soon whir, whang, and clank around the room, out of control. First the man who was being questioned answered, but at his third or fourth answer the other witness corrected him; then the first went on, the second interrupted again, somebody else disagreed, others put in their opinions, somebody else suggested a new theory, here and there two men started arguing with one another, and somebody called out to the district attorney what he had noticed particularly about the visitors that evening. When they were told to be quiet, they would cease for a minute, but they were so excited they'd pipe right up again. I think that the only people who weren't talking finally were Mr. Smith, whose brain was gone, and an alcoholic who'd been brought in the night before, who fortunately was in the sodden, stuporous state that alternated with raving.

When I looked up and saw several of the women from the other ward peeking around the doors, I suggested to the resident and the questioners that we move our informants to the lounge and continue the questions there. This involved detaching some tubes and wires and wheeling the two men's beds into the sunroom and closing the door. Only then could the district attorney proceed.

The memory of Frank Murphy was as evanescent as he was. The ward men talked some about the death, and more about their own perceptions and speculations for a few days, then the uproar subsided.

When the trial finally took place I was on an entirely different service, and the whole episode had faded in my memory sufficiently that I could be only moderately helpful myself. The fact was that I hadn't paid much attention to the men who had visited

Mr. Murphy, and I couldn't make a positive identification. The prosecution's theory was that it was a small-scale gangland killing, that Frank Murphy, who'd been dealing in a bush league way, had simply been put out of commission. The two "friends" might be indicted later on drug charges, but murder couldn't be proven. They were acquitted.

Al Whittaker had been especially delighted with the temporary excitement but was not doing as well as his good spirits suggested. Lying in one position for so long and being so emaciated, he was developing an awful bedsore. The nurses did their best, moving him to different positions, keeping his skin clean, and padding him, but it was no good. There were several ulcerated places on his bony rear end, and one spot was getting raw, oozing a serous mixture of serum, blood, and pus in spite of bandages and ointment. I was getting worried about him. Tough little geezer though he was, he would once in a while announce to the ward that his ass was red, white, and blue and hurt like hell. I called in a surgical consult.

Two surgical residents came over, took a careful look, and told me he needed to have the whole area opened up, debrided, and left open to the air. To debride is to remove pus and dead tissue to get down to the pebbly, red tissue that is raw and bleeds when you get to it because it is growing.

When I told Al, he groaned, but the next day he went spunkily enough. Everybody had to rub his foot extra well before his bed could be pushed out of the ward. A surgical orderly came down, and he pushed the bed while I walked beside it, holding Al's lightweight body to the bed as we negotiated ramps and the elevator on the way to Surgery. Hs operation was scheduled for 2:00 P.M., the last case on the OR schedule, because it was an infected case, a "dirty" operation. Al enjoyed getting out of the ward; he complained that the elevator ride to the ninth floor was too short.

They didn't get started until 4:00, and he lay in

the corridor all that while. I checked him a couple of times, and he always seemed cheerful. The operation lasted a half-hour.

Al came back from Surgery in worse shape than when I sent him over. His backside had been almost flayed open, and he was in a great deal of pain. A framework for a big tent around the area was attached to his bed, with a regular light bulb inside, to help healing.

But the huge areas of exposed skin became infected nevertheless.

I gave him antibiotics intravenously. I had to keep ahead of his infection, fight it down, return him to his observant, lively self. I had to rescue him from the danger I had helped put him in by calling in the surgical consult.

Often during the day I would check the IV solution; once a day I would check the blood count. I would quickly inspect his wound—the large area of raw and oozing flesh that was so tender you could hardly have breathed on it without causing him pain—but of course you wouldn't breathe on such an infected wound. Every time I walked into the room my eyes would turn involuntarily to the fifth bed and the angular outline of Al's body and his tent. He lay either on one side or the other to take his weight off his mutilated buttocks. Everyone else in the ward would follow my eyes and look grave, reminded again of Al's peril.

Al's temperature shot up. The infection was so virulent that he smelled fetid. Now he'd have to be put in isolation so he couldn't contaminate the others.

In his feverish weakness he protested. "Don't put me in isolation, please. Please don't. I'll be lonely." He was crying feebly.

I apologized to him, quietly and sincerely. I knew he would be lonely. But maybe we could get him recovering, and he could return to the ward. I disconnected his call button and light switches, put his meager possessions from his bedside table onto

136

the foot of the bed, and started to roll it away. "No, no," he whimpered.

Then the other men on the ward began calling out encouragement and, as before his surgery, they all requested the good-luck sign, so I wheeled him around the ward some so the bedridden could reach out and try to touch his foot. They grasped it tenderly and protectively.

Then we approached one of the isolation rooms. He moaned, "I'm gonna die in there."

"No, you won't, Al," I replied.

"I'm gonna die," he said quietly, breathing shallowly and trembling with fever.

After I got him installed in the isolation room, he just lay there. He was flushed with the power of the fever and weakened by his pain. He looked at me helplessly and said nothing more. Though I checked him often and stayed with him as much as I could, he simply lay on his side, one leg drawn up. He was falling into the fatigue of the fever. When he opened his bloodshot eyes he gazed straight ahead.

He said he was going to die and later that night he did.

The ward was very depressed and quiet and some patients and a nurse or two cried. The patients' pain was harder that day; we gave out more pain pills than any day before. I managed to get through the rest of the afternoon competently but without enthusiasm.

I learned later to believe people when they told me they were going to die, and when I got home at last I cried, too. I cried for a long time.

October

Emergency Room

PART III

October

Emergency Room

17

By now I knew the hospital well. It had seemed at first like a challenging puzzle, a set of stubbornly interlocking spheres that did not include the real world. Now I thought I saw the hospital as a complex living organism in which each part was different and necessary. I sensed myself as a smoothly functioning part who fitted with other parts, whether friendly or indifferent.

It was the Emergency Room that seemed to me to let the outside, hostile world in through its suddenly opening swinging doors.

On the Emergency Room rotation you were on for thirty-six hours, off for twenty-four, then on for thirty-six hours again. In other words, if you started at 8:00 A.M., you would be on around the clock and through the whole next day until 8:00 P.M.; then you'd go home and sleep for a whole day, maybe eat a little. Your next duty would start at 8:00 P.M. and go around the clock three times to let you off at 8:00 A.M. two days later. This schedule threw off our circadian—or twenty-four-hour—rhythm, and we were experiencing jet lag all the time.

Until 4:00 P.M. most general medicine problems were handled by the walk-in clinics next to the ER. Yet somebody could come in without an appointment, with a minor bronchial ailment, and be seen by us. Some people might even come in at 2:00 A.M. with belly pain or a urinary problem that had bothered them for two weeks. An Emergency Room doctor was frequently used as a general physician. However, most of what we saw at night was what I would call the hard stuff.

During a late afternoon off-hour—before the evening's injuries came in and after the bulk of the day's outpatients—when half of the doctors had gone to dinner and the others were busy with patients, I was the only doctor available when a young man was brought in by his coach. He was bundled up in the man's overcoat in spite of the warmth of the evening. He was sweating and ashen with pain. The boy had dislocated his shoulder during basketball practice.

The arm had to be popped back into the socket. I looked at his tall muscular frame, saw the pain he was in, and realized that I didn't have the strength to do it for him. I had him sit on the table in the fracture room while I called an orthopedic surgery resident, Dr. Fallon, who returned immediately from his dinner.

He came in, washed his hands vigorously, and burped. "Sorry," he said cheerfully. "Ginger ale. Now let's see." Dr. Fallon was handsome and well built, with light brown hair and eyes. He looked as though he played basketball himself.

"Oh God, Jackson," he said to the young man, "you're in again. I never knew a man looser than you are."

He tested the young man to make sure there was no nerve damage. Then he gave him Valium intravenously to relax his muscles. "Well, you know what we've got to do." Dr. Fallon was brisk. The boy lay down on his stomach and, gasping, let his dislocated arm hang down over the side.

Dr. Fallon told me I could help.

"I've never seen it done, but I'll do what I can," I offered.

"Hold his shoulders down. Now really do it," he warned. "This is going to be a big pull."

I thought I should just hold his body steady, but Dr. Fallon stooped, grabbed the arm, and yanked it down and forward with such force that the young man's body almost jerked out of my grasp. The boy groaned and fainted. The shoulder had been fixed. My own hold on him was no longer necessary.

"Okay," said Dr. Fallon, swinging his own arms like windmills. Catching my appalled stare, he grinned and beat his chest a few thumps. "Give him some smelling salts," he told the nurse.

I expected Dr. Fallon to leave, but he stayed while the patient recovered consciousness. Even with the muscle relaxant, he must have still ached. Then he got control over himself, held his arm tenderly, and turned over. Exhausted, he lay there grim-faced.

Dr. Fallon said, "Yep. You know as well as I do . . ."

Jackson shook his head.

"Yes, you do. Listen. I've been in this hospital for three years now, and during two of them you've come in seven times with this shoulder dislocated. As far as I can see, it gets more painful every time. Most people won't come in more than six or seven times with this. They get to be afraid of it happening. You know you're not doing the joint any good letting it pop out and be snapped back in again all the time. I can imagine what that cartilage looks like by now."

The boy smiled grimly. "You're just tryin' to get yourself an operation, Doc."

Dr. Fallon smiled. "You've been here often enough, Jackson, to know all about us surgical residents and our bloodthirstiness."

The young man laughed and sat up, dangling his legs, trying not to be dizzy and covering it up with weak laughter. "I'm goin' home and get some sleep."

Dr. Fallon put his hand on the patient's knee to prevent his getting off the table yet. Turning to me, the resident said, "This is an interesting case for you. You said you'd never seen a dislocation put back in before. Mr. Jackson here—*Andrew* Jackson, if you can believe it, Old Nonhickory here—has a history of dislocations of the shoulder. There are people whose joints are too loose, just as there are people whose joints are too tight, and both extremes are liable to injury when they engage in active sports, like the star basketball player here." He tapped the young man on his knee, and Jackson made a lazy modest gesture with his good arm.

Dr. Fallon continued. "He's getting to be less and less of a star because he's more and more of a risk." I watched to see how Jackson responded but he was getting logy, and maybe he didn't hear very much of Fallon's lecture. "The operation will prevent further dislocations, but there is a risk that so much scar tissue will form that he might not be able to play basketball." Fallon was brutally direct, it seemed.

There was a silence. After a moment Jackson said, "Thanks, Doc. I'll be going now. Catch you later."

Dr. Fallon kidded him then about basketball, took care of the discharge, and sent Jackson off with his coach with friendly good-byes.

I liked Dr. Fallon. He was an honest and capable doctor. I asked him why he'd handled the patient in this particular way. He came to our little lounge and poured himself a cup of hot, thick coffee.

"He's a kid," said Dr. Fallon, "only eighteen. He'll graduate in the spring. His shoulder's been getting worse, and no college will offer him an athletic scholarship, which he needs. Too much of a medical risk, and he knows it. It's a hard thing for him because he's put all his love into basketball and being the best at it. That's why I say he's young, you know? He doesn't have any idea that he could be something else instead, that there are alternatives, that the day after tomorrow could be different."

"I wonder whether teen-agers have any sense of time passing," I said. "I get the impression that they don't believe anything but now exists."

"You may be right," he acknowledged. "That would make sense, since they've only been who they are for such a short time. Their childhood is so near, and yet so far away."

It was good to have such a conversation with an observant doctor. It felt very comfortable.

He went on. "He'll decide on the operation, some-

144

time. It's just a matter of how many more dislocations he's going to have to go through, and how much the fear of its happening will build up and invade the rest of his life. I'm betting he'll have it done next summer. But that might be overoptimistic."

We chatted for a while longer. I was very impressed with his gentleness—everything he said seemed humane. He didn't wear a wedding band. Well, it didn't make any difference anyway, since I was going with Dennis, but I filed Dr. Fallon in the back on my mind for later, just in case.

Several days later I was on again at night. It was 2:30 A.M., the slow time, and the nurses were giving the male doctors massages. When I first came on the ER I hadn't realized that this was one of the nightly procedures. I don't think it was a custom at University —or at least I never saw it. I think it's a nice idea, but no one ever offered to massage me. When I first heard the nurse suggest it to the resident, she pointedly ignored me. "It's been such a hard night so far," she said. "You must be exhausted, Doctor. Wouldn't you like a little help to relax?" She led him off like a little boy. From the tone she used I imagined they were going to screw in one of the examining rooms, but it turned out to be only this massage business.

On this particular night at 2:30 A.M., each of the men was on a table in a different examining room getting his massage while I minded the store up front. Suddenly I heard a commotion outside, voices calling, and I rushed to the door. Before I got there, in came a man and woman. Dressed in coats over pajamas or nightgown, bare legs and sockless feet looking bony in their shoes, they were holding a ten-year-old boy, writhing and shrieking, his eyes screwed tightly shut. If his arms hadn't been held hard, he would have been hitting out. As I accompanied them to an examining room, I decided that he was not suffering an epileptic fit. He continued screaming and jerking.

In agitation the mother told me, "The child woke up suddenly, screaming that his brain was being cut

145

—it was being sawed into—and he has been scream-ing and holding his head ever since." They seemed afraid that he was swiftly dying from a sudden dis-ease. Then she crossed herself. "Do you think he could be possessed?"

I got the child onto the table and strapped him down so I could examine him. His pupils were nor-mal, so was his color, and, except that he was hoarse from screaming, so was his breathing. I was holding his head still and looking into one of his ears with the otoscope when I saw a thin black growth of some kind.

Startled by this horror, I peered at it carefully for a long moment. Then I straightened up.

"Oil!" I commanded the nurse. "Bring me oil, and a towel!"

"What kind of oil?" asked the perplexed nurse.

The parents were astonished by my behavior.

"Mineral oil," I said sternly. When she brought it, I turned the boy's head and carefully poured some of it into his ear.

His parents gasped. There was a moment of silence.

"It stopped!" cried the boy. "It stopped sawing!"

I smiled majestically. What I had seen in his ear was a mosquito that was definitely alive and struggling to get out of the canal. Its noise must have been terrifying. Looking again into his ear, I saw the carcass of the mosquito, drowned in the oil, rising toward me where I could triumphantly pluck it out with tweezers.

"Your son had a mosquito in his ear," I said to them.

"Mosquito!"

The boy had perked up considerably. "You can see it?"

I nodded.

"It hasn't got into my brain yet?"

"No, absolutely not." I showed it to him. "Do you want it for a souvenir?" I asked him. When he said yes, I had the nurse put it between two glass slides.

As the boy got up to walk out, his mother made a motion to cuff him on the ear with vexation, but thought better of it, and instead thanked me profusely. Relieved, they departed from the magician who had saved their boy.

If only all emergency procedures were so successful and offered such opportunities for hamming it up.

One morning it turned very cold. I hadn't thought to put on any warm outerwear, so by the time I reached the hospital I was freezing. My hands were icy.

I walked into the ER, hung up my jacket, and grabbed the clipboard for the first patient that day. Shivering still, I walked briskly toward the examining room, taking no more time to read the information than to see that the presenting symptom was perineal sores. The perineum is the pelvic floor between the pubis and the coccyx, or tailbone.

Well, I thought, as I breezed into the doorway of Room 6, it's a funny place to put her. It wasn't a GYN examining room.

Lying on a benchlike examining table against the wall with legs stretched out, darkly tanned shoulders leaning against the wall, and with a tiny white towel covering his genitals was one of the handsomest nude men I'd ever seen. He was giving me a lazy half-smile.

I came to a dead stop.

"Oh." My voice squeaked like a changing boy's. I went on swiftly, "What's the problem?"

He lifted the towel to reveal his genitals. Trying to cover up my confusion, I strode forward briskly and took his penis in my ice-cold hands.

He yelped and jerked back. I let go.

"Oh. Ha, ha," I said, "I should have warned you." I rubbed my cold hands together as hard as I could to warm them up, looking like a witch in greedy anticipation. (I learned later to run my hands under hot water.) "These sores," I continued in a professional tone. "How do you think you got them?"

"Well," he said, reassured that my hands were warm enough as I began to examine him, "I've just been on

147

vacation. I spent a lot of time on the beach and now I have these little bumps. I thought they might have come from the sand. Bugs, or something."

For the life of me, I couldn't find any bumps.

But I slowed myself down, and as soon as I relaxed, I *could* see a few little things like bites on his testicles. I didn't recognize them, though. I knew I should check his upper pubic hair for crabs or other insects, too, so I did that as fast as I could, turned, and dashed out of the room, saying, "You can get dressed now. I'll talk to you outside."

I pretended to be very busy with other patients, but as I rushed from one examining room to another, I saw him, clothed, leaning against the counter at the nurses' station.

I went over. "Well," I said judiciously. "It's possible you have some sand bites. On the other hand, have you been having sex with anyone new recently?" I looked down, prepared to write something on his chart.

"No," he said mildly, "just the same old woman." I looked up; he was smiling again.

"Well, then," I said briskly, "what I'll do is give you a prescription called Quell, and, uh, you can use it and, uh, it ought to take care of the problem."

I had only heard of the medicine in medical school, had never seen it prescribed, and didn't know what the specific directions were. Such ignorance is, in fact, a common problem in the ER, so I retreated behind the nurses' station and got out the PDR (*Physicians' Desk Reference*) to look it up.

My patient stood leaning over the counter, grinning at me, while I tried hurriedly to find it. I recalled it as a powerful specific for body lice. Quell, Quell—it just wasn't there. I went down the *Q*'s three times. Surely they hadn't withdrawn it in the year or so since I'd heard of it.

A nurse saw my haste and confusion. "What are you looking for?" she asked loudly.

"Sssh!" I hushed her. "A medication called Quell," I whispered. "I can't find it."

She shrugged. "It's right there," she said.

"Where?"

"In the *K*'s, of course!"

Of course they'd spell it in some jazzy, illiterate way. There it was: Kwell. I had to decide whether ointment or shampoo would be better for this handsome man to put on his testicles. I tried to forget where it was going to be used and decided on shampoo.

I scribbled out the prescription and sent him off to the pharmacy as quickly as I could.

Five minutes later I got a call from the pharmacy. "Say, this prescription you just wrote out. It doesn't say how the stuff is to be used, you know?"

No, I thought, my stomach sinking; how do *I* know how it's supposed to be used?

"I'll call you back."

I got out the PDR again and pondered the recommendations. I called the pharmacy back. "Shampoo twice a day," I dictated. "Lather well; do not rinse for five minutes. Then rinse thoroughly." Trying desperately to visualize head hair, I hung up.

Several minutes later I saw my patient heading toward me again.

"Say," he asked, "what about a reappointment? A follow-up?"

"Oh. Uh. Yes. I think you ought to see Dr. Mallory. He's the best dermatologist in town."

He nodded as if he understood, smiled, and said good-bye. I watched him walk away. I had been unusually rattled by him. However, it delighted me to note that apparently there were so many good-looking, pleasant men around. The world was generous.

When I happened to be watching TV with some other staff people one evening and saw my patient's handsome face on the screen, I was surprised and amused. No wonder he'd been able to be so cool: he was a news commentator.

18

One case I had changed two habits of mine. A woman came in because of painful urination and vaginal irritation and discharge. She was heavy, weighing about 200 pounds for a height of five feet four inches, and had a sharp querulous manner. Her skin had the dingy look of ill health and infrequent washing, though her fingernails were clean enough and she was neatly dressed. She was a picture of neglect just barely rescued for the occasion of coming to the doctor. No doubt she had ignored her condition and postponed coming in for some time.

I took her history and found that she was living alone with two young children. The eldest was an adolescent girl who had run away. Her latest sexual contact, she told me abruptly and with hostility, had occurred three months ago and then he had moved out, so although her last menstrual period had occurred two months ago, she couldn't be pregnant. After I'd asked everything, I had her lie down for the pelvic exam.

The sour, irritating vaginal odor should have warned me. She had a yeast infection, at least. She might also have gonorrhea, which doesn't smell.

I inserted the speculum and locked it open, getting a stronger whiff as I did. As I visually examined the vagina, I could not see all of the cervix because of a mass of pus and a greenish-white discharge, which I tried to clean off. She probably had two or three infections. After getting a smear and culture, I put in the fingers of one gloved hand to do the bimanual exam. At the end of it, as I was removing my fingers from her vagina, there was suction and a plop. Some of the discharge came out along with my hand and spattered my face.

I was appalled. It was almost without a doubt the discharge of gonorrhea, and my eyes could be in serious danger. While the nurse took over, I quickly washed up and hurried to Ophthalmology.

Immediately they removed my contact lenses, bathed my eyes in water, and applied an antibiotic ointment. The ophthalmologist on duty, a pleasant, serious man, said, "You know, I strongly advise you to wear glasses on duty. Save your contacts for social occasions."

"I've never thought of it."

"Well, that's what I advise. I'd get all doctors to wear glasses as a protection if I could, whether they need them or not! But some of them are too vain." He smiled. "They might also accuse me of empire-building if I got everyone in the hospital to wear glasses."

I did wear my glasses on duty from then on.

This experience also changed something else. Until then I'd been on the pill. It had been an effective and useful method of contraception for me and I'd had no bad reactions to it. But the pill gave me no protection from infections, and the men weren't using condoms. Dennis Danes—though I was sure he was clean and would be careful of himself, especially since he was a gynecologist—had gone to bed with every good-looking, willing woman in the hospital, and probably some of his willing patients as well. I was not going to take any chances, however remote. It was not a matter of trust, it was a matter of primitive safety. I'd gotten a terrible scare.

I changed to a diaphragm, and I placed a prescription penicillin tablet within it before I put it in place. From then on I always did that before a date, though I never told Dennis.

It was superstitious of me, and foolish in a way. Though I know I was not allergic to penicillin, I could have sensitized myself by my habit. I wonder whether a man who *was* allergic would have had a reaction. And many strains of gonorrhea are resistant to penicillin. Short of massive prophylactic doses of anti-

151

biotics before intercourse, which of course is out of the question, the only real protection from venereal disease is to know whom you're going to bed with, know that he's clean, and then to go ahead and check to make sure he isn't infected. Some men drip pus, and a prostate massage and milking the urethra will produce either clear, healthy seminal fluid or pus from an infection.

A man came into the Emergency Room in great distress.

He'd been a cancer patient and had had a colostomy. The upper right colon had been provided with an opening through the abdominal wall, and feces were discharged into a disposable colostomy bag. He was taking a medication to regulate the consistency of his stool. Now he'd been vomiting for twenty-four hours; he was dehydrated, with low blood pressure, and had a fast pulse. Beads of sweat stood out on his upper lip and forehead, and his hands trembled.

"Do you think I'm having a reaction to the medicine?" he asked anxiously.

"It's possible," I replied. "We'll check it."

When I examined him and looked into his mouth I was startled by the odor that issued from it—it smelled just like shit. I asked him about it.

He flushed and said, "I brush my teeth and I gargle . . ."

When I stuck my finger in the opening to see if it was open or blocked, it came out yellow and sticky.

He began to heave. I couldn't give him the bowl in time, and he vomited all over the floor. It looked like regular vomit, but with yellow curds, and the stench was horrible. He groaned, saying, "Oh, God, I'm sorry. I spattered you." Indeed he had, I realized, as he began vomiting again. After he was finished and I was helping him into the next examining room while the orderly cleaned up, he said shakily, laughing, "You know, it's funny, the vomit all tastes like shit."

Then I knew. I asked him a few more questions and discovered that he'd taken too much medicine. It had made his stool gluey, and after a while he had simply gotten stopped up; the stools had backed up and had had to be vomited up. The more vomiting he did, the more dehydrated he became; the more dehydrated, the harder the stool—and the more vomiting.

He needed an enema through the colostomy hole. As I busily prepared for the procedure, I wished for a second that I could get someone else to do it for me— it was literally shitwork. I got him positioned, began the enema, and in no time at all the shit came oozing out with increased speed. As his bowel gradually emptied, he couldn't help sighing with relief. I got smeared with shit, and I wished I'd thought of wearing a rubber apron as well as rubber gloves.

It took ten minutes to clear the large bowel enough to relieve the stoppage and the pressure on the stomach. Then I gave him liquids to help unglue the food affected by the medicine. At last I took him to a treatment room for intravenous hydration and a little rest after such an exhausting experience.

He looked weak but happy. As I was wheeling him, he started giggling. He murmured something about how funny it was. When I got him settled, he confided in me what he had realized. Shaking his head and smiling weakly, he said, "Funny. You know it's really funny, but it looked like shit, it smelled like shit—but I couldn't believe it, it really *tasted* like shit."

It was a very busy Saturday night in the Emergency Room: several drunks, three victims of an automobile accident, and a heart-attack case. There were also less serious cases, like a man who choked on a bite of food, coughed it up, and came in to make sure he was out of danger; a couple who got into a fight and ended up socking one another; and a baby whose diarrhea had become so bad its pediatrician had told the parents to bring it on in for rehydration and monitoring.

It was 12:30 A.M. when a group of ten people escorted by two policemen came through the doors, excitedly talking among themselves. Having been in a very minor auto accident, they insisted that each of them be completely checked over for injuries. Each car had held about five people. One car, driven by a woman named Rosalita Rodriguez, had sideswiped the other car at a stoplight. Since the other car had been stopped and hers was slowing down for the light, the impact of the collision had been slight enough that the passengers were not really injured, though the cars' fenders had been badly crumpled. Rosalita Rodriguez had begun to act strangely, as though she might have had some trauma, and the police were anxious to have her certified okay, so everybody else had gotten worried about themselves as well.

A woman in her late twenties or early thirties, but so heavily made up that she looked older, Miss Rodriguez was wearing very high platform shoes and staggered loose-kneed, whether because of them or because of some equilibrium problem it was not clear. She clung to the policeman's arm with both her hands, moaning and wincing as she walked. The other intern, Michael Kraft, got her.

I was starting to check one of the other victims when there was a sharp shriek from Michael's examining room. He rushed out of his room and past mine. "She's gone blind!" he hissed, his face white with alarm.

After I'd reassured my patient, I went into the examining room where Miss Rodriguez was. Slumped down on the examining table with her head in her hands, she was groaning. Michael had brought in Dr. Abel, our chief resident, who was talking to her.

He said loudly, "What is it? What has happened to you?"

She raised her face, her eyes wide with horror, and sobbed, "I am gone blind! I can't see! My eyes! My eyes!"

He examined her eyes very carefully, then equally carefully looked in her ears for blood. He grunted once in a while.

"What? What?" she asked anxiously.

He didn't reply.

"Lie down," he ordered.

She seemed to collapse onto the table, falling back

154

with a shudder and a long faint moan. She appeared to be inert, almost unconscious.

Dr. Abel unzipped her slacks in order to examine her abdomen for a ruptured spleen, liver damage, and any other visceral problem. As he was palpating the lower abdomen, her hand come up and brushed his hands away. He tried again, and again her hand lifted up to push his away, as we imagine a sleeping gesture. He tried several times, but was never able to feel long enough to make a definite judgment. At last he must have thought he'd felt enough, because he stopped trying.

"Well," he said in a loud voice, glancing at the clock behind him. "She's had an accident. Very interesting." He walked out of the examining room, still talking loudly. "She seems to be unconscious now. She has lost her sight. In twenty minutes she'll wake up, and she'll be able to see again." Standing in the hall, he called to her friends in the waiting room. "Your friend," he said, still in his best stentorian voice, "is unconscious. She will be unconscious for twenty minutes. You must stay with her for that time so that when she wakes up she will be able to see again. She will not be able to see before twenty minutes is up, so you must stay with her." He arranged for her to be taken to a holding area where her friends could fit in, too, and as he was supervising this, he repeated two more times the crucial details of twenty minutes' unconsciousness and her regaining her vision.

Then he left them all together by themselves.

As I followed Dr. Abel away, I could hear their low voices whispering to one another as they stood guard over their friend.

"What did you do?" I asked, when we were safely out of range of their hearing.

He shrugged. "You saw. She's having a hysterical reaction. She isn't blind, but you can't tell her she isn't; she thinks she is, and she truly cannot see. But she isn't unconscious. So I gave her permission to be blind for twenty minutes, and then I told her she would be all right. You'll see. Hang around for twenty minutes."

Sure enough, in twenty minutes, right on the dot, I heard a raising of voices from the holding area, and one in particular, full of joy: "I can see! Oh, thank God I can see again!"

I was impressed with Dr. Abel.

It was about 6:00 P.M., and still light, a few days later when the ambulance drove up (the driver usually turns the siren off within a block of the hospital to avoid disturbing the patients) and discharged a small group of people who were unusually upset. You can detect a quality of distress or fear in the people who come into Emergency from the way they hold their bodies. It's mostly the lay people who show it; the staff is too busy to show anything but careful haste. But this time the ambulance driver and the technician were upset, too.

I wasn't on the team, but I stationed myself where I could see into the room where they had taken the stretcher. A child was lying limply, eyes open but glazed with shock. The doctors lifted the blanket, and I saw that it was a little boy, about ten years old, with a bandage around his loins that looked like a diaper. They turned him over; his body seemed awkward and stiff, as though his muscles were tight. They removed the bandage, and I saw that his anus was bloody. It had been ripped open about three inches in a jagged wound. "We'll get him up to Surgery right away," someone said in a grim, tight voice.

He'd been raped. A rapist's erect penis is really a blunt instrument, I realized with horror. Troubled, I went back to the waiting room, where the sight of the boy's parents stopped me. Dr. Abel was talking to them. The mother was white-faced and red-eyed, the father looked completely stunned. Woodenly he got up and walked to the water fountain. As he passed me I could smell his sour breath; it smelled like vomit.

They spent three hours repairing the boy's rectum and anus.

Everybody was appalled at this brutal case of child molestation. It was the only case of child rape that I

156

saw, though I was told that in the summer months there were quite a few. I had heard that in prison the rapist is the criminal with the highest reputation, the child molester the one with the lowest, and I had often wondered at what age a girl-child became a woman and thus by her victimization raised the status of her attacker from animal to hero.

19

A woman came in one day with vaginal bleeding, sometimes heavy, that had been going on for days. It was not time for her period.

"I think there's something in my vagina," she said.

"Have you felt it with your fingers?" I asked.

"Yes, I did investigate, but I can't really tell. But it feels funny. It hurts."

She was also having some cramping. When I examined her I saw something protruding from the cervix, but I couldn't tell what it was. There was a possibility that she was aborting. Dr. Abel was in fact a GYN resident, and I asked him to look at her.

"Aborting," he said.

"That can't be," she insisted. "I'm on the pill. I'm not pregnant."

Dr. Abel replied, "Come, come. You probably forgot to take it."

She flushed.

He felt inside, and said, "You *are* aborting. I can feel the tissue."

"I'm not pregnant, I tell you!" she said.

"Aw, come on. It's all right to get an abortion nowadays," he replied.

"Listen," she said. "I'm not pregnant!"

"God," Dr. Abel said in exasperation. "You women are so insistent on your cover story . . ." He reached in and put a clamp on the protruding mass and tugged.

She interrupted him with a shriek.

"I'm just going to help it along," he said.

She screamed with pain.

"Just calm down," he told her. "Keep it quiet. You'll get everybody else uptight."

"It hurts! Stop it!"

"It'll be over in a minute."

"You get the hell out of there!"

He didn't answer but kept on tugging, and she kept on crying out. I grabbed her hand—she gripped it so hard my fingers hurt.

In five minutes he straightened up with something in his gloved hand that for sure was not a fetus. With great chagrin he slammed it into the steel receiving bowl and stamped out of the room. "Get her up to the OR," he told me. "They'll check for the rest of it."

He had been pulling on a polyp that had been growing on the uterine wall. While he pulled she had been in excruciating pain, until he'd finally managed to get part of it off.

She was fighting mad. "I should have closed my legs on the bastard," she apologized to herself. "I should have gotten right up off the table. I should have walked out of here and gone over to University." She was taken up to Surgery.

I checked on her later in the day. They'd found another polyp inside her uterus and removed it. Then she had a D and C, and the bleeding stopped.

Dr. Abel seemed to handle many GYN cases the same way, irritably and tyrannically. He was quick and curt. When he went into private practice, he'd probably be able to make the $100,000 a year some gynecologists expect because he would run the cases through so fast.

I noticed the young women who came in on weekends. Abel invariably diagnosed them as PID (pelvic inflammatory disease) secondary to gonorrhea. For the first time I was impressed with the magnitude of the epidemic of venereal disease that I had read was occurring among young people. But what puzzled me was why patients seemed to come in only on Friday and Saturday nights rather than during the week. Did gonorrhea flare up only on weekends?

The next Friday night when he got such a patient, I stopped Dr. Abel before he went into the GYN examining room. "May I observe your technique?" I asked deferentially.

He flicked a glance at me. "All right," he muttered.

He went hastily into the room and I followed him quietly. Since he didn't introduce me to the patient or ask her permission for me to be there, I did. I stationed myself by his side so I could see what he was doing.

He glanced at the young woman's chart. "Student, huh?" She was a *graduate* student. "Okay. What's your complaint?"

While she described her pelvic pain he looked hassled, as though he might leave the room at any moment. His questions were staccato. She said the pain came and went, that it didn't last for days at a time, but it had been occurring off and on for months and she was frightened. He asked her whether she was engaging in any "Sek-sual activity." When she said yes she lowered her eyes, so she missed the curt nod and significant look he gave me.

"All right," he ordered. "Lie back, get your feet in the stirrups, move your ass on down here, spread your legs. Come on, spread 'em."

Perhaps it was fortunate that the pelvic exam he gave was so brief. Every once in a while she'd grimace.

He straightened up and said, "That's it. Get dressed. I'll take care of you outside." He quickly prepared the smears.

"Uh," I interrupted. "May I examine the patient?"

"Oh. Sure." He stepped aside.

"Do you mind, Miss Gallatin?" I asked.

She shook her head no.

159

First I looked with the aid of the speculum. There was no discharge from the uterus as there probably would have been if it was gonorrhea. I could see nothing really abnormal. Then I tried to examine her, but for an unexperienced doctor like me, finding the ovaries was like feeling for two grapes inside a pillow. I couldn't feel them. What I could feel was a cervix that seemed pulpy; the perimeter area on both sides of the uterus was tender, but not hot.

"Seen enough, doctor?" Abel said impatiently.

"Oh, yes. Thanks." I thanked the patient, too, before I followed Abel out the door.

"Well?" He gave me a tight smile as if to encourage me to risk an opinion.

"I don't think she has gonorrhea."

"You have a crystal ball, Doctor?" he sneered. "You felt the tenderness. You heard her complaint. If you want to wait for results from the culture, you'll just delay medication even longer." He leaned back against the wall and crossed his arms, as if waiting for me to wake up.

"I'd like to interview the patient again," I persisted.

He laughed. "Dr. Donnan, your reputation has preceded you. I thought I was going to get off easy this month, but you were just holding off, weren't you?"

I didn't reply. Up yours, too, I thought to myself.

"With your permission, Dr. Abel," I said calmly, "I'm going to interview the patient again."

"Oh, by all means, Doctor. Be my guest." He pushed himself off the wall and bowed.

I went back into the room where Miss Gallatin had finished dressing. "Would you mind letting me ask you a couple more questions?"

"No, of course not." I had her sit on the stool while I leaned against the examining table.

I soon had enough information to give me a diagnosis that made sense of these weekend PID emergencies. They were probably sexually active young women who experienced excitation and intercourse but seldom or never came to orgasm. The whole vaginal and cervical area became engorged with blood

160

and the nerve endings excited unbearably because there had been no relief. Prostitutes sometimes suffer the same problem. In a way, it must be useful for a prostitute to turn herself off, since apparently the condition is exceedingly painful. It must be comparable to "blue balls," the common name for the ache a man feels in his testicles when he doesn't come after arousal.

I told her what I recommended: orgasm, or a hot bath and then the knee-chest position to drain the blood from the pelvis. Then I gave her a prescription for an antibiotic in case she did have gonorrhea; we wouldn't know for several days. She looked like a different person now that she was enlightened.

When I told Dr. Abel my diagnosis he scoffed at it, but she didn't have gonorrhea, and we didn't have to see her again.

However, the next week when I was just coming on, I saw that another intern had had a PID the previous night, diagnosed as secondary to gonorrhea.

"Hey," I said, as he was leaving, "are you sure about this one?" I showed him the chart.

"What do you mean?" He was exhausted and irritated that I was delaying him. "That one? Some chick screwing around, that's all. What's so unusual?"

I told him my theory.

"Yeah? Possibly," he said wearily and without interest. He started to go.

"Listen," I said, in my fresh, early-morning earnestness. "Next time one of those women comes in with inflammation and pain, why don't you at least consider excitation without satisfaction?"

"All right, all right. I'll consider it." Without another word he left. I don't know whether he ever did.

I began to try to get such women assigned to me. When a good-looking female came in and I took her, the male interns complained, but Abel was willing to let me have these cases. Michael Kraft thought I was too aggressive. "How can you horn in on those GYN cases, after all?" he demanded.

"Abel lets me," I contended.

"He's probably avoiding a fight with you."

I laughed. "Probably."

"Boy," Michael muttered, "you just want a penis!"

I wouldn't let him get away with that. "Yes, indeed!" I laughed. "Regularly and often!" It used to be common for men to accuse an ambitious or successful woman of penis envy, but I don't hear that particular statement much nowadays.

He blushed.

Later that week I was at a dinner party talking with a woman, the wife of a medical school professor who herself had just become a social worker. She asked me whether I would be interested in joining a women's consciousness-raising group. I started to ask her about it when a man interrupted us; he began an argument with another man about whether women's liberationists were neurotic and hysterical, whether women were equal to men in creativity, and about the moral dangers of quotas.

Finally, after ten or fifteen minutes of discussion swirling around us without our ever having been asked an opinion of our sex, I opened my mouth wide and sat there with it open. It took a full minute for one of the men to notice my expression. He was startled. "What is it, Phyllis?" he asked.

"Amazement," I said.

"Amazement?" he repeated.

"Amazement," I replied. Several people laughed and the debaters shut up. I never knew whether they had gotten the point or not.

When there was a very urgent emergency, in order to alert the team, the ambulance driver turned on a siren a moment before he arrived. We sprang through the doors to receive the patient. The ambulance backed up, and the medical technician inside opened the door from his side as I pulled from mine. "Suicide," he gasped, and he turned to help get the patient.

Filling the stretcher was a gray, obese woman like a

bag of badly broken limbs. The technician was telling us that she'd jumped out of a fifth-floor window and had very little heartbeat but was still breathing. No bones were showing through her flesh although she'd splintered and shattered her feet, legs, pelvis, and back.

Her ribs had punctured the pleural space and shredded the lung tissue, so her breaths were pumping air into the rest of her body tissues. She wasn't obese—she was puffed up. When I touched her to get a pulse her skin popped softly. It was blown up thin, like a roasted chicken's, and it felt crinkly, like crepe paper. As you listened, you could hear a queer, random, popping sound from the skin's inflating into little air bubbles. Dr. Abel was cutting down through the inflated tissue to the veins in her legs to get IV lines in; someone else had intubated her and was breathing her with the Ambu bag. The more air that went into her, the more the rest of her body inflated —it was like blowing up a balloon. We came to a halt in the fracture room, a large, well-equipped emergency room just off the entrance, and for a moment the silence was absolute except for the sounds of her body as it bloated.

Then her heart stopped. With a quick incision, Dr. Abel sliced open her chest, broke an unbroken rib, and reached in to grasp the heart and massage it, pumping blood for her.

I gazed at his hands working on her heart with such strength and persistence, and with so little hope. He held her live heart in his hand and made it beat.

He called on the first-year resident to spell him. Abel was sweating with the tension, but after a few minutes' rest he went back to the heart massage. I don't know how long he kept it up altogether—maybe ten or fifteen minutes, though it seemed longer. It was clear he was doing her living for her. The air that pumped into her spread through her body; she was bleeding out through damaged vessels into her torn tissues, and she could not live. Finally, Abel just stepped back and let her go.

Since she had committed suicide, she would have to be taken to the hospital morgue and held for the medical examiner's report. "You'll have to tell the family," I heard someone say, and then Abel's tight voice replied, "I nominate Phyllis to do it."

"Take Mabel with you," he said as he disappeared. Mabel was an older ER nurse, completely reliable and very experienced. Perhaps she'd had occasion in the past to help the family of a suicide. I didn't know why Dr. Abel wouldn't do it.

I looked out into the waiting area and saw a man leaning forward tensely. He had to be the woman's husband. I went to sit on the bench beside him. Mabel sat on the other side and leaned toward him protectively, so as to take him in her arms if he needed it.

I told him his wife was dead. He cried out loudly, "Can't you keep her alive?" but Mabel said something I didn't hear. He turned to plead with her. After a moment I had to get up and go to my next case. I was so tired I couldn't think about what had happened. I just knew that, again, the nurses had been our mainstays.

Something else interesting was Dr. Abel's behavior. He'd worked so hard to save that suicide's life; he'd been patient and clear with the hysterical woman. Why was he so cursory and irritable with women with minor problems? I think there were at least two reasons. One was a reluctance he shared with many doctors, I think, to let people need them except for medical care; with Dr. Abel that willingness was limited narrowly to emergency medical care. The other reason, I think, was that he disliked women and could forget their sex only in emergencies, when they were human, not female.

It was unfortunate that he had chosen to be a gynecologist.

20

We got a phone call that an ambulance was bringing in accident victims from a hospital halfway across the state—three woman law students. One had been killed, another was still unconscious, and the driver's foot had gone through the floor. Most of the bones might be lost. Healing would be difficult in this area and there might be a lot of bone infection. She was going to require sophisticated orthopedic work. Both survivors had facial cuts that needed prompt plastic surgery.

Both the ER staff and the orthopedic chief were quickly ready. When the ambulance arrived, the unconscious woman was taken immediately to X ray and then to intensive care. The other woman, Marianne Carter, was first taken to the fracture room. Fuzzy from the painkiller but conscious, she kept murmuring, "Oh, God."

I stood near her head while the surgeons, having draped her, took a careful look at her foot and leg. I caught a glimpse—it looked pretty bad. They were going to clean it up, debride it to get more of the mangled muscle and tendon out of the way, and take her right up to X ray and into the OR, where the films would be sent.

"We might as well knock her out right now, then," said the surgeon, and the anesthesiologist nodded.

"When was the last time you ate?" he asked her.

She looked puzzled.

"I vomited," she muttered.

"Good," he said approvingly. "Now, Marianne, I'm

going to give you morphine. You know what its effects are and how quickly it works.

"Don't worry, my dear." The surgeon came over to look down at her, replacing me by her side. He took her hand, squeezed it and patted it. "Everything's going to be all right."

"Kim," she pleaded.

"She's going to be all right, too. I don't want you to worry."

"Are you sure?" she asked, hope brightening her voice.

"Yes, of course. Now don't worry." He nodded to the anesthesiologist. "Okay, Doctor."

I thought Kim was the other student admitted, but she was the one who had died.

When they turned the cart to wheel her out I got a look at her injury: the foot seemed connected to the leg only by the deep, underlying tissues. The broken, large legbones were showing; the foot was misshapen, contused, and lacerated, with small as well as large tears and again white bones and tendons showing. Fear rippled through me, and as they wheeled her away relief made me sigh.

I went about my duties for the rest of the day, repressing the impact of the accident on my imagination as though it were a strong wrestler who had to be pinned to the ground yet heaved again and again under my grip, even under the weight of my whole body.

Everybody in the hospital knew about the two women and their progress. Their facial lacerations were being carefully stitched by plastic surgeons. Fortunately, Marianne's ankle joint itself was intact. The first metal plates were introduced on either side of the break to prepare for reconstruction of the bone. She was going to need several operations on her foot and leg.

The other woman regained consciousness and began a simple recovery. But Marianne Carter was not recovering well. Three days after the accident she learned what she must have known intuitively, that her friend had died. Morphine was not strong enough to dull that pain. I was told that she cried out once.

166

The next day I happened to be walking past her room, and found that I needed to look in. She was not alone in her private room; two visitors were there, a middle-aged couple. All three figures were sitting still and silent. Marianne was gazing at the ceiling, on which traveled reflections from automobile windshields in the street below.

The next weekend I was off for twenty-four hours, so I called to make sure Dennis and I could get together. He was playing tennis that afternoon, unfortunately, and wouldn't break the date. I would just have to wait until he called me back.

It was interesting which medical people got involved in sports. Most of the interns got their only exercise walking down blocks and blocks of corridors, taking patients here and there. I got another kind of workout whenever I could—during intercourse—and I hoped I would use up at least three hundred calories per act.

By the time five o'clock rolled around and I hadn't heard from Dennis I was horny, and I felt very aggressive, even hostile, about it. It wasn't like me. I drank a glass of wine to smooth myself out. Since I didn't drink very much, or very often, one glass was usually very effective.

Soothed and feeling happier, I was about to pick up the phone and call him when it rang. Startled, I stood there a moment. I hated to pick up a phone on the first ring; on the other hand, I hated to stand by and listen to it. On the third ring I picked it up.

It was Dennis.

"We're having a couple of drinks at the tennis club. I won't be able to pick you up until seven."

"Oh, okay," I said unconcernedly. "Say, why don't we have dinner here? I can cook you up something really good, you know."

"Really?" he said, in what I assumed was mock amazement. I could hear his smile.

"Of course. I'm some woman."

"I know that."

"Good. But you'll have to be here by six-thirty."

"Well . . . I suppose I can cut this short."

"Yes," I said.

"All right. See you then."

"Good-bye, lover," I said in a hothouse voice. He couldn't reply to that because he was calling from the bar of the club. I liked to make him a little helpless that way.

I let him in by the back window, as usual, and had him sit down while I pretended to be fixing him a drink.

When I emerged from the kitchen, I was dressed only in a pair of black net stockings held up with a garter belt, a little apron, and nothing else. "Hi!" I said. "I'm your topless cocktail waitress." I was consciously imitating Marabel Morgan's Total Woman, knowing that Dennis would get the joke.

He laughed, half rose from his seat, and grabbed me by the waist, pressing his face between my breasts. He dragged me down to the floor, lifting my provocative little apron. Undressing swiftly, he immediately entered me. As he held me by my thighs, he could move my body in rhythm to his thrusts, and soon he came. As I could feel his penis relaxing inside me, I clasped it more firmly with my perineal muscles; he settled deeply onto me, obligingly moving his own pubis so that my clitoris was excited, until quickly and softly I came, too.

"Now," he said. "How's about that dinner I was promised?"

"You've already had it, haven't you?"

"Only the appetizer," he murmured.

I laughed. We rose, washed up a little, and I went in to prepare dinner. We spent the whole evening naked, though I did use a full-length apron to protect myself from spattering while I sautéed the chicken. But we ate nude, and sat together on the sofa afterward nude, quietly caressing each other until the time came to make love again, slowly and thoroughly.

By the time we had finished I was weeping.

"Little Phyllis," he said tenderly, "what is it?" He touched a tear as it traveled down my temple.

"You're awfully good," I said.

"I am, aren't I?"

"That was really good."

"Don't cry about it."

I tried to stop crying, but surprisingly, the more I tried to stop, and the more I told myself I was just responding to a moving series of orgasms, the more I cried and the less relieved I felt—not physically, but emotionally.

Finally he said, with a trace of irritation in his voice, "I'm going to go."

"Spend the night with me," I sobbed, trying not to, trying to make it sound like just a sexy invitation.

"Phyllis, before I did that, you'd have to get yourself under control."

"All right," I said, lying back and staring hard at the ceiling at the circle of light from the lamp.

"That's better," he said after a moment. He settled close to me, putting his hand on my breast and his leg across my hip. He fell asleep incredibly fast.

I lay for a long while after that listening to his soft breathing and watching the ceiling.

When I turned out the light I could see the occasional sweep of someone's headlights across the ceiling, until my eyes became so dry that I had to close the lids. I should have been doing what Dennis was doing, sleeping. Now that I was quiet I saw what I had needed, and even why I had parodied the harem girl, the Bunny, the Total Woman. Dennis would never deeply comfort me—I really knew that. We were only physical lovers, for he didn't want to know anything else about me or be asked to do anything else for me but what he could do so expertly.

My mind filled with the memory of Marianne Carter and her peril as she sat with her fists gripping a steering wheel and her foot forcing the brake pedal down as the car began to crash and her friend began to slip through the windshield.

As her case progressed, Marianne Carter talked very seldom, even to her parents. She murmured commonplaces about the hospital and the care she was receiving. Even her friend, the other passenger, couldn't get her to open up. If I were on the floor I'd look in the room to see her propped up in bed, her face as free of lines as a dead woman's. I never went in.

A woman came in bleeding heavily from the vagina and with a high fever. She'd been pregnant for about two and a half months and was clearly having a miscarriage. I turned her over to Dr. Abel, who put her down for criminal abortion.

Like a dummy I blurted out, "What do you mean, criminal abortion? She doesn't need to do that anymore. A septic abortion, maybe. A woman who is miscarrying can get infected. But *criminal* abortion!" A back-street abortion, in other words, brought on by the woman herself or by some shady practitioner. Since the law had been changed recently, women who wanted abortions could get them in clinics or hospitals. I hadn't seen or heard of a single woman, in my last year in medical school, who'd had the dangerous procedure that had cost so many lives before.

He snapped, "Yes, criminal abortion. If a woman's septic and is miscarrying, she's put down as criminal abortion until proven otherwise."

"But she's having a miscarriage."

"We put her down for septic criminal abortion," he insisted, as we continued to walk down the corridor. She had already been taken up to GYN, where they were going to D and C her and give her antibiotics. I was just dogging him back down the hall.

"But she *wanted* to get pregnant," I persisted. "She's appalled—grief-stricken—terrified because she's aborting."

He came to a stop. "Listen," he said. "You get so you don't believe *what* a woman tells you about her condition. Donnan, you're going to have to learn that, and learn it quick. I don't see how you can make it on Emergency if you don't know that. When you get up on my service, and if you get assigned to me, I hope to God you've learned at least that one thing."

I just came to a dead halt mentally, grunted, and turned away.

One evening the police brought in a man who'd been in an auto accident. They said he was drunk. His was the only car in the accident; it had been towed away and they'd gotten all the information they needed. They dumped him in the ER.

He was an ordinary-looking man, well dressed, about forty years old, with thinning hair. He looked to be in good physical condition. He was acting drunk: he was very agitated, with quick, nervous motions of his hands and head, unable to sit still or look at one thing for a long time, or form his sentences coherently and consistently. He'd hop up and try to move away, which must have been what made the police call him "unruly." I didn't think he was drunk.

"Mr. Denning, what happened to you?" I asked.

He didn't reply.

Loudly, I repeated my question.

His attention caught, he gazed at me for a moment, then murmured almost unintelligibly, "I don't remember."

"Had you been drinking, Mr. Denning?"

He made a noise like a whimper and started off the chair.

"You can sit back down now," I said, again loudly. I grabbed his arm and gently pushed him back down onto the seat. I checked his ears, nose, and throat for blood, and his nose for any clear spinal fluid. I was worried that he'd had head trauma. His confusion was not alcoholic, but more like concussion.

I examined him very carefully and gently to check for a ruptured spleen or other damage to the viscera. There'd been no drop in his blood pressure to indicate internal bleeding, but we wanted to be extra sure. Then I ordered a whole series of x rays on him—cranial, thoracic, and abdominal. The x rays showed no breaks or cracks and all the lab tests were normal, but I was still suspicious.

I kept him in a holding room for observation. Slowly

171

he regained control and became more oriented and focused. When, after four hours, I went in to check him again, I noticed that the muscles in his neck were stiffening. That was bad; they were going into a kind of muscle spasm and it was going to be quite painful for him.

"Can you remember what happened now, Mr. Denning?" I asked.

He wrinkled his forehead in puzzlement. "I don't know. I really don't remember."

"Where is your car?"

He looked amazed and troubled. "I don't know."

"The police say you had an accident."

"Something hit me?" he said, startled. He frowned. "Look, I've got to get home. I was on my way home. I'm expecting some people for dinner tonight. What time is it?"

When I told him it was 10:00 P.M. he groaned. "I've got to get home!" he said in a panic.

"Your guests surely would have gone home," I observed.

"No!" he insisted. "My wife—they're with her! She must be frantic."

I suggested he phone his wife. Calming her alarm helped him become more rational, and after he talked to her he seemed more controlled. She was coming down right away to get him.

He was very eager to go home. I was reluctant to let him go, but without a visible injury, since he was now so lucid, and with someone to be responsible for him, I had to let him go. I warned him that he would probably have much head and neck pain and prescribed Valium. I made sure he understood that if he felt nauseated, dizzy, or lightheaded, he should come back to the hospital immediately. When his wife arrived, I carefully instructed her similarly before I let her take him home.

I was worried about him, but he was intelligent. In fact, two days later, when he started feeling nauseated and began having involuntary spasms and hesitant

172

movement on his left side, he got himself back to the Emergency Room in a hurry.

The new, exotic symptoms he had on one side of his body suggested a subdural hematoma—a blood clot under his skull pressing against the brain. It's a common late complication of head trauma, and a major reason why such patients should be followed very closely for several weeks after an accident. He was taken to the OR right away, and the blood clot was found and drained.

His prognosis was excellent and I was relieved. When I went up to his room to visit, I could see he was in good spirits. He even joked about the accident and being whammed, bounced, and spun around by a hit-and-run driver. He was eager to get back to work. He supervised a lab for a large pharmaceutical company, and at the moment they were working on a fascinating research project.

I realized that my detailed attention to Mr. Denning's case was simply what I should be doing as a doctor, but I was conscious of a deeper fervor, as though I had a special responsibility.

Jerry Carter, who'd been my medical resident, was a kind and supportive man. So it was especially frightening when he came into the ER one night with a stab wound in his back.

He'd been off that day and had gone by bus out to the suburbs, where he often rode horseback. Returning, he had walked from the bus stop back toward his apartment near the hospital around 9:30. It was dark and quiet along the street bordering the slum that the hospital itself sat in the middle of. He was confidently strolling along, aware that someone was walking behind him and that another man was on the other side of the street, but being an athletic man and over six feet tall, he thought nothing of it.

Suddenly he heard a few running steps behind him, and something whipped into his back with a sharp pain and remained there. He walked on for a few moments, as if stunned, until it occurred to him to turn around. He saw a figure running away from him, and he realized he'd been stabbed.

"Huh!" Jerry grunted, standing there with his mouth open. He reached behind him and felt the knife protruding from his middle right back. Oh, Jesus, he thought, that doesn't feel right. And he pulled it out.

He must have been in a kind of mental shock because he shouldn't have removed the knife; as a doctor he should have remembered that. He should have gotten himself to the Emergency Room by making somebody who lived there take him or by calling the police. The knife should have been carefully removed in the OR after x rays and precautions to stop bleeding.

But he did pull it out. Because he thought a knife didn't belong there.

He did walk on, dragging his feet, the two blocks to the hospital. By the time he got there he was panting, his back was bubbling blood, and the pleural cavity was filling up with blood. He was having a hard time breathing.

The team was instantly mobilized—cleaning the wound, getting blood for typing, and starting the IV. Though Jerry knew his own blood type, his blood, like everybody's, had to be cross-matched at the moment of crisis to make sure there were no new or temporary antibodies.

Michael Kraft knew we'd have to put a chest tube into him to get the air and blood out, but though he was stronger than I he couldn't do it. Jerry's chest was thick and muscular. To get a chest tube in, you'd have to hammer it in with more strength than had been used to stab him in the first place. None of us would do it.

"Come on, come on, you guys," he said drowsily, beginning to lose consciousness.

"I can't. I just can't do it," Michael said.

We called the chief of surgery, Dr. Cohen. The great man came and listened briefly to the story. He walked up to Jerry's large, supine form, took the pointed tube, lifted it high in the air, and with all his strength rammed it down onto the right chest just below the thick pectoral.

I saw poor Jerry's astonished expression as he realized the chief was going to stab him again.

The tube went in right between the ribs, just deep enough to begin draining.

Then Jerry was taken to the OR and sewn up.

When someone working in the hospital gets sick or has an accident, everybody is intensely concerned. It's like policemen, who are especially energetic in hunting down someone who had endangered one of their number. Jerry was a relaxed, popular guy, too. The only thing extraordinary about his quick recovery was the number of his visitors.

We were all struck now by a new danger, and we became very careful when we had to walk through the area. Jerry figured that some kid had stabbed him on a dare, since no one had robbed him; but from then on, if I heard someone running behind me, I'd twist around and leap out of the way, even in daylight. Kids playing tag didn't know what to make of me.

We hadn't had trouble in that neighborhood before. It was what you would call a slum, yes, but a coherent place in a sense. If there was a drug traffic, it went its own way; if there was prostitution, there wasn't much cruising—it was a well-organized territory and the whores worked in apartments or hotels; if the police were suspicious of most of the inhabitants, they didn't bust many. I do know that people from areas that had been cleaned up or redeveloped had been relocated elsewhere and that the area around University Hospital had quite dramatically declined. Months ago, Hasselblad had told me that a security guard from one of the new apartment complexes had come into the ER, pistol-whipped with his own pistol.

By the end of the month on Emergency, I was even more exhausted than ever. I hadn't thought that was possible. But the tension of knowing that a new disaster could burst through the doors at any moment, and the demands you make of yourself to be swift but accurate—no mistakes, or you'll push the patient over that thin line between life and death—work on you while you're not even sure whether it's night or day. Time is incoherent; a month felt like a year.

I'd been conscious of the sense of transience that seemed to pervade the Emergency service. A patient, a doctor—everyone passed along except the nurses. Even life seemed so temporary. It was a good thing we doctors didn't have to provide continuity, for by the end of the month I was feeling depressed and I didn't know how the ER nurses could stand it. There are doctors who are now beginning to specialize in emergency care, but I think a doctor who spent all his time on Emergency would have to be heroic, or crazy. I was overjoyed to be finished. And I was especially lucky that I got my week's vacation for the year just then.

What I did first was stagger into bed, intending to sleep the whole week if necessary. However, I awoke after about fourteen hours. It was eleven o'clock in the morning. When I pulled the drapes, moist gray light tumbled into the room. I was famished. Scrambled eggs, I thought with delight; toast—whole wheat toast; bacon—yes, bacon flavoring the new air of my little apartment!

I flung open the refrigerator door and groaned. I should have known. When had I last bought groceries, after all? There were a couple of jars of leftovers covered with pale green fuzz. There was a plastic bag full of rotten, brownish lettuce. A cucumber had dark bulletmarks of rot. The milk was sour, and the orange juice smelled as if it had turned to alcohol.

What was still edible was some margarine, a couple of bottles of tonic water, and box of dry fudge. With canned goods—soup, peanut butter, coffee—I could find something to eat, but not my ideal breakfast. This disappointment was a peripheral, unrecognized liability of internship.

I closed the refrigerator door, unwilling to begin my vacation by cleaning out spoiled food. I sat in the kitchenette and gazed at the rain. A weird time for a vacation, I realized. Whoever heard of a vacation in November? I was too hungry. I opened the refrigerator again, averted my eyes from most of the contents, and fished out the box of fudge. I crawled back into bed, ate about half a pound—I thought it was delicious —and snuggled back down to fall asleep again.

This time when I woke up it was 1:00 A.M. Filled with energy, I got up, brewed some coffee, turned on the radio, and cleaned out the refrigerator. Then I cleaned the kitchen. I cleaned the bathroom. My activities must have awakened some people in the apartment building for I heard a couple of toilets flush. So I couldn't use the vacuum cleaner, though I was dying to get at the rug and the upholstery. I was like a junkie needing a fix, and while I found more and more extra things to do to eke out the time before I could turn on the blamed noisemaker, it was more than I could stand.

I went out.

The streets were wet, but it was no longer raining. The gutters were clogged with leaves. In the early grayness the streetlights were pale. A car passed slowly. Several yards beyond me the door on the passenger's side opened; someone tried to get out. Brakes squealed and the car stopped. A woman got out, yelled, and started running toward me.

For a moment the car paused, then it sped away. It didn't occur to me to take down its license number until it was too late. The woman reached me, held my forearms in a desperate grip, and sobbed, tears streaking her face, "Oh, thank God, thank God."

I knew—I had known the moment the door opened while the car was still moving—that she had been raped.

"I'm a doctor," I told her. "I'm going to take you to the Emergency Room."

"Oh, thank God, thank God," she kept murmuring.

I took her back to my apartment to get my car keys and called the police. She desperately wanted to wash. I understood her feelings, but I had to prevent her; the police and doctors had to see her first. Partly to give her something to do, I asked her to take a pad of paper and write the answers to my questions as we drove to the hospital. It calmed her down and made her angry at her attacker, rather than afraid.

The ER staff was willing for me to take the case even though technically I was off—it saved them work. I wanted to do a complete exam and make careful note of each and every bruise. Often a woman feels she's being re-raped when a resident uses a speculum on her. Often, too, a policeman had to be there while the exam is being done. There was a woman resident, I was told, who was interested in the problem of rape, and I called her. She was Annabelle Zabriskie, chief pediatric resident. She lived in the suburbs, but was willing to come in.

I had to call the police station a second time to hurry them. We waited for half an hour, and I was about to call again when they finally arrived.

Helen Washington begged me to stay with her during the questioning.

"Who are you, a friend?" one of them asked.

"I'm her doctor," I snapped.

"Now, let's see," he began, "you know this man?"

"I . . . Yes, I do."

"Um-hm. He your boyfriend?"

"No. He lives somewhere in my neighborhood."

"I see. You ever go out with him before?"

"No."

"Last night was your first date?"

"I didn't . . . I wasn't on a date last night!"

"Are you a virgin?"

I interrupted. "What does that have to do with it?" I demanded.

"Well," he said, turning to me, "if you're a doctor, you know yourself that a virgin is tight, whereas . . ."

"I'm glad to know," I told him sarcastically, "that you've never raped a woman!" He looked startled. "If you had, you'd know you have to lubricate yourself with KY-Jelly or something." That was not true, as a matter of fact; a virgin is usually moist enough—like the inside of one's mouth—for rape to be possible, but not moist enough for rape to be painless.

He continued questioning her for a few minutes in

a skeptical manner, polite yet insulting, until she told him that after the rape the man had driven her around for hours while he talked, attempting to have a conversation. Suddenly the detective became serious. This was the *modus operandi* of a man who'd recently raped several women. Now he believed her. The rapist had penetrated her three times, but ejaculated only in her mouth. This pattern too was typical. There were bruises on her arms and shoulders where he had held her down, but he hadn't beaten her. There was a scratch on her cheek from the awl he had threatened her eyes with.

Helen Washington was trembling with the re-creation of her fear by the time she had finished telling her story, but fortunately the questioning was over and I could proceed with the physical.

I took smears from her vagina and her mouth. Semen will reflect under ultraviolet light, and it can be dried and saved for identification. In some people it will reveal blood type. I wasn't taking any chances of pregnancy with the small amount of semen that might have been discharged into her vagina, so I gave her the morning-after pill. The di-ethylstilbestrol, which she was to take twice a day for five days, would make her violently ill, so I prescribed some medication for the nausea. Several lacerations of the vagina were not serious enough to require stitches, fortunately; antiseptic ointments would suffice. But she also had to be tested for gonorrhea and put on antibiotic pencillin as prevention.

By the time Annabelle Zabriskie finally arrived, I was exhausted but confident that I had done everything I could for Helen Washington. When I saw Dr. Zabriskie, I wondered whether I shouldn't have called in a psychiatric consult instead. She was a tiny woman, pretty, with short, ash-blond hair, and she had a small, soft voice like a girl's. She let me speak to her only briefly in the corridor before she went into the room where Helen Washington was.

"Ms. Washington," she announced as she walked in, "I'm Dr. Zabriskie. I was raped once myself." She went straight to her and held out her hands in such a way that the woman had to sit up to grasp them. "I know how you feel."

Helen Washington burst into sobs. Dr. Zabriskie stood beside her with her arm lightly around her shoulder. She murmured words that I couldn't hear. Then she said, "I bet you could draw me every detail of the interior of that car!" and the woman laughed, tearfully.

I had been eavesdropping, in effect, and I realized I should go. I felt that I was leaving a better doctor than I with my patient.

I then went shopping and bought magnificent food and wine it turned out I would never get around to eating. I met a woman who'd been a technician in the same lab I'd worked in while I was married. She told me that a mutual friend had a play opening Off-Broadway that weekend. She and her husband were going, and if I could come, I was invited to the cast party afterward. As I walked out of the supermarket wheeling the cart full of groceries, I suddenly decided to fly to New York.

Two days later, comfortably seated next to the window of a jet flying in brilliant sunlight above the clouds, I caught my breath and thought about my vacation. I'd cleaned my apartment, bought groceries fit for gourmet cooking, and bargain-hunted through boutiques and department stores. My vacation activities had been enthusiastically "feminine." I chuckled.

The man who sat a seat away from me looked up and smiled.

"Going to New York?" he inquired.

"Yes," I acknowledged, and turned to the prospect of a pleasant conversation and male companionship.

I had thought vacation would be a time to pause, reflect, and understand. But it wasn't. I found that I became a hectic tourist in a foreign country, taking in activities and people as if I might never return to them again. One night, I dreamed of a long and narrow street shining like linoleum, and someone who must have been me walking silently as though on wheels, the sound of my wheels a soft *whissh, whissh,* like a nurse's nyloned thighs. Then Dennis drove me around for hours in his sports car until I burst into a room shouting, "Trick or treat," tremulous with apprehension but bold—daringly bold. That was one dream. There were others. I dreamed them with fascination, as though I were watching particularly compelling movies.

PART IV

November and December

Obstetrics

21

Our first day on OB was full, for we were being introduced to one floor, where the antenatal and postpartum cases and the nurseries were, and to the floor above, the labor and delivery sections of the surgical floor. They are together because some complications of labor or delivery require surgery. Along with several operating rooms for OB-GYN, there is always an emergency OR available for Caesarean sections.

In spite of my hectic expenditure of energy during vacation, and in spite of the fact that I couldn't prevent my anxious dreams, I came back to work strangely calm. I looked forward to Obstetrics being a joyful service. I expected it to erase unpleasant and painful medical memories.

One of the pleasures that greeted me was the discovery that I would be working with another woman intern, Amy Paredes. I wondered why she hadn't started in July with the rest of us. As soon as there was time, I suggested that we take a break and have some coffee, for I was very eager to get to know her.

She seemed very young, though in fact she was a little older than her fellow interns because she'd dropped out of medical school a few months before graduation, in March. She told me she was just picking up her internship now, in November.

Remembering my friend who'd dropped out and not wishing to embarrass Amy, I simply said, "You *are* back."

She looked relieved that I didn't ask questions. I don't know whether she understood my emphasis.

"You've been on for a week already," I said. "Tell me what it's like." She'd been working while I was on vacation.

"I like it," she said. "The chief of service, Dr. Lefkowitz, is famous, of course; the chief resident is very capable; the other residents on our team are good . . ."

I interrupted her: "I can't believe it. There must be something wrong with it!"

"Well," she said, "I haven't seen anything." Then she laughed, as if ironically.

Amy was extremely intelligent, with a wry sense of humor and a stoical perseverance. Coming back to an internship in the middle of a year was to waste the time, because she couldn't get credit for a program except from July to July. Thus she'd have to repeat nine months of her internship, beginning all over again next July. She was willing to do that, and her willingness was very beneficial to the hospital staff. The hospital had lost several interns from the program since the beginning of the year, and was very glad to get someone to fill in. Apparently they were politely testing her, too, to see if she'd survive.

After a week or so, Amy told me her story. She'd had a nervous breakdown in the spring and spent about six weeks in a psychiatric hospital, then was an outpatient for another two months. In therapy through the summer, she'd studied for her exams, and her medical school let her take them in September. They'd professed themselves amazed at how well she did.

"I'm suspicious of such remarks," I said.

"Yes?" she smiled.

"Sounds patronizing."

"True, true," she said airily. "But you can't fight city hall."

"Amy," I said, *"you* are the dangerous woman."

She looked taken aback. "What do you mean?"

"Well, me," I explained, "everybody can see what I'm thinking . . ."

"Which is hardly true," she observed sardonically.

"Let me finish," I demanded. "It's someone like you, accommodating, who's the subversive. When you sneak into your medical school with a round black bomb in your hand everybody else will be appalled, but *I* won't be surprised."

She was a little embarrassed that I'd detected the resentment beneath her apparent meekness.

I grew to like Amy a lot, and from the very beginning we depended on one another for understanding and cooperation. One of the hassles on the delivery floor was scrubdresses. We'd strip to our underwear and put a scrubdress on in the morning. For a delivery, there were plenty of sterile paper gowns to put on over that, but the scrubdresses were scarce, and the nurses didn't appreciate our stealing their allotment. The male staff was provided with cotton trousers and shirts, the nurses were provided with their own scrubdresses; but the laundry couldn't seem to remember that there were two extra woman doctors up here, and they were forever forgetting to send up additional gowns. When we made a request for more, they were unwilling to add them to the regular allotment, apparently suspicious that we'd want to wear them more often than necessary. Unbeautiful, faded blue-green sacks that they were, we needed them on the delivery floor, but there was no temptation to consider them clothing.

We had to make a friend of one woman down in the laundry, and either Amy or I would go down each day to pick up extra gowns that our co-conspirator saved for us. Then we kept them in our room so they wouldn't be used by anybody else.

One night, early in our rotation, we were both on and observing a normal delivery. We hadn't gotten used to the rhythm of nighttime OB—periods of hectic activity alternating with periods of boring waiting—and we were tired and frazzled. At 4:00 A.M., dazed and wrinkled, we stood side by side in our faded gowns when the obstetrician, exhilarated by the birth of the baby and punchy with the late hour, cried out to the mother, "A girl! A baby girl! Isn't that lovely!

187

Wouldn't you like your daughter to grow up to be a doctor, like these two?"

The woman took one revolted look at us and said, "Oh, no, I want my daughter to grow up to be a lady."

It was funny how the hospital had provided for two woman doctors to sleep on duty. I had shared an on-call room with men on Private Medicine and had been able to appropriate a little single room on the Ward and ER. Now, however, with two women, the hospital had decided they couldn't ignore the issue entirely. They gave us a windowless closet with metal bunks; we called it the Cot Closet. The walls were full of shelves and empty, glass-fronted cupboards. I had to marvel at their surrendering so much storage space, because the halls in the labor and delivery wing were cluttered with equipment and carts of supplies.

Perhaps there is a delight in giving birth that is contagious, but obstetricians seemed to go into a kind of high in the delivery room, as if they'd succeeded in actually giving birth themselves. They laughed and made lewd jokes, and this transformation of the doctor they'd been going to for months shocked some women.

One obstetrician, seated between a woman's up-raised legs and looking closely at her perineum while he stitched up the episiotomy—the cut often made to prevent tissue from tearing when the baby is pushed through—always asked, "How big is your husband, Ruby?"—or Mary, or Franny—as though he could stitch the opening of the vagina to fit. (The last stitch of the episiotomy was called "the husband's knot.") I saw one woman turn red from head to foot with embarrassment.

This particular obstetrician always made his patients' bottoms very tight. I told him that it was probably uncomfortable for his patients. "Aw," he said, "they get it all stretched out soon enough."

"Well," I responded lightly, "maybe so. But I've never thought it was pleasant for a man to try to screw a Coke bottle."

I think he did loosen up a little on the stitching.

The first night I was on, I got to assist with a not quite ordinary case.

The patient was fifteen, and she had had such a long labor that in order to reduce the possible danger to the baby in its slow, agonizing passage through the birth canal it had been delivered by forceps. The obstetrical forceps is a pair of long metal tongs ending in oval rings that act as a helmet to protect the baby's head. The baby is drawn out of the vagina using this protective device. Because of the tight fit of the baby, there had been many vaginal lacerations. She was going to be sore afterward, but not in agony, because the vagina up high has hardly any nerve endings. The baby, though bruised, was in good shape. The mother was now out cold on the delivery table and her body was tipped so that the presenting view was of her vagina.

The doctor was sewing up all the tears, and my job was to hold the retractors and keep sponging in order to maintain a clear view. The woman's vagina looked like mincemeat. The doctor went about his stitching very carefully and competently; it took two hours, though it seemed longer. (It sometimes takes longer to do a vaginal delivery than a Caesarean.) He kept up a running commentary on his patient's sex life, her probable excitability, generalizations about the sex life of teen-aged girls, and his theories of the subtle variation of the stages of female sexual excitement.

I shifted from one foot to another.

"Ha-ha!" he chuckled. "You let your hands relax, Doctor. Keep the field open, now, keep it open. You know how to do it."

"Yes, I do," I said.

"Ha-ha-ha!" he laughed. "I bet you do."

When the operation and repair work were finished I was glad to get out of there. Afterward the doctor's manner changed radically, and when he emerged from the Surgeons' Lounge dressed in his street clothes he looked self-contained and powerful, and he nodded and bowed to me as though he didn't quite recognize me. It was not uncommon for doctors to have a distinct operating room personality that was very different from their "public" one. This man's transformation went from boor in the OR to courtier in public.

One of the odd duties of an obstetrician is to circumcise the boy babies—you would think that a surgeon or a pediatrician might be the logical choice for this task. Amy found it one of the most difficult spectacles on OB, though I didn't share her reluctance. It was the resident who usually did it, at "circumcision time" each morning, but we interns were required to learn how.

The men on the staff almost always joked about circumcisions. The second time that I was being supervised by my chief resident, a man named Burke, he suddenly said urgently, "Watch it, watch it!" and after a moment, "God, I was afraid you'd take the whole thing off!"

Gazing at the incredibly tiny penis of the infant below, I responded, "Are you kidding? I wouldn't do that. These kids are just the right age: I might need them in fifteen to twenty years!"

Poor little boys, they cried of course at the beginning, but strangely, they all stopped crying at some point before the procedure was over. I'll never know why.

*

I detected no cycle of busy and light days on the delivery wing. Susan Freeman, a nurse, thinks there is a major thirteen-day rhythm, with a smaller counterrhythm of eight days. I wasn't sure how serious she was in proposing such an esoteric system because Adela French, another delivery wing nurse, laughed. She said, "There's *no* rhyme or reason to it. The only pattern I can see is emergencies come when there's not enough of us around to deal with them."

I had stopped in the Nurses' Lounge, a small room with an even smaller locker room off it. There were a cracked vinyl and chrome sofa, a chair, and a telephone. It was an appallingly ugly little room.

The telephone rang with the announcement that Dr. Lefkowitz was admitting a patient, Mrs. George, the daughter of the director of the hospital. She was going to deliver twins. Twins are an important event because so many complications can occur, what with the different presentations and the possibility that one or the other's cord could be compromised during the labor. Both Susan Freeman and Adela French, being the best and most experienced nurses on duty at the time, were to assist at this delivery.

Susan grimaced as she got up. "My feet are killing me."

"I keep trying to tell you, woman," said Adela, "to get yourself some space shoes, like me." Adela, a strikingly beautiful woman, wore incredibly ugly shoes. She got kidded about them, but paid no attention.

"Too expensive," Susan replied.

"And too ugly?" I supplied.

"Yeah," Susan corroborated. We were walking down the hall.

"I don't care how they look, momma, I just want my feet to feel good!" Adela declared. In fact, she'd had to get a letter from an orthopedist and special permission to wear her shoes. Nurses were tyrannized about their clothing. They had to wear a certain kind of nylon stockings. If they wanted to wear support hose, they had to wear them *under* regulation stockings. In contrast to their regimentation, I could look awful because I was a doctor, but I tried to minimize my greater freedom. I'd prefer to wear socks, for example, but I wore stockings. However, I did wear comfortable, broken-down slippers.

Everybody on the OB staff wanted to work with Dr. Lefkowitz on a twin birth. A dignified man in his sixties, he concentrated on teaching and on fertility research, and he could seldom be observed actually delivering a baby in his famous grave manner. One story about his coolness was famous. He was majesti-

191

cally beginning a straightforward Caesarean section, passing the scalpel over the pregnant belly of the patient in the long incision, when a spout of urine welled up. Somebody hadn't catheterized the bladder and he'd sliced a full bladder open. Without blinking he put a sponge down on the place and said airily, "Sometimes one gets carried away!"

Adela and Susan were lucky to be on duty when Mrs. George came in. They were hoping that her labor would go fast enough so the babies could be born while they were still there. I wished I could be in on it, but interns seldom get to do anything important with private patients. I shuffled off. In the next hour several women were admitted in various stages of labor, and soon everyone was well occupied. I was given Mrs. Flannery, a woman who'd come to the clinic a few times during her pregnancy. She was now laboring with her sixth baby. Her brown hair was graying and she had blue-gray eyes with freckled, pale skin.

She'd had no trouble with any of her previous deliveries. This labor was going smoothly: effacement, or the thinning of the cervix, was occurring speedily; the fetal heartbeat was fine; and Mrs. Flannery was working away, knowing exactly what to expect and not at all intimidated by it. She was a strong, well-built woman with a pelvis you could drive a Mack truck through (that was the witticism obstetricians used to describe a wide birth canal through the pelvis). She was overweight, so I had no idea how big the baby was. We talked a lot when I came in to check her. I kidded her about not waiting long enough to get a Thanksgiving baby. She laughed and said, "My kids are fighting about whether I should have a girl or a boy. Whichever way it turns out, some of them are not going to thank me."

She told me about her kids, all of them twelve or under. Her husband was out of work and on disability right now, having hurt his back. When I asked her how they managed with such a large family, she replied cheerfully that she had worked part-time at

192

Sears, until her seventh month. Her husband willingly supervised the children, and her twelve-year-old daughter was a great little mother.

In about five contractions Mrs. Flannery approached full dilation. I was surprised at how fast it went. I got ready to take her quickly into the delivery room so she wouldn't push the baby out onto the bed. Our delivery room was next to the main event; Mrs. George was about to be taken also. I began to get excited.

The nurse with me was a willing, cordial worker, but she was new and didn't speak much English. Our hospital had an exchange program and sometimes had Filipino nurses. She told me her name was Señora Assunta Consuelo Navarro, which she pronounced beautifully and swiftly, but it was too ornate for me to hear or use. I told her I would call her "Nurse."

It was to be a straightforward delivery for Mrs. Flannery, and with the drain on the rest of the staff, there were only the three of us in our delivery room: me, the nurse, and a nurse-anesthetist to monitor a spinal after the anesthesiologist had given it. A spinal anesthetic blocks all sensation in the pelvic area; a woman can't feel her contractions and so she doesn't know exactly when to push. Therefore we kept monitoring the contractions so we could instruct Mrs. Flannery when to exert herself. The baby's head was down so fast that I was guarding the introitus, feeling the head with one hand and smoothing the introitus with the other, while on the other side of the draping the nurse felt the abdomen for the contractions. When the nurse got excited and called out something I interpreted it to mean a contraction, and so I shouted to Mrs. Flannery, "Take a deep breath and for ten seconds: Push! Push! Push! Push! Push! Push! Push! Push! Push! Push!"

The contractions were coming every two minutes, lasting for a minute, and at each contraction I would count the seconds off with "Push! Push! Push!" for ten, yell "Take a deep breath and Push! Push! Push!" for another ten, and on and on. I felt the baby's head pressing. I felt the force of the mother's muscles. I yelled and she pushed, and I could hear the nurse saying something that must have meant the contractions were over; Mrs. Flannery gasped, "Jesus Mary!" and we were all able to pause and rest for a minute. The nurse swabbed off Mrs. Flannery's sweating forehead and face. I peeked at her over the draping between her upraised legs and encouraged her: "You're doing great, Mrs. Flannery, the baby's almost here."

"I can't feel a thing!" she mumbled, tired from pushing. The nurse looked up at me.

"Here comes another one!" I shouted, dropping back into my position and calling "Push now! Come on, that's it, push, push, push it out! Whoops, here it is!" The baby had slipped into the world easily and needed no episiotomy to get through.

It was a small baby girl, perfectly formed, probably of good birth weight, but too small, suspiciously small, for a sixth baby from a woman of Mrs. Flannery's size. Uh-oh, I thought. After I clamped and cut the cord and checked that she was breathing all right, I gave the baby to the nurse. Then I looked into Mrs. Flannery's vagina and thought I saw another bag of waters! Twins!

I said to the nurse, "Hey, run out and see if there's somebody in the hall who can help!"

She turned from her work on the baby and looked at me inquiringly. She hadn't understood me. "Can you speak Spanish?" I asked the anesthetist, who herself could not leave the patient. She shook her head no. It would take too long for me to get the nurse to understand she should give the baby to Mrs. Flannery and go get someone to help with twins. Hell, it was good to have Spanish-speaking nurses on, and this one *was* a good nurse, but I hoped she'd learn more English before long or that I would learn more Spanish.

I'd have to do it. Everybody else was otherwise engaged anyway. The nurse-anesthetist could help if necessary with a breech. I ruptured the membranes. What I felt then was not a head but unmistakably a pair of feet. Not only was I going to get to deliver twins, this was going to be my first breech delivery, and a double footling one at that (in which both feet are presenting instead of buttocks).

"What's the matter?" Mrs. Flannery asked.

"Nothing at all!" I cried, delightedly. "Mrs. Flannery," I announced, grinning, "you are having twins!"

"Twins!" she wailed. "Oh no!"

"Quite a surprise, eh?" I added fatuously. With the nurse's signal I said, "Okay, here's the contraction; now, come on, Mrs. Flannery, let's have another pooosh! Push! Push!" If I'd been loud before, I was twice as loud now as I encouraged her with a cheer, and without having time to worry whether I'd be able to extricate the baby if the head were too large or the position was odd, I found myself catching the infant. A boy following his sister.

"Twins!" I gurgled. "A girl and a boy! You're the mother of twins, Mrs. Flannery!"

She was laughing weakly. "Oh no!" she kept saying. She looked foolish and bewildered.

When I'd taken care of everything and Mrs. Flannery had gone to her room to recover, I went to the other delivery room, poked my head in the door, and started to say "Guess what?"

Alex Winton, the first-year resident, looked up and said, "Be quiet!"

The great Dr. Lefkowitz turned his head toward me. "Was that you, Doctor," he asked in a deep, firm voice, "in the next room not so long ago?"

"Yes, sir, it was," I said jauntily.

"And now you are presumably no longer *in* that room?"

"That's right. I'm finished."

"Good. Let me be the first to congratulate you on being finished."

The two men turned back to their work. Adela's eyes were looking at me above her mask and smiling as though she were tickled to death. Later she told me that my shouts of "Push! Push! Push!" had been

195

heard in Dr. Lefkowitz's delivery room. They had been very disturbing to any rhythm Mrs. George might have been working on, and had irritated the doctors.

By the time I looked in, they'd just delivered the first twin, breech, and the second one was presenting vertex, or head down; they were doing everything slowly and safely. I left them to their work and happily went to complete my own twin baby papers.

The next day Mrs. Flannery had time to take in her achievement. "I can't wait until I get my hands on that priest," she threatened. "I didn't even want another *one,* let alone two! Now I got seven!"

She took the babies to her breast very lovingly though.

"Your kids won't be disappointed," I noted. "A girl and a boy—something for everyone!"

When I spoke to her about contraceptives she said she wanted her tubes tied. She didn't want and couldn't use any other method. I made arrangements for her to have it done in six weeks. "What the priest don't know won't hurt him," she said.

22

When I was walking down the hall one morning I saw a man I recognized. Mr. Monroe was a prominent museum director from whom I'd taken an art appreciation course once when I was married. I remembered the pleasurable envy I'd felt when I contemplated what I thought was a kind of human perfection and happiness. Mr. Monroe had a thriving career making the art museum lively and successful, enjoyed a great deal of prestige, and was confident and considerate.

He was handsome, tall, and athletic. He gave a course each year somewhere in the city. I think he had inherited wealth and he must have been well paid, too. He drove a Rolls.

Mrs. Monroe also seemed to enjoy the American dream. She was so beautiful, she had been a model. She was intelligent, sophisticated, and kind, and had many friends and admirers. She was very active on the boards of various organizations, and it was known that she was dedicated and energetic, not a society figurehead, when she got involved.

She was in to have her third child, by natural childbirth. When I saw Mr. Monroe walking down the hall I said hello. He'd been heading for his wife's room, but he stopped to say a relaxed hello to me.

"I'm flattered that you recognized me," I said.

He smiled, "Of course I recognized you, Doctor. There weren't many women in that class, after all."

I laughed.

"Are you going to assist with my wife?" he asked politely.

"Well, I haven't been assigned her," I answered, "but I'd be very happy to. Let's see if I can arrange it."

Eagerly I went to ask the resident and her private doctor whether they'd mind putting me on Mrs. Monroe's case. Burke, my chief resident, was willing for me to volunteer for an extra case any time. Her doctor said, sipping his coffee, "There's not going to be anything to do, Doctor. She's doing it natural, you know. But if you want to stand around and watch, that's okay with me."

When I went back to tell Mr. Monroe that I would be there, he was with his wife. The nurse told me that she was well into active labor and wanting to push the baby already. We should get her to the delivery room. She was working hard, grunting with the pain and effort and panting throughout the long expulsion contractions, the most painful in the whole labor. She gripped her husband's hand so fiercely that it must have been difficult for him.

We whipped her into the delivery room and I quickly scrubbed and put on my gown and booties. Dr. Parker had not yet arrived; he was just being informed that she was into precipitate labor. In a moment between contractions when I asked her how she was doing, she smiled weakly, murmuring, "Okay." When I looked, I could see that the baby's head was crowning, becoming visible at the vaginal opening. My excitement mounted. Maybe if Dr. Parker didn't arrive in time I could deliver her.

Unfortunately he came striding into the room at exactly that moment, calling out to her heartily, "Well, well, well. Thought you'd sneak by me, eh?"

"Oh too bad, Dr. Parker," I said. "I thought you'd let me do it."

He laughed, saying, "Someday, maybe."

Mrs. Monroe was trying to push, but lying flat gave her no leverage. "Get your wife's shoulders up," I told Mr. Monroe, who was standing at the head of the table, calmly watching everything—or so it seemed.

He nodded to me as if he understood, but he did nothing. I couldn't tell whether he'd heard me or not. There was a lot of noise, as there often is in the delivery room, with Mrs. Monroe whining and growling as she pushed her baby down and Dr. Parker talking to her steadily, smoothing the introitus around the baby's head and stretching the skin. I tried to get Mr. Monroe's attention. Finally I had to go to him and show him how to put his shoulder and back under hers to lift her to a better angle. Now I was no longer sterile and couldn't have helped Dr. Parker if he'd needed me. All you needed to make this position possible on a delivery table was a wedge-shaped cushion, which some delivery tables in other hospitals had. Mr. Monroe followed my advice, but a bit reluctantly, I thought. Now he couldn't see anything unless he twisted his head around.

Soon Dr. Parker was helping the baby through the perineum, and Mrs. Monroe, feeling it come, cried out "Whuuup!" and the baby was born sunnyside up, its face and eyes looking up to the ceiling.

"Ah!" I said, craning to see the baby as it tumbled out.

Dr. Parker held it for a split second, glancing over it for abnormalities as OBs do. The infant boy had screwed up his face, pulled the air into his lungs in a couple of gasps, and let out a little cry. He was breathing fine.

Dr. Parker looked at me, nodded, and cut the cord.

"Ah," I said to Mrs. Monroe. "You have a beautiful son!"

She smiled perfunctorily, trying to watch the baby and whatever the nurse was doing to it. Her husband seemed very tight and inexpressive. The nurse held the baby, tilted, for Mr. Monroe to see. "See? Isn't he a lovely boy?" she beamed.

"Hey!" Dr. Parker kidded, "boys don't get called 'lovely.'" She took the baby to the corner where she put the drops in his eyes, cleaned off the vernix caseosa, or the cheesy-looking substance that covers the skin of the fetus, and began to footprint him.

"Boys are just as lovely as girls when they're first born. It's only later that they lose all their attractions," the nurse repeated defiantly.

Mr. Monroe had not said a word. He looked pale. "Are you all right?" I asked him. "Do you want to sit down?"

His wife looked at him anxiously.

Mr. Monroe looked haughtily at the corner where the baby was being cared for. "You don't know what he's like inside."

Chilled by his ominous words, I went over to the nurse. "Is the baby okay?" I asked in a low voice.

"Yes, of course," she said in a normal tone.

Mr. Monroe left his wife's side and came over to us. "You don't know," he said accusingly.

"Well, uh, sir," began the nurse.

I left the room and went to the nearest phone. "Get a pediatric consult over here right away," I instructed the operator. "Delivery Room Four. We've got a problem baby."

The chief of pediatrics himself, Dr. Gates, came

199

within a few minutes. I had waited for him in the hall and explained. Without a word he went straight in, scrubbed, and in another minute was in the delivery room talking quietly to Mr. Monroe as he carefully examined his newborn son.

In the meantime Dr. Parker was delivering the placenta and stitching up the episiotomy. I stayed outside, looking in, sensing that there were many people in that room, taut and quiet, listening to Dr. Gates talk to the father.

When Mrs. Monroe was finished I accompanied her to her room and got her settled there. It was unusual that she was not falling asleep, for women invariably did so after their exhausting work. But she looked tense and anxious. Her husband had not come with her, but had prevailed upon Dr. Gates to do a more thorough cardiac exam and had gone with him to await the results.

I was worried about Mrs. Monroe. She was frightened. I called Dr. Parker, hoping he had not yet left the hospital. He talked with her while I hovered outside in the hall. When he came out I motioned him to come with me into the lounge.

"What's the problem?" I asked. "The baby's fine, isn't he?"

Dr. Parker nodded yes. "You see her chart?" he asked.

"No, I just came on at the last minute."

"Ah, yes."

"Mr. Monroe let me," I said.

Dr. Parker tipped his head. "Her chart would have told you the story. She's been my patient for almost twelve years, during which she's had nine pregnancies. This is her third live birth. Their first baby was a boy with a heart defect that showed up after a couple of days. He's had several operations, and he's only eight."

"The second child?" I asked.

"A girl, normal. Now the third is a boy, and they want to make sure he's okay."

"Is there any doubt so far?" I asked.

"No. I have every reason to believe that he's normal too." Dr. Parker sighed. "I thought that the best way to handle it was to ignore the fear. Once she'd made it past the first trimester she was home free. I thought their plans to do natural childbirth were a healthy sign. They both seemed fine."

"She didn't want any drugs?" I said.

He nodded. We both realized she must have feared damaging the baby, for he went on as he got to his feet. "All this propaganda against drugs! I can't count how many women I've delivered healthy babies to who had all kinds of drugs. Hell, most of these women who come in expecting to be able to drop a baby like a cow get Demerol at least." Demerol is a narcotic analgesic.

"Well," he said briskly, "she's getting herself sterilized. We'll give her a tubal ligation. She won't have to go through all this agony again." Abruptly, he left.

I went to the door to Mrs. Monroe's room. Her roommate looked up and started to speak, but I motioned her to hush. Mrs. Monroe was sleeping, curled up on her side, with her silky hair partially covering her smooth face. One finger was touching her lips.

The baby turned out to be fine and Mrs. Monroe quickly lost her anxiety, but her husband was still suspicious and cold, as if he feared to love the child yet. She joked, teased, and played with him, partly to get him to relax. He treated her as though her strength and vivacity were amazing, almost incredible. I supposed that when he finally realized the baby was healthy, he'd behave more comfortably with his wife, too.

I took care of Mrs. Monroe for the week she was with us. They'd insisted that the baby stay that long, so she did, too. She was completely recovered in a few days except for some perineal itching from the stitches. She overrode the fourth-day depression, possibly buoyed up by the relief that her son was normal. I don't think I've seen anyone so pleased to go home.

When they left, she was gazing up at her husband with adoration, and he was actually smiling.

Betty Lester came to the prenatal clinic just before it closed one afternoon. Her husband dropped her off on his way to work on the night shift somewhere. They expected her to deliver soon, and since this was her fifth child, they were both somewhat blasé about it. It was alarming, however, that she had a little vaginal bleeding.

The resident on duty got an IV into her and sent her up to the labor floor to be examined since there was a possibility she had a placenta previa—that is, the placenta partially covering the os, or exit from the uterus—and she'd have to have a Caesarean. She was to be my patient, with Jeff Donaldson, a second-year resident, supervising.

She was sitting in a wheelchair, her IV bottle inverted on the IV pole, by the nurses' station, talking cheerfully. She leaned on one arm of the wheelchair as if to take the weight of her pregnancy off her rear end. I had no doubt that after five children she had a bad case of hemorrhoids.

She looked up at me. "Oho!" she said. "They got women doctors now, too?"

"Yes, ma'am," I said. "I'm Dr. Donnan."

She eyed me with some amusement. "What will they think of next?" she asked the air, winking at a nurse.

"I'll take you down and examine you now," I said.

"Say, Nancy," Mrs. Lester said to the nurse. "You ever let a woman doctor do you?" Nancy had three children.

"I have the same training as a male doctor, Mrs. Lester," I assured her, knowing that women about to deliver can get very alarmed about things.

"I never had it done by a woman doctor," she said, smiling. "I guess I can afford to try it."

I started to wheel her down the hall and around the corner to the labor wing. "Say, put me in Three, will you?" she asked, craning her head to look up at me.

"Okay, let's see if it's free," I said.

"I had my last one in Three. A pretty little girl. It's good luck for me. I have two girls and two boys; now I want another boy. You know Susan?" she asked.

"Susan Freeman?" I replied.

"Yeah. Can I have her? I had her for the last three, she's a good girl."

"She's not on right at the moment, but if you deliver after she comes, I should think she'd be happy to help out."

She clucked her tongue. "Okey-doke," she said, settling down for the last minute of the ride and singing under her breath. Then the nurse and I helped her onto the bed and got her ready to be examined.

I noticed she had winced when she moved to the bed. "You have some pain?" I asked.

"Aah, just a little bit."

"Where?"

She touched a place a little low and to the side of her belly. "Its nothing," she said. "But I've been having a naggin' backache."

First I listened for the fetal heartbeat. I had had the bell of the stethoscope in my hand for the past two minutes, so that it would be warm when I put it to the woman's skin. As soon as I put it on her belly and started to listen, moving it around after a few moments, she said proudly, "Oh, he was quite active two or three hours ago. This one is surely a boy. He's kicked and kicked. He gives me no rest!"

"Sssh!" I hushed her.

Usually I could hear the fetal heart in spite of the mother's talk, bowel sounds, and noises in the room. But this time I could pick up no beat. I moved the stethoscope around, pausing and straining to hear, feeling with my hand for any protuberances that would clue me in to the baby's position in the mother's abdomen.

"You can bring the monitor over," I instructed the nurse casually. As my hand touched the place Mrs.

Lester had indicated was tender, I felt the uterus contract in hyperactivity, and she sucked in her breath in sudden pain.

"Boy!" she said. "Either you got some witch's touch, or that baby just gave me a terrific pinch!"

"Hm," I grunted. The nurse came over with the monitor, a box that looks like an FM tuner with a paper strip coming out of it; it's attached to a belt that can be placed around the woman's belly—often to her annoyance—to pick up the baby's heartbeat through ultrasound amplifiers and the uterine contractions through a pressure gauge. "You know the monitor," I said to her. "I'll just move the belt around a little."

I listened all over, but the machine could pick up no heartbeat. The baby was dead.

I straightened up. The baby's head was far down. The uterus was irritable. Mrs. Lester was bleeding. Everything suggested that she had had an abruption—a premature detachment of the placenta—that killed her baby.

"What is it?" she asked anxiously, her previous cheerfulness gone.

It's not fair not to tell a patient the truth. I said, "Your baby is dead, and I think your own life might be in danger. I'm going to break your bag of waters and get your labor started right away."

She sucked in her breath and turned her face away.

Jeff Donaldson examined her. The cervix was three centimeters dilated and the water was intact. So we ruptured the membranes; dark, wine-colored fluid started dripping out.

We looked at one another quickly. It *was* an abruption. We'd have to get her delivered soon.

"I can feel the water leaking out," Mrs. Lester called out.

"Yes, that's right," I told her, coming to her side. "We're going to make sure you go into labor. We'll start a pitocin drip, here through your intravenous, and watch you very carefully." Pitocin stimulates the uterus to contract and is used to induce labor.

"You watch me for sure," she warned. "I go fast."

"Good," I told her. Jeff and I quickly agreed that I was to follow her progress and he'd check with me in an hour.

At 8:30 that evening, when I was walking down the hall toward Mrs. Lester's labor room, my buzzer went off. I stopped right outside her door to take the call, which was to go to her room immediately. She'd started hemorrhaging.

I rushed in. Blood was pouring from her vagina. She'd started to bleed from the IV site. Her blood pressure had plummeted and her pulse was rising. She wasn't clotting. The rapidity of the deterioration was appalling.

Susan Freeman was with her. We got another line into the IV to measure central venous pressure. We called for some blood units that had already been cross-matched and started transfusing her immediately.

Mrs. Lester was frightened and in pain but she was silent. She'd been in satisfactory labor for several hours, but now she was worried. "I never had it like this," she murmured. Susan took her hand and clasped it.

"You'll be all right," she assured her. "We'll take care of you."

"I know it," she murmured, and gasped as another contraction came. They were getting harder.

Dr. Burke, the chief resident, arrived. He, Jeff Donaldson, and I stood in the hall and discussed the gravity of her situation. It was probable that a clot, developing behind the detached placenta, was using up the clotting factors in her blood. This meant that any incision would erupt into more bleeding. So we couldn't risk a Caesarean, for instance. Even an epidural anesthetic, administered by needle within the vertebra but outside the dura of the spine, could not be risked for fear of hematoma or blood clot in the spine. She was a compromised patient. If her condition didn't improve, and delivery didn't take place so the uterus could clamp down on the bleeding, we'd probably have to risk a section, anyway.

The most delicate problem was to keep her stable,

205

so Burke and Donaldson took over that job. The pitocin was continued and now blood was being transfused, with clotting factors and narcotics to keep the pain tolerable.

Then she went into tonic contractions—fierce, continuous pain—and she began screaming. "Make it stop! Make it stop!" she screamed. Susan Freeman sat close to her, telling her it would soon be over, making her feel that Susan at least believed it. Mrs. Lester yelled at Susan, "Shut up! I hate you, you liar!" She cursed the baby, she cursed the doctors, begged our forgiveness, pleaded with us to save her. She was half out of her mind with pain and the narcotic Demerol. Her torment was awful.

At last she was ready to deliver and we moved her into the delivery room. Since Burke and Donaldson were still carefully monitoring the inflows, it was my job to deliver her.

On the table, her legs up in the stirrups and draped, she was still bleeding out as fast as the blood was going into her. Then a huge contraction robbed her of her breath, her uterus expelled the baby, and her body pushed it down in one great heave. Through my waiting hands and into my lap fell the dead infant, the placenta, a large clot, and a panful of spattering blood.

She uttered a long high moan and began at last to breathe normally. "It's over," I heard her say, as I bent over the contents of my lap in a near faint. Immediately I pulled myself together, realizing that she was still bleeding copiously. Susan was massaging her belly already, to make the uterus clamp down, and I saw everything was under control—the other two doctors were dealing with the bleeding—so I turned around and gave my burden to a nurse. After I checked for lacerations, at last I could leave the room.

I changed my gown before I went to see Mrs. Lester in the recovery room so she wouldn't be alarmed by the dark stains on the blue. By that time her bleeding had subsided, and she was experiencing the normal uterine contractions that follow delivery.

"I don't hear the baby," she murmured, exhausted.

Her pain, the drugs, or the relief had made her forget.

There was a silence, then, "Your baby is dead," Susan told her again.

"Ohhhh," she cried out, grabbing Susan's hand and looking up at her. Mrs. Lester started to cry. Susan brushed the woman's hair from her forehead, and I saw her cry, too.

"She's stable now," Dr. Burke said. "Let's move her."

I suggested that she be put on GYN instead of on the postpartum floor. "Sure," said Dr. Burke, and Susan and I took her down.

Since Mrs. Lester was transferred to a GYN intern, I didn't see her regularly. I did stop in her room a couple of times, but our conversations were polite and perfunctory. She depended on Susan Freeman to stop in to talk. I asked Susan about her spirits. She told me that Mrs. Lester was depressed, yes, but after she went through the grief she would be okay. Susan didn't elaborate.

When I was on call in my third week, I was awakened for a delivery at about 6:00 A.M. I rolled out of the cot, put my shoes on, and ran to the end of the hall where the ambulance crew was just bringing the patient off the elevator. They were relieved to see me, for they hadn't wanted to deliver her themselves. She was a woman whose pregnancy seemed overwhelmed by fat.

A tremor passed over her body and she grunted. Her contractions were coming fast.

"What is your name? Have you come here for prenatal care?" I asked quickly before another contraction took over. Mrs. Meacham had come to the prenatal clinic and her chart was at the desk, so I could grab it and take off down the hall with her.

The nurse came after us. "Do you still want your tubes tied, Mrs. Meacham?" she asked. "You signed for it before."

The woman gasped at the end of the contraction

and said, "Lordy, yes. This 'un'll be number nine. I don't want no more."

We were in the delivery room. In the middle of our trying to get her onto the delivery table, she grunted out, "Baby come!"

"No, no!" I cried. "Don't do it!" I took a deep breath and told her, more quietly, "Don't push, Mrs. Meacham. Just keep calm. Breathe rapidly. Take little breaths, like this." I showed her how. "Now don't push yet."

I did a pelvic exam. The cervix was fully dilated, the bag of waters was still intact, and the baby's head was not down in the pelvis yet. "Mrs. Meacham, the baby's not coming yet," I told her.

"What'd I feel then?" she asked me suspiciously.

"Well, just a normal impulse," I said confidently. "Don't push. We're not ready yet." I didn't want her to push because the baby's cord might drop down before the head when the membranes broke, and then the oxygen and blood supply to the baby might be cut off. A push or a contraction might send the cord down. I was going to needle the membranes, as we called it—break the bag of waters carefully.

When I pricked the membranes gently the clear amniotic fluid began trickling slowly out of the cervix, and as the waters trickled out I could feel that the baby's head was lower than I had at first thought, so since it was already somewhat engaged I wouldn't have to worry about the cord after all. Mrs. Meacham's sensations had been more accurate than my theories, apparently.

"Okay," I said encouragingly.

"Okay what, girl?" she asked scornfully; then, as the next contraction came, she dragged a huge amount of air into her lungs as though she was taking a long drag on a cigarette, held it, and pushed.

Along with a great fart, down the birth canal came the baby. I had to impede its progress to make sure that it could pass through the perineal exit, which it did without any trouble. If I hadn't been there, it might have come sailing out.

"Well, Mrs. Meacham," I said, rising from my receiving position, "you have a lovely girl."

She grimaced. "Hope she do better than me. Now, when you gonna get to them tubes?" Since she'd been definite and signed for it ahead of time, it could be done right away.

"In a moment, in a moment. It won't be me who does it. The nurse is rounding up the right doctor now." I wanted to show her the baby. Both white and black babies look pretty much alike at birth—kind of purple and a little ugly. But this baby's features were regular and delicate.

When she saw how beautiful her new daughter was her face softened appreciatively. "Can't tell her skin color for a while yet—she'll probably get as black as the rest of 'em," she observed. "But everything else is okay, ain't it?" We smiled at each other.

I checked for lacerations. Her delivery had been so fast, this was the first chance the nurse had to get an IV into her. Then I tried to massage the uterus to encourage the delivery of the placenta. The placenta is a jellyfishlike organ attached to the uterine wall that usually detaches as the uterus shrinks. The space it occupied is no longer there, so it simply shears off and is expelled. The average wait is eight minutes; it could be a half-hour. As an intern, I was not allowed to explore manually for it, so I just had to wait. It wasn't until after the placenta was delivered that they could give her anesthesia, make the abdominal incision, and tie the tubes.

We waited and waited. The baby was all set, Mrs. Meacham was starting to snore on the delivery table, and I was sitting there at the foot of the table, waiting. The nurse continued to massage her belly to help the uterus contract. It's amazing how swiftly the uterus does shrink after delivery—from full size down to an eighth of that almost at once!

By now it was 7:15 A.M. and I could hear people out in the hall, on their way to rounds.

I looked down again and saw a large amount of

blood oozing from the vagina, but the placenta wasn't coming out.

"Hey!" I yelled at the top of my lungs. "Whoever's out there, help!"

Mrs. Meacham woke up with a jerk. "What's 'at?" she complained.

Alex Winton, the first-year resident, rushed in. "What the hell's going on?" he demanded.

"I can't remove this placenta," I told him.

"Hell, Doctor, why didn't you get the nurse to come out and get me? Why this big, hysterical yell? Look what you've done, you've alarmed your patient!"

"Now don't you pull that shit on my doctor!" Mrs. Meacham surprisingly came to my defense. "She just deliver me a beautiful child!"

He turned to me and said curtly, "What's your trouble here?"

"It's been forty-five minutes and the placenta hasn't delivered yet, and now we're getting bleeding. I need your permission to go after it."

"Sure," he said, and he turned and walked out.

A fat lot of supervision I was going to get from him. I'd done this only twice before, so I began hesitantly. Since the cervix was still dilated, I could get my hand all the way up into the still-enlarged uterus. Expecting to work my hand in and around the edge bit by bit until the placenta came away, I placed one hand on the abdomen to hold the uterus and one hand inside. I realized with a sinking feeling that the uterus had clamped down and that I'd have to work against the force of this tough, strong muscle. It wasn't going to separate easily at all. Mrs. Meacham was grunting again and cursing now. It was becoming very painful for her. After a few minutes I seemed to have separated a good bit of the placenta, but some of it would still not budge. Then I saw I was getting more bleeding.

"You get Dr. Winton," I said to the nurse, and when, in the next moment, the blood started flowing more copiously, I yelled out just as loudly as before, "Hey! We need a resident in here! Hey!"

Alex Winton came running back in, saw the blood that was accumulating under the table and on my clothes, and without stopping to scrub threw a gown over his street clothes, put on a long glove, and quickly examined her. He tried to finish the removal so that the uterus could clamp down all the way and stop the bleeding, but the placenta wouldn't come.

By this time Mrs. Meacham was screaming with fear and pain, and the delivery room looked like a disaster area.

"Shut up, you!" he yelled at her. "I can't think!"

She didn't shut up—she screamed louder.

He withdrew his hand and arm, stripping off the blood-smeared glove. "I bet it's a placenta accreta," he said quickly. "Call and get an OR. We're going to do a hysterectomy right away." He ran out of the room, while the nurse had already picked up the phone to get an operating room freed up. The OR schedule began at 7:30 and I hoped we'd be just in time, otherwise all the ORs would be in use and we'd have to do it in the delivery room.

Now that he'd stopped tugging Mrs. Meacham was in less pain. She didn't know how heavily she was bleeding because she was draped, but it was clear from all our activity that her condition was serious. We got her onto a cart, with lots of bedding wadded up and jammed against her bottom to absorb the blood, and dashed down the corridor, around the corner, and into OR 3.

I saw them lift the patient we'd displaced off the operating table as we wheeled Mrs. Meacham in.

Somebody got another IV into her, drew blood studies, and sent a tube of blood down to be cross-matched. Chief Resident Burke had been notified and along with Alex Winton, was scrubbing hastily. I asked permission, which was curtly given, and I scrubbed, too.

The anesthetist had gotten Mrs. Meacham under already while a nurse was scrubbing her abdomen and somebody else was draping her. She was already being transfused with O negative blood since we hadn't cross-matched her yet and she'd lost so much.

It seemed that in a moment Dr. Burke was opening her belly. I couldn't see very much of what was going on, but they went in fast, talking all the while and clamping off uterine vessels. As it happened, she was transfused five units of blood and they were talking about whether she was going to make it or not.

The placenta had grown entirely through the uterine wall and might have embedded in the bladder, but fortunately it hadn't gone that far. They did a complete hysterectomy on her and, consistent with the tempo of everything else up to then, it was the fastest hysterectomy I think I will ever see.

The next day I told her about it. She was sitting up in bed, dazed by the morphine, and just nodded, so I made sure to tell her again the next day when she was clearer.

She had her tiny daughter in her arms and was about to nurse her. She looked up at me with a troubled expression. "Okay, honey," she said, "but what you-all done about my tubes?"

"Oh, you don't have to worry about that, Mrs. Meacham—" I began.

She interrupted. "You know I don't want no more kids. I got my man out of the house so I don't need his permission, and I want my tubes tied!"

"Mrs. Meacham," I said, "without a uterus you'll never have another pregnancy. You won't have periods either." I've known hysterectomy patients to come back in very worried that they weren't having their periods anymore, not realizing that menstruation is the uterine lining sloughing off.

"You sure I won't get pregnant?" she asked me suspiciously.

"I give you my word," I pronounced solemnly. "If you have another baby, I promise you I'll adopt it!"

She broke into a big smile. "Honey, I'd be doing you a favor." She looked down happily at her daughter, still the most beautiful baby in the nursery.

It took me a while to explain it to her, but I made

sure she understood the reproductive system, and that in spite of the fact that she still had her ovaries and tubes, she couldn't get pregnant without a uterus. Sperm couldn't get to an egg, for one thing.

"Hm," she said, in her big, deep voice. "About time."

She left the hospital seven days postoperative, having recovered beautifully, happy as she could be: no more pregnancies, and her last one was a beauty.

One of the favorite topics of conversation in the Doctors' Lounge was sex. The humor medical people often use with one another is like locker-room humor, mocking and earthy. Our intimacy with bodies—not only nakedness, but also the indignities and dysfunctions all flesh is heir to—and our reliance on our own bodies' reflexes and stamina make us joke about sleep, for example, and bowels, and what we look like, and sex. We are teamworkers, and our humor is a kind of companionship, too, as we make advances and trade insults that attach us to one another, pungently, maybe because our connections are so temporary. It's hard to represent the humor, because its success depends a lot on being in the situation and caught up in the rhythm and flow of the badinage; and if anyone thinks badinage is what you put over a wound, he could be right.

There was a lot of sexual kidding and a lot of sexual gossip. I heard a fascinating story in the lounge one Saturday afternoon as we waited for various patients to deliver. There were two plastic surgery residents in the hospital who were great friends.

"In fact," said Jeff, "I've heard they'll share a woman."

"So?" I said, in my worldly-wise manner. "What's so special about a woman having two lovers?"

Jeff laughed. "You've got it backward."

Amy and I were entranced. "You mean two men make love to a woman at the same time? Wow! Terrific!" I was enthusiastic.

213

"I've always wanted two women to make love to *me* at the same time," Jeff said dreamily.

"Yeah," said a medical student. "That would be something."

"Do you mean to say," I pursued, "that there are two men in this hospital who would be happy to make love to me together?"

Jeff got up and came over to me and pressed down on my shoulders as if to prevent my rising out of the chair. "Hold your horses," he laughed. "If I understand my informant correctly, they do it seriatim."

Amy frowned. "One after another?"

"That's not so bad, still," I said, unabashed.

"She said they both start out all hands, undressing, and then one of them has sex very quickly while the other one looks on."

"That sounds like fun," I said, my own exhibitionistic impulses tickled.

"It sounds creepy," said Amy.

"Well," said Jeff, still smiling, "my informant didn't think it was so bad. Apparently several women have been willing. My friend didn't do it again, though. She got into a normal relationship with one of them, and it lasted a year or so until she met somebody else."

I was called to a patient. Getting up, I said, "I still think it could be terrific."

Jeff retorted, "I'd rather have two women than be one of two men. Hey, how about you and Amy?"

Amy looked pityingly at him. "I'm not sure you're worth the effort," she said witheringly.

He was not dismayed. "We don't have to tell anyone," he cajoled. "You can be Doctor X," he said to Amy, and looking at me, "And you can be the other Doctor X. Hey, you two together can be Doctor XX."

Females are characterized by having two X chromosomes. I laughed.

"Hey, we'll nickname you Doctor XX!" Jeff was enchanted with his idea.

"You better not," Amy warned him, getting up to push me out the door.

"Why not?" I asked her. "I thought that was pretty witty."

She informed us, "XX also means double-cross." She stuck out her tongue at Jeff as we both left.

23

In the middle of the night I was waiting for a patient to deliver and Amy was with me. One of the private obstetricians had brought in a little Sony on which to watch the pro football game. He always took it home afterward, knowing full well it would be stolen if he left it. Ironically, that very morning at about two, when he was in the delivery room and the rest of us were either asleep or at work, somebody did steal it.

He was sitting smoking, watching the *Tonight Show*. Amy and I had wandered in for coffee, and one of the residents was dozing in a chair. I told Dr. Bancroft that his patient was beginning to be distraught and giving the nurse some trouble. The patient's weeping had sent her husband out of her labor room in a big worry, and he was looking for someone to page the OB.

Dr. Bancroft sighed. "She's a candidate for a section," he said as he rose.

"She been in labor long?" I asked.

"Fourteen hours. *Prima gravida*. Hasn't dilated." He stubbed out his cigarette and left the room. *Prima gravida* meant a first pregnancy.

"Do you mind if I turn this off?" Amy asked irritably, going over to the TV.

The resident woke up, checked his watch, and said he was going to look in on Mrs. Mirabile. Amy and I got our coffee and sat down. I sprawled, I was so tired.

Amy didn't. She looked neat, and tense. Something was on her mind, and I guessed she'd bring it up now that we were alone.

"Johnny Carson," Amy said. "Boy, what an aged fraternity man he is." She was scornful.

"True, true," I laughed. "He does neat tricks with a pencil, though."

"Listen, Phyllis," she said. "Something's going to have to be done about the bathroom."

There was one bathroom for all of the doctors, male and female; the nurses, of course, had a different john, at the other end of the floor. Ours had one toilet in a little area where you could close the door, a sink, a urinal, and a shower.

"Okay," I said, ready for adventure.

She continued with fury. "The other day I was in there, on the john, and somebody comes in without even knocking, pisses in the urinal, takes off his clothes, and starts to take a shower."

"Well, why didn't you tell him to wait until you were finished?"

She sighed and didn't reply. It wouldn't bother me to announce my presence, but apparently Amy had been too embarrassed to say anything. She'd stayed locked in the toilet stall, silent, until he was finished with his shower.

"Let's put a flowerpot in the urinal," I suggested.

"I'm not going to stand for it!" she announced fiercely.

"Good," I said.

"I'm going to get a lock put on that outer door!"

I laughed. I had expected her to think up some esoteric arrangement for privacy or an elaborate revenge. Instead she'd come up with a simple solution.

She burst into tears.

"What it is?" I asked, going over to her, but she got up and went to our Cot Closet and closed the door.

To change clothes for the operating room, Amy and I had had to use the locker room off the Nurses' Lounge while the male doctors, residents, and interns used the dressing room off the Surgeons' Lounge.

(The latter was different from the Doctors' Lounge, where we waited, talked, and snacked.) The Surgeons' Lounge was large and comfortable, the Nurses' Lounge was small and mean. There was a status problem, too: Amy and I were required to change with the nurses.

We'd planned a small adjustment.

I'd measured the signs on the lounges, gone to an outside agency, and, for ten hard-earned dollars, ordered two signs stamped in white letters on black plastic.

That night around eleven o'clock when the shifts were changing and no one was near the OR's, Amy and I had crept down the hall to the lounge area. Stealthily and silently, we'd unscrewed the signs and put up our own, using unidirectional screws and epoxy glue so they couldn't be removed. They read Women's Changing Room and Men's Changing Room.

We'd waited for a reaction the next day, but none came. I'd guessed that's what is meant by a quiet revolution.

I had been misled by Amy's resentment and her gameness for one subversive act into forgetting that she might be especially fragile. I bulled my way through an outer layer of prejudice in order to get the medical training I wanted and to keep the atmosphere around me light rather than oppressive. I could do it because I was becoming more and more assertive, not to say aggressive; but Amy seemed to be having a hard time of it, and I began to see how she really could have cracked under the strain before.

I had become interested in natural childbirth. To me, it combined contradictory elements. It idealized motherhood; the breathless glorifications surrounding it were as romantic and fulsome as any late Victorian praise of motherhood. Yet it was unconservative in wresting control over the birth process from a paternal obstetrician to the woman herself. It partook of the back-to-the-earth movement, which repudiated modern technology (and, consequently, labor-saving devices that could be said to have freed women from drudgery); such women seemed to be earth mothers or pioneer women doing traditionally female things fiercely, in a spirit of self-sufficiency that was quite un-"feminine."

Amy Paredes and I discussed natural childbirth. As interns, we were not allowed to assist at any but spontaneous vaginal deliveries; we could use a forceps only when the resident was present, giving permission and directing us, and we definitely could not do any complicated deliveries. But we did work with many uncomplicated deliveries, and among them were a few women who came in wanting to give birth naturally or who almost inadvertently did it the old way. Amy and I were struck by the power of giving birth.

One day a young couple named Haney came in. The woman had started labor and said she was going to deliver by natural childbirth. They both gave their occupation as graduate student. Linda Haney was in a master's program in botany; Greg Haney was in a Ph.D. program in biochemistry. I have since had occasion to think that it was good they weren't in the same department.

He let her talk for a while, answering questions that only she could answer, but whenever I got to a point that he could have an opinion on, he'd answer for her. She let him.

I asked him to leave the room while I examined her, and he said, "Hell, you can go right ahead. Linda's as familiar to me as I am."

Of course that was true. Nevertheless, at that time I was accustomed to having only a nurse or another doctor in the room while I did a pelvic exam. Later, I began to let husbands stay in the room. But he annoyed me so much that I said, "I'd like you to leave the room temporarily."

"Oh, all right," he grumbled, and left.

Her membranes had ruptured and she was already about two centimeters dilated, so she was just starting her labor.

I straightened up and stripped off the glove, asking, "Are you in much discomfort yet?"

She grimaced. "They told us in the class that it was like menstrual cramps," she whispered. "I've never had cramps like this! How long can this go on?" She looked uncomfortable and was beginning to be afraid.

I approached her bedside closely and told her that it was different for each woman, and that the generalizations she had learned in her maternity course might apply to her, and then again might not. I told her medication was available.

"Oh," she whimpered, "I don't think Greg would let me."

"Greg! *He's* not going through it."

"No, well, no, but he feels very strongly for the baby, you know." She sounded miserable.

"Hnh! Well, we'll just see about that!" I was ready to do battle with this Greg.

I stepped out of her labor room; he was waiting just outside. He took me by the elbow—an intimidating, masterful gesture—and said, "I'm not going to have any of this shaving business."

He caught me off stride. "Prepping is a routine hospital procedure," I informed him. The fact was that I too thought shaving was unnecessary, a defeminization.

"And no episiotomy," he said.

"What? How many children has your wife had?" I inquired with sarcasm.

"What do you mean? She hasn't had any. You know that."

"Then there's been no stretching," I explained.

"Listen. She'll do it the way nature intended."

"Yeah. Nature also used to kill off two out of five women in childbirth."

He snorted in disbelief.

I walked away. I consulted Burke about medication and the episiotomy. He said that Mrs. Haney's wishes would be followed if possible. She was so dominated by her husband that she would never contravene his wishes. She'd suffer.

And suffer she did.

Her labor went on for twenty hours after she came in. It was steady, grinding, and slow, and exhausted all of us as well as her. She wanted to scream but her Protestant stoicism wouldn't let her, and after a while she was just sleeping in between pains. Her husband sat at her shoulder and coached her with every contraction: "Come on, now, breathing one-two-three-four . . ." counting off the seconds and making sure she was taking the short shallow breaths that were supposed to relieve pressure on the contracting uterus. She had ice chips, she sucked sourball candy, but in all that time she had no other nourishment, and she was weak.

"Let me give her something," I pleaded with her husband.

"Are you kidding? Don't insult us." He glared at me with deep, sincere hatred.

"Greg," she gasped, "I can't stand it much longer."

"It's not pain, honey," he said to her. "That's your fear talking. Don't let it get you."

He talked to her repeatedly in that fashion. It gave me the creeps. In the month I had been on Obstetrics, I could see for sure that what most of these women went through was *pain,* no two ways about it, and I had been struck by how hard delivery was. I could hardly stand it just waiting beside a patient who was suffering agonies and not doing anything about it, and I often asked the doctors to give an epidural long before they were willing to. I realized that the pain was temporary, unlike suffering some sick patients go through. But I never blamed a woman in labor for making a fuss. Many doctors and most nurses don't want women to scream. It *is* rather nerve-racking to hear, but if she wants to scream, I say let her.

Greg Haney, the bastard, was pep-talking his wife about suffering he didn't have to go through and didn't even credit. He thought he was heroic to stay awake the whole time while she, on the other hand, dozed between contractions for a minute or two at a time.

Finally she was fully effaced and dilated, and she should have been pushing with the long, stage two contractions, but she had no strength left.

"She needs a spinal, or even just local Novocain now," I told him. The Novocain could be injected at two points deep in the vagina.

"She's also going to need a forceps delivery," I said. It was awful that I talked only to him, not to her anymore.

Greg Haney said, "No."

I notified Alex Winton that I was having trouble, and asked him to take over. If I'd thought Greg Haney would respond better to an authoritative male doctor, I was mistaken. When Alex told the man that his wife would need a forceps delivery, since it was going to take too long for the infant to pass through the birth canal and it could get into trouble, he refused. "I will not have instruments used."

"We may *have* to intervene," Alex said stiffly. He was offended.

"Oh, come on," Greg Haney said. "You just want to get it over with and get out of here." Alex bristled and turned red at the accusation. "The baby's still okay, isn't it?" Haney challenged. He was referring to the fact that the fetal monitor showed the baby's heartbeat was still regular. "When and if that baby gets into trouble, *then* we make the decision," Greg Haney announced emphatically.

The only thing I could do was to show him how to get under his wife's shoulders to give her more leverage to push. It took her three more hours in the labor room to move the baby on down until the head crowned. Then, at last, we could take her to the delivery room.

She was on the table and Alex was watching carefully: the perineum wasn't stretching enough and she started to tear. Alex almost crowed in triumph.

He picked up the scissors, announced, "We're going to need some help here!" and just as Greg Haney was protesting, "Now wait a minute!" Alex whisked the scissors in a cut that looked to me like a longer episiotomy than necessary.

The baby slipped out, covered with blood, and with its poor head elongated by its slow passage through the canal.

It was a little boy.

There was the usual fuss and activity—getting the baby to breathe, clamping and cutting the cord, and cleaning the baby up. He was given immediately to his mother, who was barely strong enough to take him in her arms. Like many women right after delivery, she had been shaking hard for a minute or so, and then she went to sleep.

"Give it the breast, give it the breast," her husband urged, so meekly she roused herself and put the baby to her breast, wincing as it took the nipple and gave a couple of hard sucks. I hoped she'd prepared her nipples beforehand; this baby was going to suck vigorously. Then both baby and mother went to sleep.

A conflict, a competition for control over Linda Haney, had swiftly developed between Alex Winton and Greg Haney, and the poor laboring mother had been forgotten. I was convinced of it later, when I was checking her stitches and saw that Alex had cut the anal sphincter. Though cutting into the rectum is not considered bad, in his haste to make the forbidden episiotomy Alex had cut what might be called a generous one.

There was one appalling case that I, fortunately, didn't have to work on. It was, in fact, Amy's patient. Everything had gone smoothly for Mrs. Kent, it seemed, until she delivered. The baby, a little girl, was missing her left hand. In all other respects she was fine, both organically and neurologically, and she was even prettier than some babies are at first, with a lot of silky brown hair. She was alert and responsive and breathing vigorously.

When Mrs. Kent had been told that her daughter was beautiful and healthy, but had this one deformity, she started screaming and had to be sedated. The doctors had thought her husband would be able to help calm her down, but when he was told, he just sat with a look of horror and disgust on his face, then he said grimly, "Well, we'll talk about it." He didn't want to look at his daughter.

They waited for a day to let the parents get accustomed to the news. The nursery nurses made a special effort to assure them that Baby Girl Kent was charming, which apparently she was, but they received no response. Mrs. Kent was depressed and her husband looked grim, if not angry.

I learned the rest of the story from Amy, who did the scutwork on Mrs. Kent and whom the obstetrician enlisted to try to persuade the mother to respond to her child.

"Last Tuesday," Amy told me, "I took the baby in to her. She was wrapped up in a blanket and you couldn't see her arm, you could just see how cute she was. I talked to Mrs. Kent and offered her the baby, and just as I was about to lay her in her mother's arms, I could see that if I let go of her her mother would drop her. Drop her. I stopped, right in the middle of holding her infant out to her, and I couldn't let that baby go! It would have been like *me* dropping her.

"Mrs. Kent must have seen the look on my face, because she sneered and said, 'You can't do it, can you? Maybe you're smart not to trust it to me.'

"Phyllis, I've never heard anyone sound so bitter as when she turned her face away from me and said she wasn't going to keep the baby anyway and it was going to be put up for adoption."

Amy said tremulously, "Can you imagine? I got the baby out of there as fast as if the place were contaminated, and I let that woman see how I felt."

"But I'm not sure it's all her fault," I said. "I think I heard her husband say something like: 'See what you've done,' or 'You can't even do that right.' It's unbelievable." Amy shuddered and made a disgusted face.

The whole situation was a source of misery on the

floor, a very ugly thing. It was especially painful for Amy, who told me the details of every encounter she had to have with the Kents. She repeated each scene obsessively until she enabled me to share her feelings of outrage and impotence at the unnatural reactions of the parents who repudiated their daughter.

We were glad when they left the hospital. The baby was taken for adoption soon after.

A few weeks later, I learned the explanation for their behavior. Her patient had told Amy many details of her past, and only later could Amy unburden herself of the knowledge.

Lydia Kent had been an adopted child herself. I'd known adopted people who considered themselves "chosen" children, but that had apparently not been the case with Mrs. Kent, perhaps because she'd been adopted by her great-aunt, a fifty-five-year-old widow who'd taken her on as a family duty. She was a bitter and parsimonious woman. They had slept together in the same old double bed until Lydia was a grown woman and had married.

Perhaps Lydia Kent had been too grateful to her husband for marrying her and rescuing her from the old woman. Her in-laws treated her as a kind of poor relation, with either condescension or criticism. I couldn't believe such a soap-opera-like situation could occur, but the more cases I saw, the more willing I was to believe the most gothic stories.

What was monstrous was that Lydia Kent, moving from her scrawny-hearted aunt to her domineering husband, accepted all the standards and rules he and his family imposed on her. And they expected her to fail. She looked as arrogant as anyone else in the Kent family, but some of the things her mother-in-law said to her about producing a defective child might well have humiliated her. I watched her when she was being wheeled down the corridor to the elevators, away from the beautiful child she'd abandoned—no doubt to a more loving home than she could have provided. She was as taut and still as a perfectly drawn bow.

224

The woman I had been with for several hours had bled very heavily on the delivery table with the detachment of the placenta and had been transfused two pints, but the bleeding had subsided as her uterus cramped down in size, with the aid of ergotrate. I was helping by rubbing her belly and I'd been rubbing for a long time.

A woman in her late twenties, she'd had two previous children. Every once in a while she would complain that she'd never had problems before. Then she'd doze. Her face in repose was gaunt and sallow. She seemed exhausted and her body lay inert, being moved only by my massage. Now and then I could feel the enlarged uterus ripple below the surface involuntarily.

She woke up with a start, crying, "Ow! You didn't have to pinch me!"

"I didn't, Mrs. Farrady. You just had another contraction."

"What the hell is this?" she complained. "I never had this before. What did that bastard do to me this time?"

"There was a problem with the placenta—" I began.

"Placenta! Jesus Christ! Can't I get any good care around here? My fucking doctor can't deliver me right, my fucking nurse can't stop my pain, my arm hurts, my belly hurts . . . I'm going out of my mind!" She began to scream as a contraction sharpened and then subsided.

I kept on massaging.

"I wish you'd stop that!" she told me irritably.

"Sorry. It helps you."

"Makes me nervous, is more like it," she grumbled.

I grunted and kept rubbing.

She moaned. "I wish I could get up out of here."

"Not yet," I replied.

"Can't you understand, you nitwit," she yelled at me, "I'm going stir-crazy. Look at my hands! See what happens when I get all nervous?"

I looked at the hands and fingers she was waggling in front of my face, and could see that she had a moderately serious case of dermatitis. No doubt her own diagnosis was correct: it was emotional in origin.

"Why is this taking so long!" she appealed without expecting an answer. "I had all this blood transfused," she challenged. "What was going on? I never had any problem before!"

"Every pregnancy is different," I responded.

"Shit," she said scornfully. "How many kids *you* have?"

I shook my head. "None," I acknowledged. They expect a woman doctor to have experienced delivery, though not, of course, a male doctor.

She sneered and looked away contemptuously. After a few minutes she began telling me about this delivery, and her other two, until after another half-hour or so she'd calmed down and her condition had stabilized so she could be taken to her room, where she fell into a sound and undisturbed sleep.

The next day her temper had considerably improved, and she was happy to see the baby she'd almost forgotten about in her dismay of the day before. I reminded her about her dermatitis, and recommended a steroid tape that she could just put over the areas; medicated, it would adhere without bulk. When she left the hospital with her baby, she thanked me for that recommendation most particularly.

"To think that, with all these high-paid doctors, I have to find out what to do about my hands from a nurse!" she claimed.

"Ah, Mrs. Farrady," I said to her, "you didn't. You found it out from a doctor!"

She didn't understand, and I let it go. Ruefully, I realized that I hadn't escaped sex stereotypes, even here among woman patients. I wondered whether Amy too felt the tiny, brief disappointment I did when a woman patient was prejudiced against me, or, as it often turned out, against herself.

Dr. Burke was doing an amniocentesis; that is, removing some amniotic fluid from the pregnant uterus to be tested for certain genetic or developmental defects, like infections. It is delicate, since you don't want to hit the fetus accidentally with the needle. I was surprised that he invited me to do it with him.

"Mrs. Spaulding," he said very formally, "this is Dr. Donnan."

The woman turned her head to give me an automatic greeting, saw that I was a woman, and hesitated, frowning slightly. She was stunningly beautiful, with dark brown hair and blue-green eyes. I was incredulous of their color.

"Dr. Donnan will do the amniocentesis," the chief resident told her. I could tell she disapproved but felt constrained not to object. I concealed my own surprise and, glancing inquisitively at Burke, began. I prepared the sterile area with some Novocain, then gently inserted a hollow needle attached to a syringe. It had to go into but not through the uterus; it should not prick the baby. The needle went through several layers of tissue, held upright by the thickness, but it jerked once from a muscular reaction, which always seemed uncanny to me.

"Hurry up, will you?" Mrs. Spaulding complained. "This is damned uncomfortable."

"I know it is," I replied. "Just a moment more."

Ah. I had gotten no blood. I withdrew twenty cc's of fluid and pulled out.

Burke rubbed his hands and smiled sardonically. "Good, Doctor, as usual. Mrs. Spaulding, we'll let you know in four weeks. You can get dressed now."

Burke was holding my elbow and pushing me out of the room. "What is it?" I asked, when we'd hastily left.

"I thought you ought to see this," he told me, his voice cold.

"What? A beautiful woman?"

"Yes, indeed," he said, turning to me. "She's beautiful, isn't she? Her beauty has everything to do with it. You ought to see her husband! A very handsome man!"

"So?" I was unimpressed.

"You know why the amniocentesis?"

"They have some unfortunate genetic problem?" I

227

guessed. "She took some kind of drug? She was exposed to rubella?" These were all reasons for a mother to fear that her unborn child might be seriously defective. Worried, dreading these perils, she'd have to wait through four weeks of agony to find out whether her child was indeed healthy or whether she and her husband would have to decide on an abortion, by which time it would have to be accomplished by saline substitution, which makes her go into labor and deliver her dead fetus. Amniocentesis is part of a painful process, not an easy one.

Burke sneered, "They want to know if their child is going to be good-looking!"

"What?" I was incredulous. We were both laughing. You couldn't tell anything about the *looks* of an unborn child!

"Who's her doctor?" I asked. I couldn't believe it.

"Some nut out in the suburbs," Burke said with the snobbery common to hospital staff. "The guy called me this morning, told me not to hold it against him, but said he had to do it."

"What would they do if they *could* find out that it was going to be ugly?" I just shook my head. I simply couldn't believe it.

Burke and I were about to separate. "You know what?" I said.

"What?"

"I must admit that I have never seen such beautifully colored eyes as hers!"

He laughed at me. "Come on, Phyllis. Haven't you ever heard of tinted contact lenses?"

Still bemused by the unusual blue-green of her eyes, I wished I could have had the chance to say to her, satirically yet prophetically, "Mrs. Spaulding, we now know that your little girl will not be more than a moderately cute baby at the beginning; however, when she gets to be three months old, her features will be more definite and you will be able to detect the beginnings of real beauty. By the time she is two years old, she will be adorable. You are to be congratulated. I'm sure you'll be very happy with your child."

I hoped the child would be very happy with its foolish parents.

But Mrs. Spaulding was not the only contriver of folly and enslavement. She made me think about perfection—first, the physical perfection most women have been taught to yearn for, hopelessly; and second, my mental association, for some reason, to doctors, as though we too had been taught to yearn for kinds of perfection—perfect calm, omniscience, immortality . . .

24

It was late at night when a call came through from the Emergency Room that a young woman close to term was coming in in seizure. Eclampsia of pregnancy is a very dangerous condition, symptomized by protein in the urine, excessively high blood pressure, edema or swelling, convulsions, and coma that can result in death. It wasn't anything for an intern to fool around with. Dr. Burke hurried down to bring her to the delivery floor.

When she arrived, everyone on the floor was alert. Though her seizure had been controlled in the ER by intravenous Valium, she was now in coma. Burke looked drained already. His face was clamped shut, and he walked quickly beside her and looked straight ahead while the patient's mother walked on the other side of the cart and spoke breathlessly to him. "I brought her in as soon as I could," she was saying defensively.

Dr. Burke said nothing. He guided the cart through the cluttered corridor toward a free labor room.

"She didn't have any of these fits before, you know," said the woman. "And as soon as she did, I brought her in. You don't have any right to treat me like some criminal. I'm taking care of my daughter!"

Dr. Burke and the nurse transferred the young woman to the bed. He examined her and realized that the baby was dead. A normal labor would continually place the patient at risk, for another seizure might kill her. He wanted magnesium sulfate in her, to control the irritability of her nervous system, and a Caesarean section right away, before another seizure. He glanced up at me; I had trailed the procession and was now ready at the door. "Get an OR lined up," he said curtly, looking back at his inert patient. You couldn't tell her age for sure, since she was so swollen with edema—abnormally large amounts of fluid in the intercellular tissue spaces of the body. The imprints of your fingers would indent her flesh for minutes afterward.

"What are you talking about, OR?" asked the mother.

I paused, but Dr. Burke barked at me, so I left hurriedly. I could hear her complaining voice as I hurried down the hall to a telephone.

Then I heard Dr. Burke's voice raised; "Woman, your daughter is going to die if we don't do a Caesarean on her right away because she cannot deliver vaginally quickly, and until she delivers her life is at risk."

I could hear argument but not words as I phoned for a crew to open up the emergency C-section OR.

"Burke is going to do an emergency Caesarean," I told Amy and Alex. "Who's to scrub with him?" I didn't want to interrupt him to ask that minor procedural question. Several nurses and a private doctor had drifted over to the nurses' station to discuss the case. We decided that Jeff Donaldson and I would scrub. Also, the visit had to be informed because of the possibility of death.

"What are the chances she'll die?" I asked.

"Last I read, it was twenty per cent. Too high," said the obstetrician.

"I heard it was down to ten," said Amy.

"You ever see it happen?" I asked the doctor.

"No, thank God. I take better care of mine than that." Obstetricians watch out for symptoms of pre-eclampsia to prevent this. Eclampsia is a disease exclusively of pregnancy: it is caused by pregnancy; its only cure is delivery, or termination of the pregnancy.

Fifteen minutes later I was standing at Burke's side holding the retractors, the instruments that keep back the edges of the wound, for a very careful, slow-moving Caesarean.

As he made his incisions and spread the layers of flesh apart, his voice—in contrast to his steady, careful fingers, was harsh with anger as he talked. "God, I hope I never see another case like this as long as I live. One's too many. This kid is sixteen, would you believe it? The woman refused to let her daughter have an abortion, never brought her in for prenatal care, and now wants her to deliver vaginally because a Caesarean isn't natural. The woman's crazy! She can't see an inch beyond this pregnancy fetish she has!"

At that moment the head of Obstetrics walked in, having come down and scrubbed to make sure everything was going all right.

"Dr. Burke," he greeted him. "Everything under control?"

Dr. Burke said, "Hello, Dr. Lefkowitz. Yes, I think we got her in time."

Dr. Lefkowitz asked the anesthetist if the patient was all right, and received a positive reply. Then he said, "Proceed, Dr. Burke. I'll just watch."

Burke couldn't control his anger. He began to tell Dr. Lefkowitz how she'd been brought in in convulsions, her whole nervous system irritated, producing bloody urine, on the edge of kidney failure with a blood pressure of 200/130, edematous over her whole body, her blood in danger of losing its clotting ability.

"Classic eclampsia and toxemia," observed Dr. Lefkowitz. "You don't often see it nowadays. Gravids are usually monitored very carefully."

"Yeah," Dr. Burke continued bitterly. "This one should have been. The damn mother maybe was punishing her daughter, making her do it all natural, as she calls it."

"You never know, Doctor," said the older man. "People are funny about pregnancy and childbirth."

"The mother should have known something was wrong," Dr. Burke insisted, as he removed the dead baby.

"Maybe she thought it was just the normal swelling of pregnancy."

"Well, at least her mother is going to have to bury that baby!" Burke spat. In fact, any fetus over twenty-four weeks had to be buried by the parents, but they could often arrange it through the hospital morgue.

"You are feeling uncommonly vindictive, Dr. Burke," Dr. Lefkowitz observed.

"Maybe so," he said. "But *you* didn't have to deal with that monster."

Dr. Lefkowitz, realizing Burke's anger, volunteered to tell the mother that her daughter was out of danger.

"And the baby?" she asked.

"The baby died."

"That operation—"

Dr. Lefkowitz interrupted. "The baby died during the seizure, if not before. Your daughter was toxemic. I warn you, any future pregnancies ought to be followed very carefully from the beginning so we can know about a potential problem before it happens." He was threatening her, for eclampsia is usually a disease of the first pregnancy.

"Now she'll have to have all her babies by Caesarean, won't she?" the woman asked bitterly.

"Yes, which is a good thing, since it will require a doctor in attendance," Dr. Lefkowitz replied stiffly. He left as quickly as he could.

When the girl, Lorna Geller, was recovering from the operation, she started screaming shrilly. She couldn't see. Her retinas had become edematous, too, and detached. We had to wait to see if they were permanently detached.

Her hysteria was very hard to control. For several days she was irrational, irritable, and very uncooperative. However, the retinas settled back into place, and she recovered from the toxemia. She became a calm and outwardly pleasant patient.

Once I overheard her mother talking to her as I came into the room.

"I want you to know that you were just terrible!" she said in a bullying tone.

Like everyone else, I'd taken a dislike to Mrs. Geller and become a partisan of her daughter. "Just terrible about what?" I challenged as I entered.

She looked at me defiantly. "You couldn't live with her while she was pregnant!" she declared.

"Ah." That was probably true. Two of the symptoms of preeclampsia are irritability and irrationality.

I took care of Lorna the ten days she was in, which was a most unpleasant experience. Her mother was critical of us and fault-finding, and Lorna was pusillanimous toward her. Unfortunately, Lorna also confided in me. Since I could do nothing about her problem, it was burdensome.

When her mother was out of the room once, Lorna whispered tremulously to me, "I know why the baby died."

"The disease," I said emphatically, knowing that she was about to embark on some superstitious explanation.

"I had the disease," she corroborated solemnly. "It was the devil in me."

I was chilled. "I can see how your imagination might—" I began, but she interrupted me.

"The devil got in when the baby got in."

"Uh-oh," I said. "Lorna, do you know 'how babies are made'?"

"I know," she said with an edge of revulsion in her voice. "That's when the devil got in, wasn't it?" she stated triumphantly.

233

"Does your mother believe all this?" I was ready to believe that Mrs. Geller was tyrannizing her daughter with this fantasy.

Lorna shook her head. Then she looked very frightened. "But it didn't work!" she wailed softly. All her words had been almost whispered, as if surreptitious. Compared to her I was shouting.

"What didn't work?" I demanded brusquely.

"When the baby was killed," she said, "I thought my dreams would stop. But I keep dreaming!" She was horrified.

"Everybody dreams."

She ignored me. "Such dreams, such evil, evil dreams!"

"Now listen, Lorna. Pregnant women dream things that might be considered horrible, but it's all normal, and anyway, a dream is only a dream . . ."

"Only a dream! I never dreamed before!"

"People think they don't dream," I said, "but they do."

"No, I *never* dreamed!" She was getting hysterical, and her mother, returning and hearing something frantic in her daughter's now louder voice, ran into the room.

"Lorna!" she said sharply. The girl caught herself and brought herself under control. "What have you been doing to her?" she demanded of me.

I asked her if we could talk in the hall.

Lorna screamed, "No! Don't you dare tell her!"

I tried to explain to Lorna that it was for her own good, but she was crying now, and her mother suspiciously refused to talk with me privately. So I went ahead and said that her daughter had been so troubled by the experience that she believed that the devil had invaded her, killed her baby, and was punishing her.

"*God* killed it!" Lorna said.

I groaned.

"You fool!" said her mother to Lorna. "What is all this garbage!" She turned her full attention to her daughter, her daughter gazed back at her, and I saw their naked confrontation from which everything else was excluded.

I was glad not to be appealed to. They were both crazy as far as I could tell. I did bring in a psychiatric consult, but Lorna was diffident, and failed to repeat her theory. When neither of them was extreme or wanted to talk, the psychiatrist left it up to me to transfer Lorna to the psychiatric ward for three days. I didn't do it; three days wouldn't have been enough.

In December I learned that the lab where I wanted to work had received its grant, and I was pleased that my next year was finally settled. The burden of uncertainty was lifted. As Christmas approached, the obstetrical service became festive. Susan and Adela got me to help them decorate. We tacked silver bells over the doorways and dangled a few plastic Santas. I bought some beautiful construction paper from which we could make paper chains. I teased Alex Winton to help us, but he said, "No, no, no. Not me. That's dumb!" I hadn't heard that accusation since grade school. Surprisingly, Burke consented to make a chain, a long, beautiful rainbow chain. He explained that he was forced to do it; otherwise the decorations would show no good taste anywhere.

I was just finishing putting up his chain, balanced on a chair, when a voice called out, "Well, if it isn't my intern!" I looked down to see a cart being wheeled along, and on it the pregnant diabetic I'd had on Medicine and whom I'd transferred temporarily to the antenatal floor.

I scrambled down to walk beside her. "Are you due already?" I asked, not remembering exactly how pregnant she'd been when I saw her. She looked large enough to be full term.

She winced as a contraction began. "No," she said, "this is eight months."

"Oh."

Her determination to talk through the contraction reminded me of her previous masterful manner. "I'm all swollen up," she said. "Too much fluid, and the diabetes is out of control again."

"You've been taking good care of yourself?" I asked perfunctorily, for I could predict the answer.

"Of course. But I've always been brittle, and all this fluid accumulation has sent me into premature labor."

A brittle diabetic can experience almost instantaneous and definitely unpredictable changes in blood sugar levels, and it was not surprising that Mrs. Jefferson had gone out of balance again, what with the additional demands the pregnancy was making on her system. As always, she spoke of her condition as though she were the doctor, not the patient.

"Do you feel worried or upset, Mrs. Jefferson?" I asked.

She grunted, her face sweating. "No," she said.

Mrs. Jefferson was assigned to Amy, not to me, but I did drop in to see her several times during the labor, which proceeded quickly. Her husband parked the car and quickly came up to be with his wife. In contrast to her determined matter-of-factness, he looked very worried and nervous. I told Amy that I thought she ought to reassure *him*.

Amy left the room with her coffee only half-drunk. "I don't have time for that," she said crossly. "He'll have to take care of himself."

Amy had become very snappish recently. I speculated that it was a good thing that her vacation was coming up. She was going to have Christmas off, in fact, with a few days before and a few days after, then she'd be back for the last several days of OB. In January we were going to be on different services. She was used to filling in wherever a hole opened up; her next rotation would be Pathology.

Apparently Amy did not spend time reassuring Mr. Jefferson, or if she did she was not very effective. I saw him wandering down the hall to go to the bathroom or stretch his legs three times in an hour, and he always looked haggard and sallow. The third time, I joined him in his reluctant walk back toward his wife's labor room.

"How is it going?" I asked, a touch of concern in my voice to let him know I sympathized.

"Oh," he said vaguely, "she says she feels all right. But I had no idea it was so painful! She doesn't let on . . . She's very brave . . . But I can tell!" He sounded bewildered and guilty.

"Don't worry," I said warmly. "I know that sounds like a cliché. But labor doesn't last forever."

"I know, but . . . !"

"Frankly, you don't sound as if you do realize that it will end. Probably sooner than you expect. It's a premature infant, a little smaller than term, and your wife should have no trouble getting it out."

I had stopped him just outside her room. He wanted to get in to her, as though the closer he came, the more compulsive his attention. The room was silent. I could see that alarmed him, though I guessed she was either dozing or bearing the pain silently. It wouldn't be like her to cry out.

"There's nothing I can do!" he protested urgently.

Maybe he'd hit exactly on his problem. Mrs. Jefferson had managed herself for a long time, and her pregnancy was another exercise she put her body through. I didn't doubt that she wanted a baby or that she would be a good mother. It was just that she couldn't abandon strict control of her potentially treacherous physical self. Her self-control deprived her husband of being able to help her, comfort her, and share the birth with her.

I suggested that he take over the timing of the contractions, which Mrs. Jefferson had been counting out loud while she watched the clock, and that he give her the ice chips one by one. She'd been serving herself when her mouth felt dry. When we entered the room, I could see that she was tiring, and judged that she'd be willing for her husband to take over these distracting minor duties.

Amy was there. She told me curtly that Mrs. Jefferson was four centimeters dilated, and she'd be getting her an epidural in a few minutes. I nodded and left. It was obvious that Amy didn't want me interfering with her case. I only hoped that there would be enough time for Mr. Jefferson to get to do *something*. He felt so futile, and, ironically, his wife might now be happy to have him help her. He wasn't going to be with her in the delivery room.

Amy took Mrs. Jefferson away in ten minutes. Mr. Jefferson stood in the hall, forlornly watching his wife being wheeled off. I sat him down in the waiting room and made him take some coffee. He didn't want to talk.

In half an hour he was informed by Amy in a cool voice that his wife had had a girl, well formed but in some respiratory distress. She weighed four pounds eight ounces, which is large for that age, but babies of diabetics are often "overweight." The baby itself was not diabetic.

I stood aside while Amy made her announcement, with the additional clipped words: "I wouldn't worry if I were you. It's common for premature infants to have difficulty breathing. She'll go into the Special Care Nursery on the floor with your wife. She'll be able to see her and even handle her—after a while."

The words were true and the facts could be comforting, but Amy's effect was chilling. Now Mr. Jefferson had another worry. He had gone pale and said nothing.

After Amy left, I saw tears in his eyes.

Every day at certain times, one might see a little grove of IV poles clustered at the window of the Special Care Nursery. There were always a certain number of women who'd had Caesareans or whose babies were put in Special Care for a day or a week, and they'd come down in their wheelchairs with their IV bottles upended to see and cuddle their babies for a while.

Mrs. Jefferson walked to the nursery and gazed through the window at her daughter, whose incubator had been wheeled over to view. Suzanne had a tube for positive pressure ventilation, to help her breathe. She could not yet be held by her mother, but she could be touched. When Mrs. Jefferson entered she stood by the incubator, oblivious to the chatter of the other women, able only to touch her child.

Mrs. Jefferson dealt with herself as strictly and impersonally as ever while she was in the hospital, but her inability to manage her daughter's health must have been terrifying. She had one of the worst cases of postpartum depression I've ever seen. Early on the morning of the fourth day after she'd delivered, one of the other women in her room notified the nurse that Mrs. Jefferson was crying. All of the encouragement and understanding words of her roommates and the nurses could not ease her. She muttered that she knew very well how to kill herself.

Amy took fright and scolded her, which made Mrs. Jefferson turn away, her face hard, and lie flat and silent in her bed. She refused to go to her baby.

"I give up," Amy told me angrily. "It's stupid to get all upset about her. She'll come out of it soon enough."

"I wonder," I said mildly. "One of my patients told me she'd been depressed for months after the birth of her first baby."

"Nonsense! She'll shape up. You know what she's like. Somebody like her letting herself go like that?" Amy shook her head. "No."

"It's not like you to be so insensitive," I said.

Amy turned on her heel and left, but not before I'd seen tears start to her eyes again. I was worried about *her* now.

Since I made sure I was in the room with one of her roommates who was my patient when I knew Mr. Jefferson would be visiting, I was able to observe a scene that reassured me and made any interference of mine unnecessary.

Mrs. Jefferson was lying, perfectly silent, with her face turned away from anyone. Her husband came in quietly, knowing something was different, walked over

239

to her, and put his hand on her head. Everyone in the room quieted down, talked softly, or read, as though we couldn't see.

"How are you?" he asked tenderly.

She didn't move or reply.

"Is Suzanne all right?" he asked patiently, without sounding alarmed.

"I don't know," she mumbled.

"Have you seen her today?" He sat down where she would have to see him, and smiled at her.

She burst into tears.

He leaned over and kissed her wet face, then placed his cheek gently above hers and cradled her head as she cried in the darkness his covering gave her.

After a while he straightened up. "She'll be all right," he told her. "She'll be just like you. She'll be able to do it."

I was so moved that I marveled for a long time afterward. How many hurts had been soothed by his one act!

She was able to handle the baby the very next day, and I saw her gingerly lift Suzanne with an expression of fear and eagerness. The baby's breathing had improved, her initial weight loss was being recovered, and soon she could be put in the regular nursery. Mrs. Jefferson went home when that happened, but she came back to the hospital for several hours each day to be with her daughter. Suzanne went home in a month, when it was clear she was stable. She was a bright, vigorous baby, though tiny, and when the Jeffersons took her home, she was dressed in a red flannelette gown with a white pompom at the bottom that one of the nursery nurses made for her because she was a Christmas baby. When the drawstring was pulled tight, she looked like a baby in a Christmas stocking.

Amy went on vacation. When she came back, both she and I had four more days on OB, but she had a bad cold with a fever, so she was told not to work. She hung around, however, instead of going home.

It was about 1:00 A.M. and I was going to try to take a nap when Amy said, "Phyllis, I need to talk."

I was exhausted, and the last thing I needed was a "talk," but I didn't say so. "Can we go to the lounge so I won't fall asleep while we're doing it?" I asked, only slightly aware of a little whine in my voice.

Amy said, "No. We'll be interrupted there."

I wouldn't sit on the top bunk in case I toppled over. So, in spite of the fact that it was as dark as a cave, we huddled on the bottom cot. It brought back memories of camp, sitting cross-legged on our bunks, talking earnestly about whatever it was that we found to talk endlessly and earnestly about, and falling asleep.

"I'm having an affair with Jeffrey Bardolph," Amy stated baldly.

That woke me up. Jeffrey Bardolph was a staff psychiatrist—not her psychiatrist, but a man who'd been on the board that voted to let her come back into the internship. He was an earnest, apparently innocent man, who could have been a minister. He'd never married and was now about forty-five. Amy's case had intrigued him, and wanting to help her back to health, he'd struck up a friendship with her. I'd thought they were close, but not sexually intimate.

"When did this happen?" I asked.

"On vacation," she said, and tears started welling up.

"Were you a virgin?" I asked, wondering why she was crying.

"No, no!" She ignored that to go on. "I spent the whole vacation with him. I thought it was going to be so wonderful!" She kept her voice down, always discreet, but agony was in it.

I was so struck that I didn't say anything.

"He asked me to marry him!" she sobbed.

I was dumbfounded. He was much older than she, and I sensed that she was frightened.

She told me that they'd gone skiing. They'd talked and talked about her. She was impressed with how tender, considerate, and protective he was. I didn't

241

know what had made her so vulnerable to the pressures of medical school, but I was suspicious of this father/lover relationship.

I asked her how sex was between them.

"Oh, it's fine," she said, vaguely. I didn't want her to tell me physical details, but I might have expected her to be more enthusiastic. "Oh, I feel so happy with him," she went on. "He makes me relax. I don't worry about being strong or intelligent or anything. It's just so comfortable. He's so accepting. All my weaknesses—he already knows them, and he doesn't care!" she wailed, not hearing the objection in her own voice to his tolerance.

I said, "Amy, do you really want to know what I think?"

"Of course."

I didn't really believe she did, but I said it anyway: "I think you ought not to do it."

"Oh, really?"

I didn't notice her tone; I just rushed on. "Frankly, I think no one can handle intimate relationships during this year. Look at Fred Manton." Fred was my resident on the ward. "He's getting divorced. His wife complains that she hasn't seen him since medical school. Look at Ted Gilman. He's got an ulcer. Tom Francis breaks out in a rash periodically, and you have crying jags.

"An intern is just not a normal person and can't have normal relationships. Amy, I think you should just cool it for now. If you still want to get married in a year or two, well, then I'd say you were making a rational decision. But not right now. I wouldn't trust anybody's emotional judgment during internship."

I didn't mention that one resident had committed suicide last year, and two years ago an intern at University had killed himself. It was *too* awful to bring up in this conversation.

"So you say don't get married," she accused me.

"Yes, that's what I think."

"You sound like those old rules that forbade anyone getting or being married until you got out!" she said bitterly.

I smiled. "You know, I think they had something there."

"Phyllis!"

"Listen, Amy," I tried to tell her. "This life right now is almost completely destructive of intimate relationships. We're run so ragged, the most important thing in our lives is sleep. You need sex to let off some of the tension, but it can't mean much more . . ."

"Maybe it can't for you," she interrupted me angrily. "I don't want to talk about it anymore, Phyllis. It's obvious we're miles apart on this."

"That's all right with me," I said. I crawled under the covers and fell asleep.

Amy regretted having brought up her situation with me. Though we were friends and had shared gossip and confidences, I was impatient and unwilling to listen to romantic rationalizations of her love affair. I couldn't understand how someone as skeptical as she could fall in love with Bardolph. It outraged me to see him encouraging her to be dependent and weak, and to take her emotional problems to him so that she wouldn't have to cope with them herself. Now I could see why she'd been such a bad match with Mrs. Jefferson, who had been ferociously independent and hard at first.

I hadn't handled Amy's wish to talk with me at all well, I could see now, and it was too late. My failure was ironically an illustration of the truth of my contention, that we had no energy left to be skillful in our own personal relationships. Unfortunately, our friendship cooled.

On the next-to-last day I was on Obstetrics, there was an unlucky birth. Mrs. Lucy Antonin was a woman in her mid-thirties who'd tried for years to get pregnant and had finally managed it. She came in in labor, but was proceeding very slowly. Her doctor, Dr. Prinz, decided to do a Caesarean, which alarmed her and her husband. They were anxious and looked very pale.

Dr. Prinz started the operation routinely, but when he saw the baby he paused. He held it in his hands for a moment as if wondering about its fate. It was a boy, fully grown and vigorous, but unmistakably hydrocephalic—with an enlarged head. The brain has ventricules, or cavities. If they are dilated, by definition there is hydrocephaly; if the baby had had this condition for some time, his chances of mental ability—and even, sometimes, survival—might be poor.

Dr. Prinz notified the chief pediatric resident, Annabelle Zabriskie, who came immediately and took the baby.

Mrs. Antonin was bewildered and worried, but Dr. Prinz told her the baby would be all right, and he let her drowse on the operating table. There was none of the joking or gay talk that accompanies the delivery of a normal child. Dr. Prinz seemed to take the last part of the operation very carefully, as if to make sure he was doing whatever he could for the mother. Then he went to break the news to her husband.

I accompanied her to the recovery room; then, after a couple of hours, I took her to her own room. She was in a semiprivate room with a woman who'd just delivered her third child and who I hoped would be helpful. Quietly I told the other woman what had happened, and tears came to her eyes. Then I closed off Mrs. Antonin's side of the room with the curtain, and her husband sat with her. He was a gaunt, sad man as he sat there waiting for his wife to wake up.

Dr. Zabriskie did a CAT scan, or computerized x ray of the brain, and found that the baby had the normal amount of gray brain tissue in addition to the dilated ventricles, so he could benefit from a shunt. Tubing would be placed from the ventricle in the brain to drain the cranial fluid into a neck vein; the tubing would continue through the vein into an atrium of the heart, where it would flow into the blood and be easily absorbed by the bloodstream. The shunt would have to be revised as the child grew, which

244

would mean many operations, but he would be able to function.

It was Dr. Zabriskie who told Mr. and Mrs. Antonin the news that he could be healthy. They were so relieved that they began to giggle and laugh; they couldn't stop. Dr. Zabriskie visited Mrs. Antonin several times, and each time not only reassured her about her son's health, but parceled out the information in several pieces so that they could take it in gradually and understand it well from the beginning. Without their asking her, she made sure she repeated what she'd already told them.

I asked her whether she thought the Antonins were having trouble understanding, as she was walking down the hall back to Ped. She laughed. "No, not at all. It's just my manner." She didn't go on to justify herself, but I realized, looking at Mrs. Antonin's joyful face as she gazed at her baby in the nursery after the operation, that Annabelle Zabriskie's careful repetitions made a solid foundation for this mother's natural love.

My obstetrical rotation was over on New Year's Eve. I wasn't on duty, so I missed what I'd been told was the tension of seeing who could delay or who could hurry to produce the very first baby of the new year. There was a small party for the staff on the floor, and a couple of the women in labor had had enough to drink before they came in that they were charmingly intoxicated during labor and delivery. Apparently, everybody was high that night.

Dennis and I spent New Year's Eve at a distant nightclub, dancing. Then we enjoyed what was left of the night at his apartment.

PART V

January and February

Gynecology

25

After Obstetrics, with its generally happy tone, Gynecology was a shock. It was a place of death where abortions were performed and where women came in with cervical or ovarian cancer. While mastectomies were done in Surgery, we got women whose breast cancer had metastasized, or spread, after mastectomy, and women whose breast cancer was now inoperable. Dr. Abel, with whom I'd had such difficulty in the Emergency Room, was going to be my unhelpful chief resident.

Since the others on my team were Catholic, I was given the primary responsibility to do the abortions. I believed in abortion. I'd seen Lorna Geller, whose mother had refused to get her an abortion. I'd seen other women on OB who were too young to care for their babies or had had too many too fast. I knew that abortion could have saved some women much agony. The early abortions, those on embryos a quarter of an inch to an inch long and up to ten or twelve weeks, were not difficult. This tiny shape could hardly be said to be alive. Up to twelve weeks, a suction abortion or a D and C, dilatation and curettage, will remove the tissue.

It was the later abortions that disturbed me. You have to wait until sixteen weeks to do a saline. The amniotic fluid is replaced with saline and prostaglandin solution. That usually kills the fetus; then the mother goes into labor and delivers the dead fetus. A hysterotomy could be performed between twelve and sixteen weeks, but that is major surgery, opening the abdomen and uterus by incision and removing the fetus, and like all surgery it carries risks. There is some risk of death from pulmonary embolism, for instance, and any risk should not be undertaken lightly. A woman who can't make up her mind to have an abortion before three months causes herself and her doctor emotional suffering.

I understood what agony might make a woman change her mind again and again about terminating the pregnancy, and I never refused to give an abortion when it was asked for. But I had terrible dreams after a while in which tiny fetuses opened their marble eyes to stare at me. They weren't alive, they weren't intelligent or ethical or reproachful, they were just there, without cause and without responsibility.

One of the first cases I had on GYN revealed a reflex in me and gave me a reputation that I got a lot of teasing about, most of it good-natured. Mrs. Marlow was twenty-eight. Carrying her triplets to term two years ago had caused relaxation in the pelvic muscles, which hold the internal organs in place like a hammock. Mrs. Marlow's uterus was protruding into her vagina and actually pressing against the introitus, causing pain and all sorts of problems, not the least of which was to make intercourse impossible. The only correction possible was removal of the uterus.

I checked her the night before her operation. She was sitting up in bed smoking and cheerfully joking with her roommate, who also was smoking.

"Look at these people!" I said, clucking my tongue at them. "Smoking in bed!"

They grinned back at me.

"I'm serious, you know," I informed them.

"We'll watch out," Mrs. Gentileschi said, quickly abashed.

"I'd rather die happy than all worried to a frazzle," declared Mrs. Marlow, poking the cigarette into the center of her mouth and puffing defiantly.

"All right, all right," I acknowledged. "It's your funeral."

"Ha! Darn tootin' it's mine! Maybe the only thing that *is* mine!"

"You seem to be in good spirits," I observed. "Any problems?"

She shook her head no.

"Any questions?"

She hesitated. When I encouraged her, she said, "Listen, sometimes I get these awful cramps, you know. Can you give me something for them?"

I asked, "You know what the operation you're going to have is, don't you?"

"Yeah. You're going to cut out my womb, right?"

"Right. Well, Mrs. Marlow, that means you won't be having any periods anymore."

"I won't?"

"No." I couldn't understand how anyone could be living in this day and age and not see diagrams, drawings, and explanations of reproductive systems.

Now Mrs. Marlow was looking worried. "I won't have my periods?" she asked anxiously.

I took some newspaper and a pen and quickly drew a diagram of the female reproductive system, life-sized. Then I gave a little lecture on how it worked. You'd have thought both of these women were innocent teen-agers. They were enthralled. I ended by asking, "Is that all clear, then, Mrs. Marlow? You're not going to have to worry about periods anymore."

She frowned. "Okay," she said slowly. "But then how are all the poisons in my body going to be drained?"

"Poisons!" I said. "You believe that menstrual blood is impure?"

"Well, isn't it to get all the poisons out?"

"No," I replied. "Anything damaging your system, and any wastes, are filtered out by the liver and kidneys and mixed with water to make urine. Any so-called poisons are voided when you urinate."

"That's it?" She couldn't believe it.

"That's it."

"Can you beat that! Pissing does what I thought the curse did!"

251

I'm not sure they entirely believed me.

I told her carefully, "You won't be able to have any more children, of course, without a uterus."

"So? Who needs more? I got three my first try. Three's enough, believe me," she said fervently.

"The important thing," I said, "is soon you'll be able to screw again."

They looked at one another, blushed, and began giggling.

Mrs. Marlow came through the operation in good shape. It was I who had difficulties the next day. The hysterectomy was to be done vaginally. My job of holding retractors was something of a feat in this particular procedure. The sleeping patient was jacked into a bottoms-up position. The legs were held in stirrups, but couldn't be spread apart really far, so the field was restricted. The surgeon stood between the woman's legs. The rest of us arranged ourselves on either side of her body as best we could. I stood by her left leg, with her leg under my arm. I could actually see only a little of what I knew was happening.

The introitus was stretched, then a clamp put on the cervix of the uterus and a cut made all around it, freeing the uterus from the vagina. The vagina and bladder were pushed aside to expose the ligaments. The uterus was pulled, and the muscular attachments of the uterus to the abdominal walls and the Fallopian tubes were cut. I was holding a retractor in one hand and a sponge in the other, arms extended over the woman's pubis, when I saw what seemed like a huge, reddish-pink organ being pulled out of the vagina.

I passed out. I had enough presence of mind to say "Whoa! Wait . . ." and lean backward before I went black and fell to the floor.

Apparently they just stepped around me and let me come to on my own, since they needed everyone on the operation at that moment and they didn't want anyone to be contaminated.

I awoke lying on the hard floor, looking up at

bright lights and the backs of green-gowned people clustered about a strangely deformed figure on a table.

In a moment I realized I was in an operating room and remembered that I'd fainted. Soon I was able to get to my feet and go out.

The surgeon, Dr. Robinson, was not going to let me get away without any teasing. "Haven't you seen pricks come out of places like this?"

"Oh, yes," I said, recovering my aplomb as a result of his challenge. "And that's where they belong!" I added.

I left the OR. "You-all come back now," he called. "Don't let a little fainting spell discourage you." He laughed. I scrubbed and gowned again and returned to the operation.

I knew I'd never live down that faint. In the hall and in the cafeteria that day, people said in amusement, "Hey, I heard you fainted in the OR today." Then they gave me advice about strong stomachs and tried to make me ill with details of gory accidents and operations. It didn't work; I didn't faint again. But always, when I saw a vaginal hysterectomy, I would feel queasy. It didn't seem right to me to see that organ coming out where babies and penises should.

In a small seminar about hysterectomies, Dr. Lefkowitz, the head of OB-GYN, discussed the indications and different surgical techniques for simple and complete hysterectomies. In a simple hysterectomy just the uterus is removed, while in a complete, the uterus, tubes, and ovaries are removed. Both can be done either abdominally or vaginally, and he pointed out the dangers of vaginal hysterectomy, although young women often insisted on this method, he said.

In the question period I asked, "Comparing the effects of a simple and a complete hysterectomy, is there any difference in the amount or kind of sexual pleasure the woman can feel afterward?"

I could feel the astonishment of the fourteen other people in the room, all of them men.

There was silence, then Dr. Lefkowitz finally replied. "That's an interesting question, Doctor, but since I've never heard any complaints, it can't be important." He laughed.

A young doctor called out, "Surely that is not a consideration, is it, sir?"

"Well . . ." he equivocated, keeping a wary eye on me, "as I said, we are trying to oblige the young ladies now by giving them low abdominal incisions, or the bikini incision, as it's popularly known."

He was changing the subject, so I piped up again. "You mean there are no studies about the libidinal effects? All these operations have been done in the past, and no one has asked the women how it affected their sexual pleasure?"

"Well, Dr. Donnan," he responded, "you must be familiar with the literature discussing neurotic reactions to the operation—the loss of biological identity, resurgence of castration anxiety, and in some cases the cessation of sexual activity altogether."

"These are all gross findings," I persisted, "and I'm not asking about neuroses."

There was some murmuring now.

The head rescued his situation by saying, "Doctor, perhaps it would be a good project for you to interview such cases as come your way. If there's nothing in the literature so far, perhaps it would be of some interest to take your particular approach to the operation."

He closed the topic the same way the ward visit had done. But apparently I had made a sensation, and for days I was teased about my gall in raising such an irrelevant question. I was beginning to be considered a nut on hysterectomies.

Dr. Robinson, the surgeon who had been doing the vag. hys. when I fainted, was a fifty-five-year-old gynecologist who had propositioned nurses, patients— any female. (It is rumored that one-quarter of all

254

gynecologists have sex with willing patients, though I'm told that a GYN examining table has the disadvantage of making the man stand on a stool to reach the woman.)

Dr. Robinson often asked for me as the intern to scrub with him. He kept up a stream of banter. While he was doing one hysterectomy and I was holding the clamp on the cervix to keep the uterus still, he asked me a nonsensical question: "Say, Phyllis, are you wearing support stockings?"

"No, why?" I replied innocently.

He giggled. "This procedure is likely to give a woman doctor some pressure on her cervix!"

"What?" I said, bewildered. "Pressure on a doctor's cervix?" I couldn't see why it should, unless I were implausibly empathetic with the patient.

"Yes," he laughed, "that's why you should be wearing Supphose."

I was speechless. Why was he making such a foolish connection? Hours after the operation, while I was walking down the hall, I realized what I should have replied. I should have said, "Doctor, the only time I get pressure on my cervix is from a good, stiff prick!" Robinson really would have enjoyed that retort.

"Now be careful there," Robinson once said to me as I was getting some vessels out of the way with my retractor. "That's the clitoral nerve. Very important, they say."

It was not the clitoral nerve at all. There's no specific nerve, but a whole network of nerves, on the outside of the body that serve the clitoral area. I gave him a look of disgust.

He took a slightly different tack. "Say, Phyllis," he said, looking eagerly at me, "how'd you like to do this hysterectomy?"

"Yes!"

"Okay" he said, taking a half-step back and startling everyone in the room. "You do the case, but on one condition. I'll trade you a hysterectomy for a fuck."

I looked at him. For a successfully promiscuous man, he was strikingly unattractive. His comment was crude and hostile. With no intention of keeping my part of the bargain but not wanting to lose out on a hysterectomy, which interns seldom get to do, I responded to the dare: "You're on."

Everyone in the OR, familiar as they were with Dr. Robinson's ribaldry, was excited at the unusual fact that an intern was going to do a hys.—and on such terms. I assumed no one believed me, even Dr. Robinson.

After a split second of timidity, I put my mind to the task and took over the operation. I constantly asked whether what I was doing was correct and whether something should come next or not. You can read all the texts and even watch many operations, but when you do your first one there is always a possibility of making a mistake. I wasn't going to be careless.

When it was all over and we were taking off our gowns in the OR, he leaned over to me and said, "You did a good job on the hysterectomy. Now when do I collect?"

"How about when I'm old and gray and really need it?" I replied.

We kept running the joke through. He never seemed to tire of it. It was good for a few more variations, such as the protest of mine to Abel: "Do you know what I have to do to get cases?"

Abel blushed.

I didn't think I could have afforded to turn down Dr. Robinson's proposition outright. I had to make a no sound like a yes.

I'd managed to work beside and under Dr. Abel in the Emergency Room by quietly avoiding his supervision when I anticipated disagreement. On GYN that was not possible. We now fought openly. I accepted his right to demand that I perform certain tasks, but I did not accept the authority of some of his opinions. As with, for example, my desire to administer the epidural earlier than the male obstetricians were in

256

the habit of doing, I had the idea that women could be permitted sex sooner after some procedures than Abel was advising them.

On GYN we saw many D and Cs. Women came in for the dilatation and curettage when there is excessive or irregular bleeding so that the endometrium, or uterine lining, can start all over again; polyps can be removed this way. A D and C will also finish up spontaneous abortions or miscarriages, and elective abortions are often D and Cs. The first time I was with Dr. Abel in his interview with a patient shortly before she went home, I was amused at his conservatism. The patient was a good-looking woman in her early thirties who'd just had a D and C because of heavy bleeding.

"Now, Mrs. Williams," Dr. Abel said stiffly, "I must advise you to abstain from relations for six weeks."

She looked blank. When he went on to talk of something else, she looked questioningly at me.

"What?" she said, interrupting him.

"What?" he said.

"What did you say 'for six weeks'?"

"Oh, ah. Relations. No relations for six weeks."

She looked at me again. "No relations!" she mouthed in dismay, guessing that she'd have to keep all her relatives away.

"Screw!" I said, clearly.

His sharp "Dr. Donnan!" came at the same moment that the light dawned on Mrs. Williams, and she broke out laughing. Dr. Abel curtly said, "I have nothing more to say here!" and he haughtily left the room. He must have thought I was insulting him.

Soon enough I felt like it. He kept advising women not to have sex for a full six weeks after a D and C and after two or three more instances, I challenged him on this point. We were in the corridor and I stopped him.

"What's the reason for your puritanical rule of six weeks?" I asked belligerently.

A battle gleam came to his eyes. A foot taller than

I, he stepped close to me, leaned over me, and said, "The reason is I said so!"

Outraged, I cried, "It's unreasonable!" He ignored me and walked away.

I wasn't going to run after him. As he went down the corridor, I yelled, "The least you could do is prescribe a vibrator!"

Even if he didn't hear it, everybody else did. All the nurses within hearing range giggled.

26

Simon Manchester was the other intern on my team. Over coffee down in the cafeteria one Wednesday afternoon, we were complaining to one another. Both of us had to spend an hour or so in the chart room before we could go home that night, trying to get the files of the patients we had discharged up to date. Abel checked our charts every Thursday to warn us to work them up before the weekend. He was the first resident we'd had who was so compulsive about charts. It had shocked us when he first made what we thought was a grade school demand.

The fact is, for all his faults, Abel's insistence on our keeping up with our charts was useful. Doctors complain a lot about paperwork, but each fact must be recorded since it's always potentially useful, and you can't rely on the memory of a patient, who will forget the most unexpected things. I admitted a woman once who told me she didn't have any allergies; if her penicillin sensitivity hadn't been on her chart I might have administered it when she subsequently developed an infection.

Simon said, "I just discharged a girl I'd seen before in the clinic."

"Yeah?" I asked. Simon was concentrating in OB-GYN, and had spent two months in the GYN day clinic.

"Yeah," he went on. "Apparently the resident down there now finally decided to admit her since he couldn't find anything and she kept coming back. Some of these girls you can't satisfy except with a hospital admission, you know?"

"How old is she?" I asked, expecting to hear about an adolescent hypochondriac.

"Twenty-three, twenty-four, I think."

"You call this a girl?"

He smiled apologetically. "Oh. Sorry. Listen, Phyllis," he explained earnestly, "she just seemed so inexperienced, I think of her as a girl."

"So tell me about this case, this twenty-four-year-old 'girl.' "

"Okay, but you promise you won't interrupt?" he said suspiciously.

I made the Brownie pledge sign, two fingers up.

He laughed; it was the Cub Scout sign, too. "Okay. This patient was in three times last year with irregular profuse bleeding. She comes in again in July with the same complaint, along with painful menstruation now. It turns out she's divorced; we all know about these psychosomatics."

I cringed. It's true that a woman's emotional state can be reflected in menstrual disorders; but a man's emotional state, perhaps more commonly, can appear also—in hypertension, heart disease, ulcers, and sexual dysfunction, to name a few maladies—and he doesn't get sneered at for it. But I was silent and let Simon go on.

"So I asked her if she was getting any sex, you know; 'How's your love life?' I asked. 'Do you have orgasm?' And you know what she did? She just clammed up. Turned bright red and clammed up. So it's obvious the diagnosis is frustration." He laughed. "Well, there's nothing I felt inclined to do about it.

So I just gave her a placebo and sent her home. That was in July."

"Now she's back again, and Lupton down there admits her for a D and C. What do you bet she'll be back in three months or four?" He paused to look at me challengingly.

"I think you're a pig."

"I could see it coming from the expression on your face," he said.

"She comes in with irregular and excessive bleeding," I said. "You don't have to be offensive and condescending."

"Well, she turned bright red, didn't she?" he said defensively.

"You embarrassed her, or she was so furious at you she couldn't talk."

"Look, Phyllis," he argued, "such questions are legitimate between a doctor and his patient. Everything is relevant, and the question of sex is especially relevant to a gynecological problem."

I yawned to clear my head, something I find useful to do before making a point, for it also disconcerts my opponent. "I suppose it's possible that she's having no sex at all, but the point is she was bleeding, and I hardly think you could prescribe a penis to stop the bleeding, which would be the logical conclusion of your line of thinking. I think it's your responsibility to maintain some dignity between you and your patient. I suppose some doctors will always laugh at some of their patients, but I don't think they should do it to their faces!"

By now, Simon was bright red. Abruptly, he got up, saying that he had to get back to work. I wondered how long it would take for him to feel comfortable with me again. I guess I *had* lectured to him.

On rounds one day, Abel motioned me to precede him into a patient's room, making a big show of being chivalrous. There were two women in the room. Mrs. Lang was very ill with cancer, which had spread to her lungs. Fluid had gotten into the pleural space and

260

collapsed one lung. Tubes in her chest drew air out of the pleural space and bubbled it through a water trap to prevent too much suction or pressure. In spite of the continuous gurgling sound of the machine, she was sleeping.

With just a glance at her, the chief resident and I walked over to the other bed, by the window. Mrs. Oliver, who'd had a hysterectomy, was a middle-aged woman. Her gray hair was short and permanent-waved. Her face, lined and sagging, had lit up at the sight of Dr. Abel. Bathed in the light from the window, she looked transformed.

"Well, Ruth," he said jovially. "How are we this morning?"

She smiled shyly. "As well as can be expected, I guess."

His conversation with her was brisk. Then he turned her over to me to check her bandages. Her animation faded when he left the room, but she tried to hide her disappointment. When I checked her bandage, I noticed a stain on it.

She was saying, "He's a really nice doctor, isn't he?"

I suppressed the traitorous thoughts that he was (1) condescending to her, (2) bullying to all his woman patients, and (3) hostile and irritating to me. I grunted a kind of yes.

She told me he had inquired after her daughters and she speculated on his marital situation. I said he was married. "Oh," she sighed, "too bad. All the nice ones get taken right away, don't they?" She giggled, wistfully.

She told me—as she had done before—how cruel her surgeon had seemed and how kind and attractive Dr. Abel had been in contrast. "He said I was a good girl to come through the operation so nicely. And to tell the truth, it was all I could do to keep from bursting into tears, he was so nice and understanding. Sympathy does that to me, I don't know why. The minute somebody starts to comfort me, it seems to make it worse somehow. I'm not being ungrateful."

I stood at her bedside, my tasks suspended, and listened. She told me again how frightened she'd been to go to a doctor when she'd started all that bleeding, how her husband had insisted she was going to get anemic if she didn't have it looked after, and how embarrassed she'd been to show her body even to her doctor. She'd had a biopsy in the office, showing she had cystic and adenomatous hyperplasia, or premalignant tumor growth in the endometrium. It had been decided to do a hysterectomy.

"And to think of a young, handsome man like Dr. Abel having to deal with an old bag of bones like me, an old hag . . ."

"No, no," I said. "You mustn't think that way about yourself. You're in fine condition, very attractive."

"I was in my younger days," she said proudly. "It's such a nice hospital," she confided. "The nurses and the doctors are generally so kind to you. I'm just very fortunate. I don't deserve it."

"Of course you do," I assured her, though I knew she wanted to be assured by Dr. Abel. I reasoned that she had let him see her body, and so she had to love him. She could accept the surgeon as a workman, and she made it all business with him, distancing him as much as she could. But the young Dr. Abel had to become something much more.

"I like the way Dr. Abel calls me Ruth. It's sweet, don't you think?"

Well, I thought, as I nodded, maybe she does get what she needs from him after all—a quick, unthreatening familiarity.

"Mrs. Oliver," I told her, "I'll have to come back with the nurse to change your bandage. I see a little bit of stain on it. I want to check to see if your wound is healing properly."

"Oh," she gasped.

"Now there's no danger. I don't want you to worry. This staining is new, and there's just a little bit. Your postoperative progress has been fine."

While the nurse and I removed her dressing, Mrs. Oliver watched us apprehensively. She clenched her

262

fists and winced as we removed the tape as gently as we could. The wound had opened in one small place and was oozing pinkish-yellow serous fluid, but it wasn't infected. Left to itself it would heal, but the scar would be lumpy there. Fortunately, I had detected it soon enough that the skin could still be closed along the original line of the incision with steri-strips; that is, adhesive strips.

The skin of the body ages more slowly than that of the face, since it is not so exposed to sun and wind. Mrs. Oliver looked at her white, soft, young belly as though she had never studied herself, and when she saw the great hysterectomy scar and stitches, she lay her head back on the pillow and didn't look again. She seemed to grieve.

"We're going to have to close that wound back up," I said. "I think steri-strips will do it."

"I want Dr. Abel," she moaned.

Unfortunately for her, I called him. He told me he didn't want tape but stitches, and if only a couple were needed and it was clean enough, he didn't want to be bothered with such a minor thing; I should go ahead and do it.

I came back in and told her, "I can do it for you right here, Mrs. Oliver, right now before it's exposed too long."

"No, I don't want you. I want Dr. Abel," she insisted.

"I'm afraid he's in the operating room and can't do it," I lied. "I'm going to get this cleaned off now, give you a little superficial Novocain, and put two stitches in, just to make sure."

She was silent. The only sound was that of Mrs. Lang's machine bubbling as I briskly fastened up the rest of Mrs. Oliver's wound. She lay with the sunlight from the window making a bar across her body and stared at the ceiling.

It was the end of Mrs. Oliver's "love affair" with Dr. Abel. He wasn't there when she saw the scar. If he had been there, maybe she could have coquetted with him and ignored it. Or he could have (she thought) reassured her that she was not ugly. But now she saw her body violated, and might have suddenly realized it was too late for even her to begin to love it. She became quiet and pensive.

The only thing Abel said was: "I'm sure glad she doesn't talk so much anymore."

"The woman is depressed," I told him.

"Ha," he said skeptically. "So now you're a psychiatrist, huh?"

Mrs. Oliver's husband was hearty and imperceptive; her roommate, refusing to believe that her own condition was serious, was unreliably cheerful; and Dr. Abel was the same curt, efficient doctor he'd always been. Only the nurses and I saw Ruth Oliver's distress, and she was sullen with me, as if she blamed me for something.

I watched helplessly as the nurses and aides tried to animate her. She seemed to sink a little deeper into her bed, to age, and to weaken until she was like a patient in an old folks' home. When a beautician came to give Mrs. Oliver a shampoo and set, I couldn't watch. She smiled and smiled. When her husband came to visit and loudly complimented her on her curls, she blushed. She left in another few days, propped up in her wheelchair like a doll.

Vaginal infections were common on GYN, especially gonorrhea. I came to understand a doctor's haste to diagnose PID—pelvic inflammatory disease—as secondary to gonorrhea. Because we saw so much of it in the early stage, and because an advanced case of gonorrhea, with enlarged, painful tubes and infected ovaries, requires a complete hysterectomy with removal of the ovaries, we didn't want to take any chances. Though it was not quite as ugly a disease as syphilis used to be, gonorrhea was dangerous. Syphilis in fact has changed through the ages, and a tertiary case no longer deforms a patient with ulcers all over his body. They were both still bad diseases, though.

Janet Wyler was one patient I saw with PID. She was getting intravenous penicillin and gentomycin.

Thirty-nine years old, she had been in the hospital several times for it. Her black hair had begun to silver. She was married, worked as a secretary, and her children were teen-agers. She had caught gonorrhea three times in the past ten years. Each time the disease had been eradicated, then she'd caught it again. It must have been her husband who gave it to her; she didn't sleep with anyone else.

I brashly grabbed her husband on his way in to visit her. "Hey, Mr. Wyler," I said. "Can I talk to you?" He was a big burly man, a foreman on a road construction crew, and he walked as though he were outdoors and had all the space in the world for his stride. Indoors, it almost made you uneasy. He turned around, and I was struck by a pair of brilliant blue eyes, curly lashes and brows, and the kind of rugged good looks that makes a man very sure of himself. He grinned at me.

"Who may you be?" he asked in a friendly, surprised tone.

"I'm, ah, one of the doctors on your wife's case," I replied, annoyingly flustered by his frankly interested gaze.

"You're kidding me! What's a girl like you doing in a place like this?" He stood stock-still, as if amazed, and grinned.

"Uh, we can talk down in the lounge, Mr. Wyler, just this way," I interrupted, starting off. I didn't pay any attention to his hamming, but led the way.

We sat down. He unzipped his jacket, and as I was leaning forward to begin speaking, I noticed with a shock the two words gleaming on his belt buckle: PENIS POWER.

"Mr. Wyler," I blurted, "I can't believe my eyes! Does your belt buckle say Penis Power?"

He laughed. "A lady is not supposed to say things like that!" He gave me what I could only interpret as a roguish look.

I sat back in my chair, silent.

After a pause he continued, "You noticed it,

265

though, didn't you?" His coy grin was still there, but it was less confident now.

I cleared my throat. "Hm. Mr. Wyler. You, uh, you've been transmitting gonorrhea to your wife, you know."

Taken aback, he turned down the corners of his mouth and tipped his head back in a gesture of disbelief and unconcern.

"I'm going to see that you get examined by one of our urologists," I said grimly.

He shook his head no. "Hnh-unh."

"Oh, yes. I'm going to get you there if I have to drag you."

He tried a reasonable tone. "Listen, I don't have it."

"Well, let's find out." I stood up and stepped over to him, prepared to try to drag him from his chair—a ridiculous impossibility since he weighed fully twice as much as I did. I stared at him coolly. "You're not going to look very dignified, being pulled at by me," I warned him.

Red-faced, he got up. It didn't occur to him to leave or simply to refuse. I'd taken him by surprise, and he was either too embarrassed or not fast-thinking enough to get himself out of the situation I'd created. In fact, I marched him down to Urology, leading him by the elbow, and made sure they took him right away.

I was really mad at this irresponsible man who even decorated himself with his boast of promiscuity. When I went into Mrs. Wyler's room, I was prepared to see her in the sympathetic position of complete victim.

"Mrs. Wyler," I told her gladly, "I'm getting your husband tested right now and he'll soon be under treatment."

She looked startled and worried, as if I'd given her bad news. "Oh, I wish you hadn't done that."

"I'm confused," I said to her. "Here you've had gonorrhea three times, it's advanced so far now that you're in constant pain, and you say you don't have sex with anybody but your husband, so it must come from him."

"You shouldn't have," she reproved me.

"Why?"

"Oh, I don't know," she replied irritably.

The other woman in the room, Mrs. Kelsey, said, "Your husband ought to get somethin' like that looked at, it might be eatin' away, eatin' away without him knowin' it." She looked genuinely concerned. She was a fifty-year-old woman in for the removal of a cystic ovary.

"It's none of your business!" Mrs. Wyler snapped at both of us.

"There you are wrong," I informed her firmly. "If he won't get himself treated and keeps reinfecting you, then—"

She interrupted, "He *does* get treatment, he *does!*" Then she realized that she was telling me he had contracted it several times. "Why do you have to meddle?" she demanded, on the edge of tears.

I paused for a moment in the face of her urgency. "I have to meddle," I said finally. "We have to interfere in a case of VD. I'm sorry if it upsets you." She wouldn't look at me, and I realized what it meant to her. My knowing and my treating him meant that I knew he was unfaithful to her, and probably often. She felt humiliated.

The next time I came into her room, I was suddenly struck with how good her hair looked and said so. The nurse had just helped her wash it that morning.

"Oh, no," Mrs. Wyler diffidently replied.

"It *is* beautiful, though," I told her.

"Oh, no," she repeated. "It's all gray."

"Not gray. Silver."

Mrs. Wyler didn't know she was beautiful, or couldn't believe that she was. I found this remarkable since she was so strikingly good-looking. I asked her how she was doing, whether she was still in pain, and other routine questions, all of which she answered meekly. From day to day she remained the same. Her condition was not improved by her antibiotics.

The only thing that would help her was the removal of her uterus and ovaries, but her doctor had been unable to convince her to allow the operation.

Mrs. Kelsey enthusiastically supported it.

"Listen, dear," she said to the younger woman, "why not do it? Why, you don't need that baby carrier anymore. It's not as though you wanted more kids for yourself, is it? No," she said soothingly. "Come on, be good to yourself, do what the doctor says. You'll not regret it, I'm sure."

"Just—just mind your own business, will you?" Mrs. Wyler answered.

"But I hate to see you lyin' there in such torture!" said the irrepressible Mrs. Kelsey.

"Just leave me alone!" Janet Wyler cried.

When Mrs. Kelsey was discharged and another woman took her place, Mrs. Wyler no longer had to contend with any motherly nagging. The doctor told me he was letting up on the pressure. "These women . . . some of these women," he amended. "You can't force them to give it all up. They've got to come to that conclusion by themselves."

I hadn't seen this before, the long suffering that a woman would endure before she surrendered. Janet Wyler would greet her IV with such hope; she'd ask for the results of each new test, and her spirits would fall when she heard there was no change. Finally, after she'd been in for fourteen days—which made a total of forty-five days from her several admissions —she consented.

I was just packing away the syringe and tube of blood I'd taken from her vein when I heard her whisper, "Tell Dr. Lefkowitz I'll let him do it."

"Ah," I said, as matter-of-factly as possible, "good. Shall I let him know in the morning?"

She slumped down in the bed. "All right," she murmured.

I touched her hand. It was thin and bony. "I think you're doing the right thing," I told her.

She smiled a twisted smile. "I just can't stand it anymore."

"You'll feel better," I assured her.

However, the next morning when she talked with the doctor, she made him promise he'd take only the uterus. She didn't want to be castrated as well. Reluctantly he agreed. He warned her she wouldn't get the relief she needed, that since her tubes and ovaries were infected she'd have to have them out sooner or later. Desperate, she insisted he leave her her ovaries.

With antibiotics, we got her inflammation smothered enough to keep the infection contained so she could have surgery. She came through the operation and the two-day postoperative danger period all right. But she was gloomy and depressed, and still in pain.

I wished I could have helped her make the better decision. A couple of months later, she did come back and had her ovaries removed. Three days later, she was feeling healthy for the first time in years. It's amazing that there's such a dramatic difference. The improvement in her health came too late for one thing, however; when she came back in, she and her husband had separated—perhaps she felt she might as well lose everything. She had made him move out, but I doubt that she believed she'd be able to survive a divorce.

Down at the end of the corridor was a patient who insisted she had nocturnal visitors. Judy Heffernan was in for surgery on an ovarian cyst. She was a huge, obese woman weighing about 250 pounds. Whenever I came into the room in the morning, checking on IVs and other things, she'd call out, "Ahhh! Here comes my sexy doctor! How are you today?"

I thought she was just an excessively jovial person, and I'd joke back at her, "How many visitors did you have last night?"

I'd laugh, but she was instantly serious. "In the evening," she told me, "there was a man who told me all about some company and its marketing problems. Marketing what, I don't know."

"Did you talk back to him?" I asked.

"Of course I don't talk to these people. I just listen."

"Anybody else?"

"Yes," she said, knowing that I didn't believe her. "Some doctor, it must have been a doctor, came in about ten or ten-thirty and started telling me about what dosage he was going to give me of some drug I'd never heard of."

"Well, now, that's interesting. I wish you'd remember."

"Oh, it lasted only a couple of minutes. I couldn't catch it."

I changed the subject and got her back onto her own health. She didn't seem troubled by these ghosts, being someone who could take her superstitions in stride, I guessed. Maybe it was because the ghosts never called her by her own name, always by someone else's.

She kept telling me day after day what had happened by her bedside the night before. I asked her whether she had any visitations during the day but she didn't know. She was out of her bed and around on the floor so much that she wouldn't have heard them anyway.

The night before she was going to be discharged, I was sitting at the desk when she came down and said, "If you're interested, I can let you hear one right now."

I went along. I was humoring her, and I was curious about what she would come up with.

When she got me around a corner, she pinned me against the wall with her body.

"You know," she whispered, "I really think you're sexy."

"Uh," I said, weakly, "thanks."

"Do you ever—you know—make it with women?" she asked, bulking large in my imagination as well as in my actual vision as a 250-pound lover.

"No," I said, "no, I don't," hoping that my answer would call her off.

"Ahhhh," she said, "you don't know what you're missing."

"Uh, maybe not, but I've *never* been attracted to it!" I declared fervently.

"Too bad," she said, and moved away.

I breathed a sigh of relief. I'd never expected to be accosted by a 250-pound lesbian, and the close shave shook me as well as amused me.

When we got to her room it was silent.

"Oh, well," she said cheerfully. "I guess we took too long to get here."

The next patient we put in that bed gave me a start. It was the second day that Mrs. Bennett was in, when I was arranging for some preoperative tests, that she complained forcefully, "The nurse came in several times last night to take my temperature," she said, "and she never did it! It's bad enough to have your sleep disturbed for that kind of thing, but for her not to go ahead and do it once she's awakened me . . . !"

I told her there must have been some mistake. Her temperature didn't need to be checked throughout the night. I assured her I'd take it up with the night nurses.

When they came on, however, they told me they hadn't done any such thing. I thought another patient had freaked out when Mrs. Bennett came flapping down the hall in her mules, her bathrobe breezing around her, and whispered urgently to us, "She's there again! And there isn't anybody there!"

A nurse and I ran back with her, and sure enough, if one of us stood close to her bed she could hear a voice apparently chatting with her as the person took her temperature, inquired about her condition, and then paused to count her pulse. When we went elsewhere in the room or stood by the beds of the other three patients we couldn't hear a thing. It was eerie.

"You can't hear it anywhere else in the room," I told her.

"I don't care. I don't want to be in this bed anymore. It's too creepy."

I didn't blame her. So we found an empty space, and in the middle of the night we transferred her bed to that room and the empty bed back to the "haunted" room.

Investigating the mystery took a couple of days until a janitor came up with the suggestion that sound was traveling down some pipes in an odd way. Indeed, if a person happened to stand in a certain place in the room above, whatever was said could be heard in that particular place in the room below.

I enjoyed standing in different places in the room upstairs and saying, in various voices, "Testing, one-two-three-four."

When I went downstairs to check with the nurses, they said they'd recognized my voice readily; they swore I could trust them never to repeat the outrageous secrets I had revealed.

The building crew came in and padded the pipes, which took care of the ghosts. Obviously, Judy Heffernan had not been crazy, after all.

27

I was standing at the nurses' station one morning, kidding with Sally and Hazel, when I received a phone call from Dr. Speir.

"Ah," I said cordially, "Dr. Speir. It's been a long time since I've seen you. What can I do for you?"

"Hello, Dr. Donnan," he replied cheerfully. "I want you to take a patient of mine. You remember Mrs. Black, don't you?"

He went on talking, but suddenly the floor seemed to drop. Then the light came back on as blindingly as if it were reflected from the snow. Dr. Speir had been telling me that Stella Black's cancer had metastasized further, to her lungs and other bone sites. Trying to respond as quickly as he could to the swiftness of her cancer he was bringing her in to have her ovaries and adrenal glands removed to prevent production of the hormones that seem to aid cancer. Without those hormones, the disease might be slowed. Cortisone would replace the adrenal hormones.

In addition, there were several small fibroids within the uterus that were causing irregular bleeding, so they were going to take the uterus out as well, particularly since they didn't want her bleeding in response to new chemotherapy.

Stella was going to be a one-breasted, defeminized castrated woman.

"It's lucky you're on GYN right now," Dr. Speir was saying. "Mrs. Black especially asked after you." He said they'd be up in about ten minutes; he was bringing her over from his office and I could do the admitting.

I hardly ever forgot a patient's medical case history. I might forget what one woman's favorite son did for a living that made her so proud, I might forget one man's opinion of the hospital, I might easily forget a patient's name, even—but most of the medical details remained vivid. As I paced back and forth between the nurses' station and the elevators, my hands plunged into the pockets of my white jacket, I automatically and precisely reviewed Stella's case: breast lump, almost immediate spread to glands in armpit, radical mastectomy, metastasis to her side and to her spine, radiation and chemotherapy, and now the swift spread to her lungs and other bone sites, and the next operation and cortisone replacement.

An elevator stopped and passengers disembarked. Another elevator came. I noted them all as they stopped and opened their doors. I was cold with efficiency and detachment. Then, at the end of the bank of elevators, the doors opened, and two men walking a woman between them got off and turned toward me.

With Dr. Speir and Mr. Black on either side of her like policemen, Stella came along as though reluctantly. She seemed inattentive to their animated talk to one another. Then she saw me and smiled, and it was as though two persons within her came together and focused.

"Mrs. Black," I greeted her, and shook her hand.

She covered my hand with her other one, looked at me, and said, "Stella, remember?"

I was shocked that she was almost exactly my height. I had remembered her as much taller. Her clear eyes like brown water gazed strongly, but her face, though tanned, looked like the face of a desperately aging woman. False eyelashes covered her sparse natural ones, and she wore an excellent wig. Her thin eyebrows were penciled fuller. Her slim, dark green suede coat framed her pallid face with a huge, grayish-white fur collar. I always admired her clothing, I realized, as though her wealth or her taste were important and enviable.

Dr. Speir, giving me instructions in his genial way, entrusted Stella's chart to me. We reached the doorway to her room. We paused there until Dr. Speir pushed open the door, and waited for Stella to go into the room as if it were a cell. Perhaps conscious of our hesitation, she walked in quickly, with small innocent steps, and in the middle of the room turned at bay.

We followed her in and Dr. Speir spoke reassuringly. "Mrs. Black, I'm sure you'll be comfortable. I'm told the nursing on this floor is the best in the hospital—you've already experienced Dr. Donnan's care here. As you know, I've got you scheduled for tomorrow morning at nine o'clock. Not too early, as these things go, as I'm sure you must realize. But I like to arrange surgery in a civilized manner, don't you agree? You have two top surgeons, Dr. Cohen, the chief of Surgery, and Dr. Lefkowitz, the head of Obstetrics and Gynecology." He told her in detail what would be happening before and during the operation. Then he shook her hand, said good-bye and that he'd be in again tomorrow. Mr. Black, saying he'd be back that evening and kissing her good-bye, went with him.

We two were left.

She stood facing me, with her arms outstretched.

"It's good to see you again," she said, without moving.

"It's good to see you," I replied. "How have you been?"

"How have *you* been?" she tossed the question back at me. Perhaps she didn't want to talk about how she'd been, not yet anyway. I had a sudden vision of her mastectomy scar, and the hysterectomy scar she would have, and the incisions in her back, and Natalie's ovaries being cut out, and a uterus being lifted from an abdomen or grotesquely emerging from a vagina.

Stella murmured, "Come, come, Doctor, how are you?" Then she turned away, took off her coat, and hung it up in the closet. She surveyed the room. "Not so nice as the other one," she observed. "Only one comfortable chair." She sat down in it and gestured for me to seat myself in the straight chair nearby.

"Tell me," she said seriously, "how have you been?" as though it were an urgent request. It was the third time she'd had to ask.

I laughed and quoted: "An intern's lot is not a happy one."

She smiled. "Ahhh." Her voice comforted me.

We both smiled.

"Stella, where did you get your tan?"

She changed gears less smoothly than she had been able to do six months earlier. "Greece," she told me. "We went to Greece for a month, just now in December. We drove into the deep countryside and through the mountains. We stayed in little market towns. The peasants we met—we would communicate only in the crudest ways, but how warmly, how hospitably, how charmingly they received us." I could imagine them giving tribute to her as she revisited the earth. The children, Miranda and Jeff, had joined them in Athens, and they had celebrated Christmas in the Greek way.

Abruptly she shifted again. "Once when Jeff was little and having so much trouble," she reminisced, "in and out of the Emergency Room or the doctor's office, I went to a psychiatrist. I went for years. It did me

275

good, really; it helped when I was going through all my fears for Jeff. But when I stopped therapy I felt freed, as if there'd been some tyranny there, some imprisonment.

"I remember leaving the office and walking out to my car as I'd done so many times before, and finding that my mind had gone blank: I couldn't get into my car and drive away. I walked past it. I wandered along the sidewalk. It was between classes, and students were rushing here and there to some destination.

"I wanted to be one of them." She smiled sadly. "Here I had my freedom, unexpectedly, and I was new again, but I didn't have anybody to be."

I didn't say anything. I wanted to get out.

"I got pregnant," she said. "Jeff was safe now. He was ten. I could try again. I had Miranda. I called her Miranda: admirable, to be admired, amazing." Stella paused.

"Well," she said briskly, "I had another child, I became another mother. I loved it, you know. I love my children and I love my husband. I'm proud of them all.

"But you see, there is a price to everything. The price I paid for all these good things was to neglect myself, and now I regret what I didn't do for myself. Do you . . ." she asked, "as a professional woman —does it bother you how little I've accomplished?"

I looked at her and shook my head emphatically. "I like what you are; you're wrong to think you're blank," but somehow I couldn't argue with how she interpreted herself. If she said she had neglected herself, then she must have somehow. Only she would know.

She went on, "I once promised Stan that we would repeat our honeymoon in Greece and I did it. I kept that promise." She told me how she had managed to reconcile her son Jeff to the family. She told me of driving Miranda to gymnastics lessons thirty miles away when she discovered her daughter's enjoyment. She told me of heading a benefit for the symphony and then the campaign of a liberal challenger for a

276

seat in the state legislature. As she spoke, her eyes were bright and her cheeks were flushed with enthusiasm, as with fever. There was a deep tension in her body, and I knew she was in pain.

"What made you come back to Dr. Speir?" I asked.

"I couldn't ignore it any longer," she said. "It wasn't working."

"What wasn't?"

"My bargain," she said.

I waited for her to explain.

"I . . . I thought that if I were good, if I used all my intelligence and energy without wasting it as I had before . . . I thought—I guess I thought I would outdistance it."

"Outdistance it," I repeated.

"Leave it behind me, get far enough away from it, the . . . cancer. That happens, doesn't it?" she asked me eagerly. "You transcend it, almost; it disappears."

"There *are* spontaneous remissions," I acknowledged.

"Yes, I know," she continued. "I've read about them, I've read everything I could get my hands on. Spontaneous remissions. Who's to say what will qualify you for one."

I wanted to tell her not to be a fool. Yet who was I to deprive her of hope? She was right. There *were* spontaneous remissions. If I told her there was no hope I would be lying. "A spontaneous remission," I echoed. "That would be good, Stella. You're right. There *is* a chance." I pitied her deeply for her hope.

She smiled, leaned forward, and clutched my hands. "I knew it!" she exclaimed. "I knew you'd agree with me. I knew I could be honest with you and tell you what I've really been doing."

She sat back again. "Now I'm ready for anything you want to do to me, you and the other doctors."

As I left her room I wanted to listen again to her and to myself, and as I walked, wishing, I realized that she was clear to me in a way she had not been before. When she'd left the hospital last summer, I'd promised her she was getting *well;* I'd ignored what

277

she told me then about dying and I'd demanded that she fulfill my promise to her that she live. Yet now, in January, her cancer had metastasized further, and I was not surprised, and emotionally I was not betrayed; I had left behind somewhere my requirement that she perform Life for me.

I was convinced now that she would soon die. In my willingness to see that, I didn't know yet that she *would* perform Life for me.

I was walking along the corridor from Stella's room when I heard a young voice saying, "Hey! Hey, Doctor!"

I looked up and saw Stella's daughter calling me. For a moment I couldn't remember her name. There was a pause, then I said, "Oh, hello, Miranda."

She came close to me and looked up at me intently. She looked ill at ease and scrawnier than I had remembered.

I asked, "What's the matter?"

She sighed in exasperation and moved restlessly as if to depart. Then she changed her mind and asked, "What's the story on Mother?"

I hesitated. I didn't know exactly what she knew, nor did I know exactly what she was asking in that abrupt, casual, yet aggressive way.

"When I was in Greece with her," Miranda put in, "she looked terrible. She looked like she could die."

I wondered whether Miranda and I both had expected Stella to be immortal. "Is it your impression that she didn't have a good time?" I asked. "From what she told me, it sounded like a fabulous vacation."

"Oh, yes," Miranda acknowledged quickly. "But I can tell when something's wrong. She was in pain, I could tell that."

"Well," I replied, "probably she was."

"So," Miranda said as if she'd proved her point. "So she comes back, and you all operate on her and take all the hurt away. Right?" Her voice was mocking, but she challenged me to say yes, to promise all.

"Come," I said to the girl. "Let's have a seat in the conference room."

"I don't want to."

"But I'd like to talk to you."

"No," she said. "I'll talk to Mother. You don't need to bother."

She turned and walked to her mother's door and went in without looking back. Perhaps she and I had always felt competitive, like sisters.

That night I was on, and before I went to bed at 11:30, I stopped by Stella's room. She should have been asleep by then, on the night before the operation, and I'd given orders for a sleeping pill, but I thought perhaps she couldn't sleep. When I opened the door and peeked in, she proved me right. "What is it?" she asked sharply and apprehensively.

"Stella," I said, coming in, "you should be asleep."

"I can't."

"Let me get you something," I offered.

"No. Wait. Just sit here a few minutes."

I turned on an overhead light that was soft.

"No, no," she said. "Just sit in the dark with me. It's easier for me to see things in the dark."

"What do you mean?" I asked, wondering if she were masochistically conjuring up fantasies.

"I had a terrible time in the islands," Stella said, referring to the part of her vacation she had spent cruising in the Aegean. "That sea is a deep aquamarine color, distant, impersonal, eternal, like eyes, like a god's eyes.

"Our boat used its sails, not its motor. In the silence I could shut out the other passengers' talk and play. Maybe I heard the sailors say things, but mostly it was silent. I felt alone.

"I'd sight an island and it was ancient, poking bare out of that eternal sea."

Stella sighed. "It's . . . it feels rather stupid to tell you this. I'm objective at the moment, and I can remember myself on that boat. I'm trying hard to be skeptical of her because I don't want her to be true."

She stopped. She'd been talking to herself, not to me, I thought. In the darkness I was able to feel part of her. Perhaps it wouldn't last for more than a few moments.

"What was she like?" I asked.

"She was like a statue," Stella said, with a kind of wonder in her voice. "She was like an air-dried clay statue. The minute something touched her, she'd crumble into dust."

My mind fought her image. I didn't want to feel that she and therefore I was a clay figure that could be so easily destroyed. Stella should be cheerful again, hopeful. At least she could have concealed herself from me, just as, I suddenly thought, many patients seemed to be able to do with their doctors. The nurses were supposed to take the brunt of all these emotions. But because I was a woman patients felt they could use me, I protested to myself, as they could ask me for a bedpan. I wished I could renege on my naive assumption that I was becoming special, quietly able to sympathize with my patients, renege on my hope that I represented the new capacities that women could bring to medicine to save it from the callousness of technology and modern, male ignorance.

I had been a fool. How could I have thought for a minute that sympathizing with pain wouldn't hurt?

Stella said, "I'm tired, and I'll sleep now. I really feel encouraged. I'm so glad you and Dr. Speir gave me this chance. It's so clear to me that it's just the thing." Her voice was bright now.

"How so?" I asked.

"Don't think I'm superstitious, but I think of this operation you're going to do as the gift to the goddess."

"Goddess?"

"Well, the cancer, you know. It feels right to give up my female organs, after all; it's . . . correct that way. Once I could be brought to give them up, you see, then it will be all right. It's them that are the . . . the thing."

Every word she spoke I heard with horror, like a mother hearing her daughter go mad.

"The operation's going to work," she said eagerly. "You all said so. It's my bargain, you see. It will work."

It was the extreme of what she'd said this morning. In the face of her sense of her life's fragility I could understand her desire for magic. I responded, "What can I say? I hope you're right." Then I said, "Bedtime."

She assented. "Goodnight," she said. "I don't need anything. I'll sleep."

"Goodnight."

Now I had to make my way through the long corridor, past rooms of sleeping patients, to my on-call room. I made the trek to my promised bunk as though I were a pale stranger walking past rows of silent, dark people. I told the late-shift nurse that I was going, I said something to somebody I passed, I waved to someone else. I saw a psychiatric resident hurrying off down the hall the opposite way from me. I heard the wheeze of an elevator door on the floor below. I heard my own shoes on the asphalt tile. When I got to my room, I automatically took off my belt and beepers, scuffed off my shoes, and arranged them ready to be put on quickly. I fell asleep.

I scrubbed the next morning. Stella seemed relaxed, even happy. When she'd been put to sleep she was turned over onto her stomach, and her middle back was painted orange with betadine solution. When everything was ready, Dr. Cohen made the incision above the kidney on one side of her spine, removed the rib, divided the muscles, and exposed the fatty tissue. I applied self-retaining retractors to hold the incision open; with one hand I could continue to follow the surgeon with a retractor to give him exposure and with the other sponge whenever necessary. The adrenal gland looks very much like the surrounding fat. He cut it out and soon was closing and suturing the incision. The adrenal gland on the other side was removed in the same way. Then she was bandaged and turned back over.

She was like a rag doll, nearly hairless, scrawny, and one-breasted. Now the organs of womanhood would be lifted from her and she would become more nearly a child again.

Dr. Lefkowitz made the incision, opened the abdomen, and pushed the bowel out of the way. First the tubes and ovaries were clamped, cut away from the sidewall, and tied off. The bladder was pushed down. Then with the uterus on stretch and held tightly, the uterine vessels were clamped and tied and the cervix was dissected from its pelvic ligaments and vessels. The last step was to circumcise, or with knife and then scissors to dissect the cervix from the vagina, and everything could be lifted out. Then the bleeding points were sutured and the vagina was sewn up, though left slightly open for better drainage until it healed into a dead end.

The whole hysterectomy took thirty-five minutes. Stella was on the operating table only an hour and forty-five minutes, and she'd had to lose very little blood.

I myself was well under control the whole time.

28

That night was crisp and cold. When I came off, I walked down the block, crossed the street, and walked another two blocks to a main thoroughfare. I passed a restaurant with its doors open, and in the dark interior I could see neon beer signs, dim lights at some booths, and the color television above the bar. The smell of tobacco smoke was strong. People's conversation hummed. I passed stores closed for the night, their display windows bright. I stopped at a filling station and asked to use their phone.

I called Dennis.

His answering service said he was at the hospital. My mind was blank for a moment. It's odd that filling station offices always seem to have a desk but seldom a chair to go with it. Boxed batteries lined the windowsill, and dusty cans of solvents and additives filled a counter on the back wall. Almost everything had black, greasy smudges except for the rack full of new maps.

Suddenly it occurred to me that I could call Dennis directly at the hospital and find out when he would be free.

Watching the attendant clean a car's windshield and, then, holding the hose to the gas tank, stand talking with the customer, I dialed the hospital and asked for Dr. Danes.

In a few minutes Dennis came on the line. He told me one of his patients was about to deliver.

"You said you weren't going to take any more obstetrical patients," I said.

"Yeah," he agreed, "and this is why. But people keep sending them to me."

"When do you think you'll be through?"

"Well, I don't anticipate any difficulties. Maybe an hour?"

"How'd you like to go out, or come over, or do something?"

He considered it for a moment, then said, "It'll have to be brief. I've got a hysterectomy tomorrow at eight o'clock."

"Whatever you say."

"All right. I'll be over."

"Call me before you leave the hospital, will you?"

"Yes."

"Good." We said good-bye and hung up.

I walked slowly, enjoying the coldness of the air.

By the time I got home, however, I'd managed to kill only a half-hour. Restlessly, I wandered around my small apartment, trying to think of something to do. Finally I decided to give myself a sponge bath, as though I were some kind of invalid. I had finished and was wondering what to put on when the phone rang.

It was Dennis. "Listen, Phyllis," he said, "it's late enough. I'm just going to come up." He was referring to my preference that he come across the roof.

"No," I started to object.

"Listen," he said impatiently. "Who cares if anybody finds out? You're being Victorian about this."

"No, I'm not," I retorted. "It's a professional consideration. Maybe it doesn't make any difference to *you* if anybody at the hospital finds out about us, but it makes a hell of a difference to me!"

There was a pause. Then his curt voice said, "Do you want me to come at all?"

Oddly, I was frightened. I gave up. "Of course. Okay, do what you want to, just come up."

There was a pause as if he were changing his mind; then at last he said, "All right."

I was relieved. "But . . . be careful, will you?" I couldn't resist asking.

"I'll take off my shoes and creep up like Dagwood," he promised.

I timed him, hovering behind the unlatched door, and when he arrived on the landing and was about to knock I let him in immediately.

The minute he was in and saw me he grinned. "You forgot to put your clothes on."

I grabbed him around the neck and kissed him open-mouthed.

He protested feebly.

I led him to the bed and quickly took his clothes off, stroking his penis; he was already well erect. Laying us down on the bed, I mounted him and moved urgently around and on him so that I felt like an umbrella, a rain shower, a great wet space opening and opening until I was coming in big gulps and grasps that were tightening and becoming defined again as I finally subsided and relaxed onto his body.

"What was that all about?" he said in annoyance after a while.

"Mmmm." I had dozed off almost immediately. I woke up and asked, "Did you come?"

"No. Get off me. It hurts." He shoved me to the side and his penis slid out of me, limp and small.

"I'm sorry, Dennis," I apologized. "Here, let me make you come."

"No. It's too irritated now."

"Well, stay and relax. We'll get it up again." I smiled.

Instead, he got up and went into my bathroom. I heard the shower start. After a few minutes he turned off the water and came into the room, toweling himself dry. Then he started to put on his clothes.

I was flabbergasted—not only surprised but also offended.

Finally, completely dressed, he said. "Goodnight, Phyllis," and started to leave.

"What the fuck do you think you're doing, being so ... *rude!*" It was the only word I could think of.

"You shut your ass, sister," he told me viciously. "You don't use me for a stud!"

"Get out!" I screamed, and he did.

Propped up on one elbow, I stared at the closed door for a moment as Dennis clattered down the stairs, vindictively making as much noise as he could. I was astounded. I'd known that our relationship was never "serious" and I'd sometimes wondered how it would end, but I never thought the definitive argument would be so brief. And yet so explicit.

I lay cold and empty.

Then I went into the bathroom, got ready for bed, and turned out the lights. I rested for a while on my back, watching the reflection of the streetlight on the ceiling.

The next morning I felt vulnerable but free. I woke up energetic and eager to get to work. I went to the hospital for breakfast, and the scrambled eggs that morning seemed delicious. I ate with Jameson, a first-year anesthesia resident, and Stein and Davison and Jeffrey, all medical students. I felt superior. I had what was to me, in my falsely euphoric state of mind, a fascinating conversation with Jameson about monitoring blood gas values with various anesthetics.

I strolled up to GYN, feeling more casual as I went.

As I turned into one corridor, however, I saw a room light go on and heard a cry for help. I ran in to see a woman thrashing around on the floor and a nurse trying to calm her. The patient in the other bed had pressed the call button. The woman on the floor was flailing her arms, jackknifing her body, and banging her arms and legs and body on the bed legs, but it didn't look as if she were having an epileptic seizure: she was too energetic, randomly. People in seizure have rhythmic convulsions.

I stooped over her and saw that she was breathing normally. I straddled her jerking body and managed to press my stethoscope onto her chest, where the heartbeat was regular and normal.

"Get a tongue blade," I ordered the nurse, in case I had misinterpreted the signs and she really was having a fit, and might bite her tongue. The nurse ran out.

Suddenly the woman reached up, and two hands grabbed my neck with a powerful grip. She began to squeeze.

The nurse was out of the room, the other patient couldn't see because we were on the floor, the woman could drag me down in a minute, and I was losing consciousness.

With sudden strength I grabbed her body somewhere and lifted, relieving the weight on my throat, and blindly slung her onto the bed.

In a moment her surprised grip had tightened again, and she was choking me with all her strength. We struggled. The stethoscope was whapping me on the

286

chest, loudly clanging on my ear, for I still had the earpieces in. In my struggle I staggered sideways, and the blue curtain that had been partway around the bed wrapped around me. I could hardly see. Everything was blue. Increasingly loud beneath the whacking sound, I was hearing ringing, louder and louder, and I used my last breath to wheeze, "You're not having a seizure! Stop it!"

"Yes, I am!" she shrieked, letting go of my throat, and I could see her roll across the bed and off it, landing on her feet on the other side, leering at me and waving something at me that she'd grabbed from her bedside table.

I staggered backward into the billowing curtain and brought myself up sharp against the windowsill. Tangled in the curtain, I tried to force air in and out of my squeezed throat, hacking and wheezing, and groped my way out of the curtain.

The nurse had rushed back in and grabbed the woman, who was still yelling at me. The ringing in my ears was beginning to fade. "See? See?" she was repeating, waving something at me.

I swayed across the bed and took it from her, focusing my eyes to read Dilantin, an anticonvulsant drug used for epileptics.

"Where'd you get this?" I whispered hoarsely.

"I was in a neurology clinic last time," she said. "See? That proves it!"

"All right, all right," I began to calm her down. "I'll check your dosage and we'll give you some." Feeling my bruises, I left the room.

I discovered that she was getting placebo Dilantin. She was a hysterical personality. Now she was on GYN for an abortion. A married woman, she had three children living with her mother, and her husband had deserted her. I wondered whether he'd left because she was crazy, or she'd gone crazy because he'd left. I was certain she was a good candidate for an abortion.

Abel was especially angry because this was her

third abortion. I found myself in the unlikely position of arguing for her. It was obvious to me that she couldn't be responsible for herself; she'd have to have repeated abortions.

"This type just uses the hospital for birth control!" Abel declared.

"Well," I countered reasonably, "it's better than having her produce baby after baby who'll turn out all screwed up."

"There are people desperate to adopt."

"Yes, but do you think she'd give up her babies for adoption? Not on your life. Don't even give her the idea of delivering and keeping a child. She'd choke the life out of it."

"Are you all right, by the way?" he asked.

"Thanks," I said dryly, "I'm okay."

I don't suppose anyone could ever feel relaxed again with someone who'd almost killed her, but she was my case, and I was bound I would give her that abortion. However, I wanted some kind of understanding. "Listen here," I told her, "if you have another seizure, you're not going to get your abortion."

"What the hell do you mean? What gives you the right to treat me like this?" she demanded angrily.

"I'm telling you you're not going to choke anybody else around here!"

"I'm going to sue you and this hospital if you refuse me the abortion!"

"If anybody sues anybody," I countered, "it'll be me suing you for assault and battery."

She quieted down, sulkily.

I did the abortion, and got her out of the hospital as soon as possible—the next day. She actually became quite respectful of me. Her friendliness was irksome—just one day of it was too much. She gave me the creeps. I didn't doubt she'd be back again in another year or so.

I was being given another abortion that afternoon. I groaned inwardly. Ellen Stokely, a very young woman —sixteen—had been so ambivalent about getting an abortion that she had delayed until it was no longer a simple matter. She was pretty, with the long straight blond hair many girls wore and large, pale blue eyes. They were powerful eyes because they seemed so open and vulnerable. Her body was slight. She had lost weight but her breasts were enlarged and her abdomen showed a slight bulge. She was four months pregnant.

She laughed tremulously when she told me that the pregnancy had been great for her figure and had given her big breasts. Sitting on the examining table, she made a poignant little gesture of lifting the new weight of her breasts with her childlike hands.

I smiled at her reassuringly, examined her, and found her to be well into her fourth month. The uterus was soft, large, and rising above the pubic bone. She would have to have a saline abortion.

I explained the procedure to her very gently. She sat with the white paper gown clutched around her, trembling with cold and fear. I got her sweater and draped it around her shoulders as I talked. Some of the amniotic fluid would be withdrawn, then with the same needle saline and prostaglandin solution would be injected into the uterus through the abdominal wall. Then she would have to wait for the saline and prostaglandin to cause labor. I didn't tell her that the fetus doesn't always die from the procedure and that the uterus might expel its occupant alive—a seven-inch-long fetus with a beating heart, well-formed limbs, and distinct facial features—but nonviable. I didn't share with her the details that filled my imagination. I told her merely that she would have to wait until labor began. Her wait might last as little as four hours, but the normal or average wait was twenty-four hours. A late abortion was a painful thing.

She was sobbing and cried out, "I don't want to, I can't do it."

I responded, "You don't have to go through with it if you don't want to."

She gazed at me in astonishment. Then she broke down again crying, "I know. I know it. I don't *have*

289

to. But I *have* to. I have to do it! I'm only sixteen ... I'm only sixteen!" she wailed.

I let her cry. I understood her self-pity and anxiety and her pathetic appeal for her youth. Finally I told her, "The very fact that you couldn't decide until now shows how upset you've been. It's going to be hard for you, I'm afraid. You can change your mind and have a baby, but you've got to decide now. You shouldn't continue this way. Pregnancy is one thing that will not stand still." I wondered what it was like to know that in your belly something was growing that wasn't you, something that took its own time, that you had to wait for.

Ellen Stokely sobbed and said, "I want the abortion. God forgive me, I have to do it."

I didn't need to know anything about her background, her family, or her situation to tell me she must be lonely and very afraid. She was also very young.

She was to be prepared for the saline procedure immediately after the routine test had been done, since it involved no anesthesia. It took place in a treatment room on the Gynecology floor. It was fortunate that Grey's didn't force women having abortions to have them performed in Obstetrics. Some hospitals did, sadistically, I thought, for it upset the women aborting; it was also shortsighted for it upset the women giving normal, happy birth.

Soon I was giving her a local anesthetic and inserting the needle. Standing beside her slight form draped on the table, I held the needle and rapidly inserted it until the clear yellow amniotic fluid came out. I was doing an obviously charitable task and steeling myself to do it, as I often had to do.

I had withdrawn virtually all the amniotic fluid when Abel walked by, seemingly on another errand, but I was sure he knew what I was doing. He checked himself, looked startled, and quickly came in.

"What are you doing?" he demanded in a loud voice. Ellen Stokely opened her eyes in terror.

"It's the saline, of course," I replied aggressively.

"Why are you doing it now?" he said, grabbing

Ellen's chart and lifting the pages one after another. "Where are the results of the Pap smear? If you dilate the cervix before you know whether she has cancer you invite it to spread!" he shouted.

The minute he had burst into the room, I had stopped what I was doing and stood, poised, with my hands holding the stilette so it wouldn't jiggle. Ellen's face was tight with her effort not to burst into tears. "I've already taken all the amniotic fluid," I protested.

"You have to stop."

I withdrew the needle, quickly put a Band-Aid over the puncture, and instructed the nurse to take Ellen to her room. Then I drove Abel out of the room, out of earshot of my patient.

As I grabbed him by the sleeve and rushed into the hall with him, he insisted in a loud voice, "You can't continue this procedure until we get those results."

I was speechless with fury at him for disturbing and scaring my patient. The probability of a sixteen-year-old having cancer was ludicrously slight, but I wasn't going to argue in front of such a nervous patient and in the middle of a procedure that frightened her. I had forgotten to wait for the results. In my own anxiety to get it over with, I had made a mistake.

As soon as Abel had exploded, he calmed down. He slowed me in my headlong rush down the corridor, stopped me by the arm, and said, "Hey, are you mad at me?"

I took a step backward, looked up at him, gasped, and vomited all over him.

29

I had seen Stella several times since her operation. That evening I stopped in at 10:00 before I went to bed. "How are you feeling tonight?" I asked.

"Crummy," she replied, with a look of self-disgust.

"What's the matter?" I was instantly alert. Anything Stella was willing to mention must surely be bothersome.

"My belly aches." It was unusual for her to be so colloquial.

"In what way? Do you mean inside, or the wound?"

She went on, "I don't like lying around seeping into sanitary napkins all the time. It makes you feel that you wet your pants."

"Ah . . ." I began to reply, but she ignored me.

"These hospital napkins are too bulky; I don't like how they feel between my legs. My incisions itch, my scars ache, and . . . and . . ." She came to a halt. She lifted her arms to her head and threaded her fingers through her hair. "Aaaaah!" she groaned. "What am I doing?"

"It sounds like you're complaining," I said.

She laughed briefly. "Yes, yes, you're right. That's what it sounds like." She paused, then continued. "It's true. All my complaints are true, you know."

"I can imagine. Do you want me to try to help you with anything?" I didn't know what I could do for her. She was on painkillers, so the itches and aches might be subjective. She couldn't wear tampons to get rid of that puddle feeling because the top of the vagina, though sutured, was open and not yet healed.

She said, heaving herself up, "I want to get out of

this stinking bed!" She almost threw herself off the edge of the bed with the violence of her movement. I held her while I reached for the stepstool with my foot. I stood by her, waiting, not because I knew I shouldn't interfere with what she was saying, but because I was helpless.

She started crying. She put her hand up to her mouth and spoke through her fingers. "I want my mommy," she whispered, with a small rocking motion. She didn't look at me. She talked to herself. "Isn't that silly? A grown woman whose mother is dead." She put on her robe, slipped her feet into slippers, and stepped down.

She sat down and motioned to the other chair for me.

I sighed. "What can I say, Stella?" I felt tired. I wanted to go to sleep.

"I'll tell you," she said. "I know what I'm worried about. Rags was here today."

I nodded.

"She's acting strangely," Stella went on. "There's nothing I can put my finger on. Her grades are as good as ever, maybe better. But ever since the trip to Greece, she's been angry—I think it's a current of anger in her. I know about teen-age rebellion, I've gone through it with Jeff, but I didn't expect it with Rags. I . . . maybe I kidded myself that she and I could be loving toward one another through this time . . .

"This afternoon, as we visited, she was . . . sneering at me, there was an offensive tone when she spoke."

Stella talked of Miranda's loving openness in the past. She began to tell me precocious things Miranda had said when she was little, projects she and her mother had had together. I listened slightly to her warm voice dancing a glowing chain through the dark. I gazed at the hospital bed, bright under the light. Finally I realized that Stella was weeping, that as she spoke, tears welled up and fell down her face as she talked steadily, smoothly, about her daughter.

"She's trying to say good-bye to me," Stella said. "She's trying to let me go."

I stood up, walked the two steps to her chair, and stood beside her.

Without looking up she reached to take my hand. I stood there for a moment, speechless.

"You pity yourself," I said.

"I deserve to," she answered simply.

That stopped me. "I suppose you're right," I said at last.

She went on. "I'm lucky to have a long time to die. I'd always wished to die quickly, in an accident, but I shouldn't have to die suddenly, all at once. I don't think we get to do it well that way."

As she spoke I felt ill.

"My dear Phyllis," she said warmly, "take advantage of this time you have to listen to me. Another day I may feel differently. That's one thing that's so awful about dying: you change your mind all the time. One day you decide you will die, you'll be able to, you'll make it into something that you *do*. But then another day you'll fight, you'll hate it, you'll be terrified and screaming with helplessness.

"But it doesn't change. It won't change. You can't change it."

"Would you like to see a psychiatrist?" I asked.

She laughed. "Am I too much for you, my dear?" I didn't answer her.

She said, "Sometimes I feel guilty for talking so to you. But I talk to my husband this way, too, you know. You're not the only person I have. Jeff and Rags get a little of it, too. It's good for all of you. It's the facts of life. Maybe that's one last thing I can teach my children."

I had no answer; it was so bare and simple. I didn't know whether I had to learn what she wanted to teach me or not. But I saw my other patients in her as well, as if she were an advocate. I started to cry.

After a moment she said, "I'm glad. Thanks."

"Glad!"

"You're a friend. You don't lie to me anymore."

Ellen Stokeley's Pap smear was normal, so I was able to continue the saline the next day. It had been all right to leave her overnight, since amniotic fluid forms again.

I was in a strange state of mind. My first reaction to losing my lover had been relief, because Dennis had not been good for me. He hadn't helped me understand myself and what was happening to me before, and we'd broken up over an act expressing my need and our failure, but still I yearned for intimacy with him, for the solace of sex. I felt abandoned, alone, as from a divorce. And I couldn't talk to anyone about it.

*

On the fourth day after Stella's operation I decreased the dosage of her painkiller. She'd asked me not to give her so much because it made her sleep all the time. When I'd come in in the morning, she'd be lying tilted up and dozing.

That morning her mouth was open, like a child's, and some saliva moistened a spot on her pillow. She was not wearing her wig, and her hair was downy and colorless, like a newborn's. Her body was thin, frail. I paused to gaze at her.

She woke up, turned her face to me, and gazed back.

Then she drew in enough breath to animate her and lifted her arms and stretched. "I feel much better today," she said happily. "Maybe the bargain will work."

"I'm glad you're feeling confident, Stella," I said, taking her thin wrist and feeling a steady pulse. I checked the nurse's notes of her temperature, pulse, respiration, and blood pressure.

"I'll let you go to the bathroom today," I told her.

She smiled. "You've changed," she said.

"Have I, Stella? In what way?"

"You're in charge now," she said.

I smiled back at her, looking down on her tiny figure. "Of what, I wonder?"

One evening soon before Stella was to be discharged, Mr. Black called me on the phone after visiting hours and insisted he wanted to speak with me privately. I met him in the lounge. When I walked in the room was dim. He was sitting next to the one light, and his face was heavily lined with shadows. The drapes had not been pulled, and we could see the lights of the city glowing on low clouds and gleaming on leftover snow and ice.

He roused himself and began to ask calm, serious questions about Stella's illness. Finally he looked away and asked, "Will she be able to . . . function . . . as a wife?"

Outraged by what I thought was a selfish question, I replied brutally, "Have sex, do you mean?"

I remembered first meeting him, and how condescending we had been toward her, like foster-parents, and I felt how different I was now, helpless in a way. The angle of his head in the light made his eyes glisten, so that I believed he wept, maybe for himself and his fears for the loss of his own pleasure, like a boy, or maybe . . . maybe for Stella. Maybe for Stella herself.

I answered him kindly. "Yes," I told him. "She still has a vagina. The mucous lining should still be moist. She has a clitoris still, and the most important nerve network. She'll be able to have sex in about six weeks. She should be able to," I finished significantly.

He was embarrassed. "I didn't mean . . ." he began, this confident man at a loss: "I don't know what I meant . . ."

In a moment he got up, thanked me politely, and said some small graceful things. We said goodnight.

Stella checked out ten days after her operation. She looked good. Energetic and cheerful, she embraced me.

"Take care," I said.

She nodded. "Don't worry. I will."

When she left, I felt as though a support had been pulled away from me. I tried to talk to Amy, but Amy was too tight and vulnerable herself. I found myself calling Kathleen, who agreed to meet me for coffee later on. I stopped by the ward to pick her up and almost had to drag her away.

"Begorra!" she exclaimed, in her mock Irish way, as we walked down the stairs. "You're in a masterful mood."

"Kathleen," I replied, "if I didn't strong-arm you, you'd be there working until Doomsday."

"I go home when it's me time," she said.

We got to the cafeteria and picked up our coffee; I bought a pastry I knew would taste like glue. I steered her to an empty table in a corner under a heating pipe.

I told her about the patient who'd tried to kill me.

Kathleen laughed. "That reminds me of something that happened when I was a student nurse. Salter was the Grand Old Man of OB then. He was a regular tyrant, hardly spoke two words to his patients, but they came to him in droves. He had a reputation of never losing a mother, you see, and at that time . . ."

"How long ago?"

"Twenty years."

"He had a reputation of never losing a mother?" I quoted her.

"Well, you know how it is. I can't help me nature. All the Irish are dreamers and liars.

"Anyway," she went on irrepressibly, "one of his patients was a poor woman with seven children already, a husband with no regular work, and herself in poor health. Salter wanted to tie her tubes, had been trying to persuade her, and finally, while she was in labor with her eighth, she agreed.

"He'd just come out to tell her husband that he had a new girl when the man grabbed his arm, glared up at him (he was a good foot shorter), made a motion to his dirty jacket pocket, and told Salter he'd shoot him if he tied his old lady's tubes.

" 'My good man,' Salter started to say, when the man pulled the pistol out of his pocket and waved it in front of Salter's face to let him get a good look at it.

'My good man,' Salter said again, not a hair turned, 'you are overwrought at the birth of yet another child, I can understand that. But believe me, I would not tie your wife's tubes if she were destined to populate the whole world!' He put his hand on the gun, lowered it, and walked away."

"Did he tie her tubes after all?" I asked.

"No, by God," said Kathleen. "He knew when a man was serious. However, when she came back in for her six-week checkup, he might have recommended what we know as 'Catholic birth control.' "

A doctor might say that a woman was bleeding so much that she'd have to have the uterus out. I didn't know how often hysterectomy still had to be used as a means of birth control.

"I say Salter might have, but I don't know that he did," Kathleen smiled.

"Kathleen," I asked, "how do you get used to the death of patients you like?"

She didn't speak for a moment. Then she said, "You don't."

"But how can you . . . ?"

"I'm not going to advise you," she said. "Each one has his or her own way to work it out, some this way, some the other."

"What was the first death you saw?" I asked, persistent.

I thought perhaps she was going to refuse to tell me; I could never predict when Kathleen wanted to keep something private and when she was willing to talk about it. She cleared her throat. "I'll tell you about it because it was good, and maybe it helped me to do the kind of nursing I need to do.

"It was my sister."

"Oh." I was embarrassed.

"Never mind. It's not a pathetic story. She'd been born premature, and my mother kept her alive in a box surrounded with hot bricks. The child spent her first month in that box close to the fire. We other children weren't allowed to come near the baby for fear of germs. But Mother's care made Bridget grow strong, and she was special for all of us, like a princess.

"As soon as she could walk she was into everything. And talkin' and askin' questions of anyone who'd listen. She must have been developing TB for some time, though, for when she was six, she was ill of it, thin and feverish, and needed nursin' again. Mother and I shared. Lots of people had died from tuberculosis in that neighborhood before, but Mother and I refused to believe it could happen in the forties. O' course, we were too poor to move or anything.

"It was Bridget herself who told us she was really and truly goin' to die. She told us not to be afraid. I don't know how she knew what dyin' was, but she did." Kathleen stopped talking.

I said, "I can't believe it. Not a child!"

"I know. It's true, though." Kathleen looked at me. "You stop and listen to your terminal patients, Phyllis, and you'll hear. Often they're better prepared than maybe anybody else around them."

"Even the ones in awful pain?"

"We try to alleviate the pain."

"Thanks, Kathleen," I said. "I've got to get back." She nodded, and we left the cafeteria.

Kathleen's confidence in a dying patient reassured me. Even when she was depressed Stella had seemed strong. Even her unlikely hope and her childish bargain had given her dignity. I had unconsciously depended on her to make sense of what was happening to her for me. Now that she had left, her absence made me feel a fear for her that was perhaps really feeling sorry for myself. For one thing, I'd have to work it all out for myself now. I couldn't even practice the distraction, for me, of trying to shield a patient from knowing. I was suspended, not wise yet in the ways of dying. But I had painfully begun to grieve.

Maybe it was a good thing that I had to cope with breaking up with Dennis and its aftermath at this time. It didn't irritate me at all to have to turn aside from a philosophical emotional issue to a social problem. Maybe the fight that broke us up was too short; we had to fight longer, and the only place left to do it was in public.

He declared war one morning when he saw me leaning against the counter at the nurses' station, looking over my patients' charts.

"Good morning, Phyllis," he said, cordially enough, I thought, and I was pleased that apparently there were no hard feelings.

"Say," he said to Pat Ziskind, a very attractive blond nurse who was there, "I'm free tonight. How's about I pick you up around seven? I can get tickets to that musical."

He stood very close to me, leaned his elbow on the counter, and ignored me. I was uncomfortably conscious of the length and volume of his body in its tasteful, well-fitting olive brown suit—like that of an FBI agent, I added satirically to make me snap out of it.

"Gee," Pat said, "I was scheduled to make dinner for my roommates." Her voice announced that she did not consider that an unbreakable contract.

"Well," he said, "trade off. They can do without you tonight."

I had gathered up my charts, a sizable pile this morning, to walk off, but two slid off the top and spilled, and I knelt down to pick them up.

He looked down at me. "Can I help you?" he asked, like a clerk in a store.

"Nope," I said curtly, sweeping all the papers into a disorganized pile that I could sort out elsewhere. He turned back to Pat.

I was furious. I considered his behavior completely gratuitous. It was designed to make me suffer, and maybe it did, but it made me mad, too. I wanted to murder him.

Though it is usually a resident who assists, it is possible for a private physician to request an intern to scrub in on his patient, as Dr. Robinson had done. Dennis began to request me. He remembered my dis-

300

may at the removal of Natalie Hoskins's cancerous ovaries, he'd heard about my fainting at the vaginal hysterectomy, and he thought he could push me a little more. He had me scrub in on three hysterectomies in a row.

As he was operating he kidded me. "Well, Phyllis," he said jovially, "are you going to go into Obstetrics and Gynecology?"

"I doubt it," I answered.

"No? You get to see a lot of women. But maybe that wouldn't appeal to you. It's a good specialty for me, however. I like women." That was either an understatement or a lie.

"I should think you'd get bored seeing women's genitals all the time," I countered. "Crotch after crotch after crotch."

"Oh, no, not at all! It's not boring in the slightest," he replied. "Let's see now, what can we find for you to specialize in? How about . . . I know! How about Urology?" Everybody was laughing.

"Oh, no," I said promptly, "I'd never go into Urology."

"Why not, Phyllis?" a medical student piped up, caught up in the swing of our exchanges.

"Because I don't want to deal with things that don't work!"

Now everybody laughed; impotency is a large part of a Urology practice.

During a vaginal hysterectomy, Dennis challenged me at length about the furor some feminists had raised about so-called unnecessary hysterectomies. He was operating seated between the patient's legs, interrupting his diatribe now and then with an announcement of each detail of the surgical procedure. He pretended he had no notion of my queasiness. I kept tight control over myself and tried not to get too close. After the uterus had been removed I was all right.

His voice changed, too, as if he knew I was out of danger. He said, generally and expansively, "What do they mean, 'unnecessary surgery'?"

I saw my opening. "You should know, Doctor."

301

That was too weak a feint; he wasn't pricked. "Why, Phyllis," he said, his eyes gleaming with pleasure, "I got a rise out of you after all!"

I looked at him and raised my eyebrows as if to say, I thought it was me that always got a rise out of you!

"Hey, Phyllis," he said, "I hear you promised Robinson a fuck for a hysterectomy. Would you do that for me, too?"

Now there would be speculation—*after* the fact—about what I had used extraordinary measures to keep secret. I could almost feel him laughing at me, and there were speculative chuckles around the room.

He began psychoanalyzing professional women, never looking up at me, his voice sounding light and good-natured. Finally, he said, "Phyllis, don't you realize that a woman trying to make it in a man's field is really just a castrating female?"

I reached back to the nurse's table and grabbed a Haney, a large, ferocious-looking clamp. My other hand in the en garde position, I aimed it between his legs. "You better watch out," I cried, "or I'll prove you right! I'll remove one the first time. That way you'll be wary of me, so that there will not be a second time."

Everybody in the operating room broke up. Dennis too was laughing. I knew we'd reached a truce.

For almost four weeks we had an unusual problem on GYN—obscene phone calls. Two or three times a week a man would call a postoperative patient and get her to examine herself. One patient told Dr. Abel that she'd received a call from the nicest doctor the day before, and asked if he would be coming in on her case. Abel had never heard of him, but thought her private doctor might have called somebody else in on her. Another patient suggested that I wasn't doing my job properly if I didn't do as thorough an examination as this Dr. Frederickson did.

Who was Dr. Frederickson? We wondered.

We soon found out that he was getting his kicks in

a strange way. He always called a woman who'd had an operation the previous day. He'd say, "This is Dr. Frederickson. I was in on your operation yesterday and found it a very interesting case. I'd like to be able to come over to examine you, but unfortunately I can't leave my office at this moment. Perhaps we can work out a compromise. If you could check certain things for me and report to me over the phone, I'll be able to give you my opinion.

"Do you think you could do that, Mrs. Jenkins?" he'd say in a straight, businesslike tone, as if it were the most common medical custom in the world.

"I guess so" would be the reply, or "I've never done this before . . ."

"You just follow my instructions, and I'm sure you'll make a competent try."

Then he'd have the woman strip and examine and palpate her breasts and report on their color and the texture of the skin and nipples, and he'd ask about the genitalia and get her to do a lengthy, precise examination of the vulva, certainly a far more careful look and touch than any doctor would need and more than most women themselves were familiar with doing.

Then he'd say very calmly, "Thank you so much, Mrs. Jenkins. You've been most thorough. I have a very good idea of your condition from what you've been able to tell me, and when I've considered my opinion, I'll let your doctor know. Goodnight."

Throughout, his voice was kind, calm, and very soothing, the women said.

We debated what to do. Finally we decided to tell the patients what had been happening and ask for their cooperation. They were shocked and excited. Some women were frightened. They were told to let us know when anyone got such a phone call and then keep him on the line (not doing what he instructed) as long as possible while we tried to trace the call. The police and phone company were cooperating, though it turned out not to be necessary.

The next woman who got a call punched her call button. She let us know that he was on the phone by

303

talking to him when an intercom came on, and we put our switchboard on alert to begin the trace. I went into her room while she was holding him on the line.

She was so funny, hamming it up, simpering, and pretending to be embarrassed and stupid.

He'd tell her to look at a certain place, apparently the aureola, and she'd say, very breathily, "Oh, where, Doctor? I'm sorry I don't know all these terms. The what? The rolleola?" Later she told him in vexation, "Oh, you'll have to wait just a moment while I try to get these pajama bottoms off. They're harem pants. I'll have to put the phone down while I get them over my feet. You don't mind, do you?" She went on and on like this, mugging at me. "Oh, I can't! Do I have to touch that?" I had to leave the room to keep from laughing. She pretended to be both incredibly ignorant and modest, and innocently seductive. I'm surprised he didn't catch on, but maybe she fit right in to his idea of women.

She kept him on the phone for at least twenty minutes. It turned out that he was a late night OR orderly who kept up on the GYN operating room schedules; he made his calls from a phone in the hospital basement.

He was arrested, of course. He wasn't jailed, but he was, appropriately, hospitalized. I had to admire his ingenuity.

PART VI

March and April

Surgery

30

By the time I got to Surgery, I was more profoundly tired than I had thought possible. My perception of what was around me was either so vivid as to be almost surrealistic or dully blurred. To see a scene, let alone a person, so precisely—the texture of the wall, the colors of a plaid jacket, the sounds of voices and machinery and instruments—was painful, and in self-preservation I tried to numb myself. I feared that if I were ever to perceive myself I would see that I was alone, and I would be so miserable that I would die.

Of course one does not die of being alone, and that's a surprise to the soul.

My breakup with Dennis, however bad he was for me, made me lonely. My being the only woman doctor on the service was lonely. Stella's approaching death threatened me with abandonment. I called my parents and talked about spending a vacation with them, but I couldn't tell them I was unhappy or frightened. They were proud of me, and for them my success had to stay intact. I tried to join a women's consciousness-raising group, but found immediately that I couldn't go because my schedule for being on call varied. Amy was not a confidante anymore, and I couldn't call on Kathleen all the time.

In a way, Surgery was a good service for me to recuperate on. It was almost entirely scutwork—the I and O sheets, IV lines, medication, bandages, and taking out stitches. I and O means intake and output, and refers to the fluid balance that a patient, especially a postoperative patient, must be kept in:

the output must balance the intake, and vice versa. We monitor the fluids, the electrolyte balance, the blood count, and the pH values to warn of trouble in advance. These figures must be checked twice a day, which means exact measurement—how much was drunk, how much from an IV bottle, how much urine was voided, how much fluid removed by a nasogastric tube—everything. The intern's first responsibility was this. We were quizzed constantly, and continually had to memorize these significant data and why they were significant: what does it mean if there's more out through the nasogastric tube than through the bladder catheter, for example. We were told to treat each patient as if he were an eighty-year-old cardiac patient. It was here that I learned the ultimate meaning of "a Grey's prep," keeping a dying patient in perfect electrolyte balance.

For our most important duty, it was tedious, picky, pedantic, and boring as all hell.

Any OR time was like a vacation, even though I only held the retractors and sponged. I became expert at standing on the edge of a group of surgeons, my outstretched arms grasping those curved metal or plastic spatulas, the retractors, holding open an operating field that I couldn't even see. I had to be careful not to let my circulation slow down, and I had to learn how to doze on my feet without losing my grip on the retractors.

Boredom and physical fatigue at least made no emotional demands, and part of me seemed to retreat or rest. The way I looked (and most of the other doctors, too) was a perfect symbol of how I felt: a wrinkled, washed-out green scrubdress, a paper cap from which my hair was escaping, and rundown slippers that made a shuffling sound as I walked.

In about two weeks, however, I had revived. One of the first things that I really remember about Surgery is walking down the hall with somebody and hearing a loud bang like the report of a gun. Turning, I heard a nurse shriek and saw her crumple up and fall.

Starting to run toward her, we were startled to see

her pick herself up, and, laughing, say, "I couldn't resist it!"

Someone had been testing a breathing apparatus and the bag had exploded.

I laughed so delightedly at her clowning that tears came to my eyes. In a way she woke me up, like a gift.

Dr. David Schwartz was another person who brought me back to life, in a way. He was a surgeon who operated not only with his hands, but also with his elbows. One scrub nurse in particular had a very large bosom, and he'd invariably manage to poke her in the chest with his elbow. Once while he was operating somebody nicked an artery, and suddenly and horribly, a spout of blood spurted up three feet high!

Dr. Schwartz doubled up his fist, slammed it down firmly on the artery, stopping the flow, turned around, and kissed the nurse through his mask. He'd broken the horror and relaxed everybody. Then he turned back and took care of the artery.

I was baited to watch a particular operation. Two plastic surgery residents happened to be sitting across from me in the cafeteria one day when Ben Kravits said to his friend John Williams, "Hey, what do you think? Wouldn't Phyllis be interested in the operation tomorrow morning?"

Williams's face lit up in a big surprised smile. "Yeah!" he said enthusiastically, and he turned to me. "You'd love it!"

Kravits said seriously, "You don't often get to see this kind of operation, you know."

"What is it?" I asked.

Ben looked at me. "Oh, I think we won't tell you. It's a big one, though." They laughed.

"How do I know I want to see it?" I said.

"Oh, take my word for it, you'll be very interested. It'll be right up your alley."

I was skeptical.

"Seriously, Phyllis," John said, trying to keep from sniggering, "it'd spoil it to tell you about it beforehand."

"Oh, sure."

"Come on, come on," Ben teased, "you scared? Everybody knows you faint when you see a vag. hys."

"Oh, that's old, " I demurred.

"Come on, are you scared? Are you afraid you'd faint in front of us?"

"Ha!" I responded. "You think I would?"

They spent a moment pretending to ponder it. "Maybe."

I snorted. "All right," I said. "Let's see what you can throw at me!"

That really made them laugh. We arranged for me to scrub with them as an observer the next morning. It was the first case, at eight o'clock.

I arrived bright and early and found Ben and John already scrubbing. They kidded me about being late and debated about whether I had left a lover in my bed, whether I started the day with a screw, and whether once a day was enough to preserve a person in good working order.

"Say, this operation now," I reminded them. "Don't you think you ought to be briefing me about it?"

"Oh, no!" they said. "It's already started. We come on second," said John.

"Look, I'll just tell you," said Ben, smiling broadly, "I myself don't often see one of these incredibly rare procedures. Why, the incidence of this operation is . . . oh, maybe point two per cent." He continued heartily with a disquisition on statistical analysis, winding up just as we entered the operating room with the statement: "Point two is high enough for me."

The first thing I looked for on entering the room was the patient, on the table and completely draped except for the genital area. I took a closer look and saw that it was a male, I couldn't tell how old.

Ben and John commented on my interest, giggled, and then Dr. Evans, a urologist, said, "Everything set?" and stepped right up and began to slice the patient's penis off!

To me it seemed almost instantaneous, but it actually could have taken ten or fifteen minutes.

310

"Hey, look out! Somebody get out of the way when Phyllis faints!" Ben shouted.

I did almost faint.

John and Ben were laughing at me. My eyes were as big as saucers, and maybe even my jaw had dropped under my mask. I felt huge, and there was the washing sound in my ears that I hear before I faint. "Why did you do that?" I squeaked, hoping to regain control of myself by talking.

The urologist, busily at work, was happy to tell me. The patient had gotten cancer of the penis. It had become excruciatingly painful, and so he had to have most of the organ removed.

A nurse commented, "Have you seen his wife? A beautiful woman!"

"Yeah," said Ben. "Too bad for her. Hey, John, how about seeing if she needs any therapy?" Now I began to wonder whether these were the two plastic surgery residents we'd heard about who had sex as a team.

The urologist, having made sure all the bleeding was stopped and the wound was clean, stepped back from the table. "Well, toodle-oo, fellas," he said, and he left the room.

"Hey!" I gulped inadvertently, giving the others still another occasion to laugh.

"It's our turn now!" Ben explained cheerily.

Breathing more easily now, I watched them begin their work. The penis having been removed, they were going to provide an approximation of one. From the lower abdomen, they took a strip of skin as long as they could technically take; leaving it attached as a flap, they made it into a tube and attached it to the scrotum. It looked like a jug handle. They told me that when most of the healing of the graft had taken place, another operation would detach the upper flap from the abdomen, and there would be an artificial penis though no longer able to communicate so much sexual pleasure; the man would urinate through a shortened urethra near his testicles.

I didn't say a word.

"Hey, Phyllis!" Ben called, "how long should we make it?"

"Hm?"

"How long should we make his penis? You're the expert!"

Without thinking I said clearly, "It's not how long that's important, it's how wide!"

The whole operating room burst out laughing.

In spite of my embarrassment and discomfort I stayed through the whole operation, musing that Ben and John's facetiousness about this particular operation had a boyishly obsessive quality about it that reminded me of all the jokes about circumcision on OB.

Two more operations could give the patient silicone implants, which he could actually pump up when he wanted an erection, and tubing, so he could urinate as usual from the end of the penis. It was amazing how much care would go into this reconstruction. I wondered whether it was more deeply traumatic for a man to lose a penis than for a woman to lose a breast.

The patient was a man in his thirties, which for penile cancer was very unusual; the average age of onset is over sixty. Apparently circumcision in infancy usually prevents it. He had a nice brown beard and blue eyes. He read science fiction all day and until he went to sleep, whenever his wife wasn't visiting him. She was truly a beautiful woman. As far as I know, he did have the complete reconstruction and has remained cancer-free.

Albert Lindner was a burly man in his early fifties who used to drive a moving van. He had dishwater-gray hair half-receded, a moderate beer belly, and a joking, kidding manner. He was in for a gastric ulcer. An ulcer personality is usually quiet, repressing anger and anxiety: that's how the ulcer occurs. His joviality immediately made me wonder whether it wasn't a valiant show.

"Ah," he said, dressed in brand-new pajamas and lying back in bed. "This is the life! Nothing to do all day but take it easy, watch the scenery . . ." He winked at me and the nurse. "And let the rest of the world go by!" He turned to the other three men in his room and appealed to them, "Now isn't this the Life of Reilly, to spend your days in bed having a bunch of women waiting on you!" He laughed. The others agreed. "Let me tell you, for a working man, this would be unheard of. I was a moving man for twenty years. Yes, sir, moved around a lot." He laughed again. "I tell you, though, that was a job for a *man!*"

"I've seen how strong movers are," I agreed. Everything he'd said so far emphasized idleness or work. I knew he was unemployed.

"Strong! What you got to lift ain't the half of it. You never know where else your strength is gonna be called for. Let me tell you the time we moved a recent widow-lady. It was the dead of winter. When her old man died, she sold her place, see, and went to her place in the mountains to live.

"Well, it was getting late, cold and windy, and there was a helluva lot of snow. The sun was just going down, see, and we still hadn't got there. God, you never seen such a road. I thought for sure we were goners once or twice, backing and filling around those curves, but we finally got to her place, and it was about the sweetest mansion you'd ever hope to see. By this time it was pitch black. We went and knocked, and she answered the door dressed in one of those hostess gowns you see in the Revlon ads.

"The house was warm and toasty, with a fire in the fireplace, and she was a knockout. Well, the fact of the matter was, she never gave the company the right idea of how long it would take to get there or what her road was like, and she invited us in and to stay the night with her. She intended all along for us to be late."

Mr. Lindner paused for a long moment, his face softened with either a memory or a fantasy of pure pleasure. We all listened quietly.

"Well," he continued at last, "there were three of us, all fine, strong men. That's what she wanted, see. Poor George, he didn't approve. I thought for a minute

313

he would spend all night out in the cold in the truck, but he slept in a little room off the kitchen where he didn't have to hear any of our goings-on. Man!" he said, shaking his head appreciatively. "She was some woman! Whooo!" He smiled sheepishly, as if apologizing for his virility.

I got him to talk about his medical history at last. "A movin' man sees a lot of injury, and he has got to take his lumps. Well, me and my buddy was movin' this piano, see, and my buddy lost his balance and the piano whipped over to the side and crushed my hand to the wall. That's the kind of injury we get all the time, mashed hands, mashed feet, mashed fingers—you don't pay much attention to it. The hand swelled up two, three times its size. My old lady made me go along to the hospital.

"For some reason, they started me on a needle, one of those upside-down bottles and stuff going into your arm. I don't know what they put in it, it was sure some Mickey Finn! The first thing I know, I'm keeling over right out of some wheelchair." He laughed. The ER doctor must have suspected his hand would need surgery, so he started an IV right away.

"Can you picture that? Me! They stick a needle in my arm and I keel over!"

"It says here you had a cardiac arrest," I told him. According to his chart, they guessed that a bottle of saline solution had potassium in it that had not been shaken up. It was only a guess, for he needn't have gotten potassium in the first place, and bottles are always shaken. They guessed that when the potassium had hit, his heart stopped. He was resuscitated and recovered well.

"Cardiac arrest!" he said derisively. "Say heart attack and get it over with. See, then the thing is, they won't let me go back to work with no heart attack. I try to convince them, but who am I? I'm no doctor. It says cardiac arrest on your record, cardiac arrest it stays." He laughed, not so convincingly this time.

"What did you do then?" I asked.

"You may well ask!" he said loudly and emphat-

314

ically. "What's a man of fifty-five gonna do? What kinda skills I got? You think a lifetime of liftin' and totin' qualifies you for anything?

"I been on unemployment, I been on job training. My real job was interesting. We got a lot of variety— different houses, different people, sometimes we got a long-distance haul, that's interesting, too. Hell, we get to help people now and then, like that widow-lady." He grinned to rob his previous words of any suffering. "We sure helped her break in a new life!"

"So," I said, "now you're here for bleeding from a gastric ulcer. They're going to take part of your stomach out, and we're going to make you stick to your ulcer diet." I looked warningly at him.

He sighed. "Well, if I got to, I guess I got to. I always thought it was just acid indigestion."

"And so it was," I affirmed.

"Say," he said diffidently, "this old hand of mine starts to ache when the weather turns wet. You got anything for it?"

I laughed. "Mr. Lindner, when I think of what that hand let you in for, I'm not sure you want anything more for it!"

"Oh, hell no. I was just kidding."

Mr. Lindner went into the operation in good shape. I held the retractors and got a good view of a simple gastric resection, in which the lower portion of the stomach was removed. The ulcer was in the upper section, but since the acid-secreting tissues were in the lower stomach, once that was removed the ulcer would heal.

Mr. Lindner recovered steadily. I enjoyed stopping in to listen to his stories. They were always ingenuously boastful, somewhat elegiac stories of his days as a mover. In a way, I guess he was lucky to have gotten so much pleasure in his job. I could understand how he wouldn't be happy in a factory or a shop. When he left, I made sure he understood he should take codeine when his hand hurt, but I doubt that he ever took it. It would have been a point of honor for him to feel the pain and to ignore it.

Mr. Franzone had been assigned to me for the usual scutwork. He and his son were in for a kidney transplant. Michael, his son, was thirty-five. He'd had kidney damage secondary to a bad strep infection as a child, and subsequently had had chronic kidney infections. The last year he'd spent on biweekly dialysis. His father was fifty-seven, and when he'd been told that in spite of his age he could donate a kidney to his son, he had eagerly prepared to do so.

John Franzone was dark-skinned and robust. The son of a fisherman, one of seven children, he'd been raised in a little fishing town on the coast. He joined the navy, young and ignorant as he was, he said, having no idea what he was getting into. When he got out, he swore he'd never go near another body of water again.

"I thought once the sea was in your blood you'd always return to it," I said.

"I go to the ocean on vacation," he emphasized, his eyes twinkling. "Don't believe all the rubbish you read about men who go down to the sea in ships. Stinking, crowded, knuckle-busting life it is, and the sea is a bitch!"

"Beautiful, though." I reminded him.

He grimaced. "I got an inland life now. My son is a lawyer," he announced with pride.

For the operation they had two tables and two teams, and everything went smoothly.

The next day, as soon as I walked into his room, John Franzone asked, "How's Michael? How's he doing?"

"He's fine, absolutely fine. You can talk to him on the phone. How are *you* doing, Mr. Franzone?"

"I thought I heard someone cry out last night."

"I don't think so. In any case, it couldn't have been your son. He had a quiet, restful night."

"Thank God," he murmured.

"Well, how are *you* this morning?" I had to prod him.

"Oh, I'm okay, a little sore maybe. You're sure he's okay? A fifty-seven-year-old kidney maybe is no joke."

Four days later, when I told him he could visit his son in Isolation, he wept silently for a moment, then knuckle-dried his eyes and asked me to get him ready. Like all visitors to Isolation, he had to wear a gown and mask. People in Isolation have told me that it's unnerving not to see anyone's face. Those who don't talk with their eyes are subtly but especially frightening.

Mr. Franzone walked to his son's room and gowned, masked, and gloved himself. Then he went in. With his first glimpse he called, "Michael!" as though relieved to find a lost child. Uncertain about what exactly he was allowed to do, he walked slowly into the room, his arms down at his sides, until his son said "Dad" softly. John Franzone went to his son's bedside, with one gloved hand grasped his son's hand, and with the other hand held his shoulder. If he hadn't been masked he would have kissed his son.

Dr. Schwartz told me that I'd gotten the highest compliment from John Frazone. "He told me he has the best nurse he's ever seen."

"Oh, who?" I said innocently.

He answered with a broad grin, "You!"

"Me! Oh, well." I smiled ruefully.

Dr. Schwartz laughed. "When I told him you were a doctor he was very surprised. 'But she's so nice!' he said."

"There's a lesson in that for *you,* Doctor," I teased. "You see what patients think of doctors!"

Unfortunately, the knowledge that I was a doctor seemed to daunt Mr. Franzone, and from then on he always spoke formally to me. I tried to joke him out of his restraint, but for the rest of his stay he was dignified and inexpressive in front of me. I wondered whether it was a class problem, that he could reveal emotions to a nurse but not to a more exalted professional, or whether he wasn't quite comfortable with the anomaly of a woman doctor. I'd had patients express their discomfort in a kind of amazement, too. Maybe there was a simple explanation: he'd been Americanized too much, and it shamed him to have let a woman see him cry.

31

On Surgery I met the fattest man I've ever seen. A call came from the Emergency Room for a surgical intern to admit a man with an incarcerated umbilical hernia. A piece of bowel was pushing out the skin of the navel. The protrusion was five inches in diameter. My chief resident said to get him ready for surgery. What neither of us knew was how fat he was.

He was lying in an examining room, overlapping the examining table. On the top curve of his high-rounded belly there was, instead of a navel, an inflamed bulge. He must have weighed three hundred pounds, and every ounce of it quivered and moaned with pain. His flesh looked dimpled, as though it were attached to what lay beneath by many tiny stitches. It seemed that his flesh was something entirely different from him, out of his control, and I found myself thinking of him and his body as separate. Unfortunately, it's difficult to operate on an obese patient because his tissues often won't take a clean incision or hold sutures well; also, fat is greasy and slippery, whether it's chicken fat or human fat.

"Well, Mr. Thomas," I said to him. "I understand you've had a lot of vomiting?"

"Ohmigod," he groaned, his eyes shut tight.

"How much vomiting?" I asked.

He groaned.

He had plunged deeply into his pain, so I stopped questioning him and instead took some blood from a vein at the inside of the elbow. When he felt the needle he screamed shortly, almost rolling over the edge of the table.

"You're all right!" I said. "Just taking blood to get your type." Then I asked him if he could sit up and walk. He wouldn't have fit into any of the wheelchairs.

"Nooo," he moaned.

"You walked in here, didn't you?" I pressed.

"No, I can't," he panted.

So, apologetically, I called for orderlies to transfer him to a cart so he could be taken up to the surgical floor. They took one look at his bulk and grunted. They usually get a blanket or canvas under the person and quickly and slightly lift from one surface to the other. Mr. Thomas did not cooperate. He lay moaning and inert, like a monstrous slug.

When they got him to the OR, it looked as though they'd have to use two operating tables somehow, to prevent his rolling off the standard narrow one; but they strapped him to the single table, and his arms outstretched on the armboards balanced him. While his belly was being shaved, washed, and painted orange with betadine, Norton and I scrubbed. Entering the OR, we saw on the table a large hemisphere of orange skin topped by a shiny nipple.

Dr. Norton told me I could do the procedure—open the abdomen, cut out the incarcerated or constricted portion of small intestine, sew the two healthy ends together, push it back into the abdomen, and sew it up. Though it's not often that an intern gets to do anything in the OR, I wasn't sure I was going to be grateful.

The minute I made the first incision, around the protrusion, the guts spilled out and started sliding down his belly. Since the intestines are like a fan, connected to the central point where the vascular supply is, it wasn't as though the intestine could unreel; but por-

319

tions began to bulge up, slip through the wound, and get in the way.

"Sally!" Norton said urgently to the scrub nurse. "Get another nurse to scrub and go call for some stools!"

"You mean things to sit on?" she asked.

"Yes," Norton replied. "We're going to need them to sit up on. We don't have a good angle here."

The intestine was coming out, the superficial flesh was shredding because of the fat, and our hands were slippery. "Oh, no," I groaned. "I can't do it!"

Norton nodded. "We both going to be hard-pressed, my friend."

We were soon perched on stools on either side of this mountain of a man, and both of us were working slowly and carefully. I took cultures of the herniated bowel tissue. The piece of intestine had died, but it hadn't yet become infected; no bacteria grew out of the cultures. Once I'd gotten that portion isolated, it could be dissected out, and the healthy intestine sewn together. Then at last we could close. For this patient we had to use stay-sutures, metal wires used in addition to the catgut stitches; they go down through the skin and the fascia and up, and are then wired together, so the wound, once it's sewn, looks like a pair of railroad tracks. Gut stitches alone won't hold in the tissues of a fat person.

There was a drain in his abdomen, a nasogastric tube, an intravenous line in his hand, and a catheter inserted into his bladder through his penis, with a Foley bag for urine. With his bulk, he looked like a failed experimental robot.

When he was being brought down from the recovery room, he murmured, "What happened to me?"

"You came through the operation fine, Mr. Thomas," I said encouragingly.

"What did you do to me!" He raised his voice.

"We took care of your hernia."

"It hurts," he said querulously. "It hurts worse than it did before!"

320

I doubted it, but I said, "You'll feel better when you've had some sleep."

"What did you do to my face?" He referred to the nasogastric tube.

I told him he'd need it in order to keep his stomach clear. He reached up to his face, threatening to pluck the tube out. I said, "Oh, no. You've got to leave that in, Mr. Thomas!" He was bleary from the operation, I knew, and not rational yet, so he'd either have to be restrained or his wife would have to stay with him to prevent his disturbing any of his artificial attachments.

By that evening he had managed to pull the tube out. It amazed me, for removing it, I should have thought, would have been as troublesome as having it there to begin with, but patients will do the damnedest things to themselves if you don't prevent them.

I explained to him, and to his overweight wife: "That tube is necessary. If you didn't have it there, your stomach would keep on discharging its secretions into the bowel, your abdomen would become distended with gas, the bowel would pop out of the wound, we'd have to operate again to put the bowel back in, and you'd simply have to start all over again."

He growled.

"I understand the tube is uncomfortable, and I'll give you a throat spray to numb your throat so it won't be so bad." I sympathize with the patient who has to endure a nasogastric tube because it's irritating, and since you can't help feeling it, it's frightening: no matter how slim a tube it actually is, you think you're going to suffocate.

Mr. Thomas managed to remove the tube twice more, so he had to be checked every fifteen minutes. He complained about the breathing machine that was necessary to keep his lungs open, and he insulted the technician who brought it in every day for his breathing exercises, calling her "Asshole" the moment he caught sight of her. He was irritated with the aide who changed his water and the man who mopped the floor. He accused the hospital of starving him. He accused me of

321

incompetence when I had to change his IV to another vein when one infiltrated. He irritated everyone.

However, one of the nurses, Della Atwood, told me that she'd gotten him launched into a jerky but powerful damnation of hospital procedures, and she'd listened to all of it. "He was full," she said. "He had every little thing sharp in his mind, like he'd been lying there brooding on them one by one all the time. I saw how furious he was so I just let him have his say. Every once in a while I even asked him a question. He must have had about ten minutes worth of detailed complaints, and that's a lot." She laughed. "I asked him what bugged him the most, and I'd see if I could get it corrected."

"Really?" I said. "What did he say?"

"What bothered him the most was having to do the coughing exercises right in the middle of afternoon visiting hours. His wife can't come at night, so it's the only time he can see her."

"Aha."

"I told him I'd try to schedule the technician at a different time, and since that was such a reasonable request, to try another. He chose getting the IV taken out so he could get up and go to the bathroom himself. I told him I'd try to arrange it with you."

That was brilliant of her, since he was due to have the IV out that very afternoon. "Hey, Della! You're a great psychologist," I complimented her.

She was pleased. "I think I did handle that one rather well," she said.

Mr. Thomas never did become friendly toward any of us. His nature was critical rather than warm: the stereotype of geniality and cheerfulness in obese people didn't apply to him. When I realized that behind some of his criticisms was a good reason, I listened more carefully and asked him for it. But he would not volunteer anything. His recovery was slow because his tissues couldn't heal as fast as usual, and this irked him. It must have been obvious to him that he'd disabled himself by his weight, and I'm sure part of his offensiveness was defiance.

When he finally left, he announced churlishly—and superstitiously—that he hoped he'd never see the place again in his life. Yet a week after he was discharged he would have to come back to the clinic to have his wire stay-sutures clipped and pulled. I wondered if he felt that was ominous.

Amy married Jeffrey Bardolph in April. I heard about it just as everyone heard about it—after it happened and from someone else, through the grapevine. I felt like rushing up to her and saying, "Amy, you didn't!" in anger and exasperation, but obviously I couldn't. When they came back from a quick honeymoon they gave a party, and I congratulated them as fervently as anyone did. I hoped Amy had more emotional energy that I at the moment. She looked glowing and worshipful.

When she came back to the hospital in a few days, she was put on OB again. The Pathology resident had complained about her falling asleep over her microscope, so he didn't want her. Then a patient on OB complained that Amy had neglected her. My heart sank. I had to talk to Amy, and arranged to have lunch.

"Amy, how are you doing?" I asked.

"Oh, I'm very happy," she replied enthusiastically.

"I heard someone complained about you on OB," I said in my blunt way.

She frowned. "I know. I was very upset about it."

"What happened?" I asked, meaning what had Amy done that dissatisfied the patient.

"Jeffrey calmed me down," Amy said. "Oh, Phyllis, he's so supportive! He told me not to worry, just go ahead and do my job, as I'm fully capable of." She looked down and said softly, "He warned me that I should be very careful of myself while I'm on Obstetrics."

I was silent, taking in his psychoanalytical implication that women having babies would be difficult for Amy to handle.

"Do you understand what he means?" she asked earnestly, as if trying to be unembarrassed or brave about the new self-doubts she felt.

"What's going to happen about you having babies?" I asked abruptly.

She blinked tears back and smiled faintly. "I don't know. He wants me to be perfectly free to be a professional woman. I don't know, he told me not to have babies just to please him."

I leaned back from her, appalled by the doubt that had entered my mind: I'd bet that he didn't want children at all, though he'd never let her know that. Why should he, when he had a daughter made to order in Amy herself? He was a little old at forty-five to be starting a family; he'd never been subjected to children's demands. I could imagine Jeffrey Bardolph "magnanimously" letting Amy make a decision not to have children, or if she decided to, letting her take full responsibility for them. I wondered which had come first, his permission for her not to have babies or her difficulty with an obstetrical patient—I'd bet his permission.

Amy and I couldn't discuss her marriage or her career anymore. She spent the rest of the lunchtime telling me how understanding and comforting he was, and I listened to her helplessly.

In fact, I expected her to drop out of medicine entirely after a while though the craziness of her marriage was not unusual. At parties, I could see the interns' and residents' wives with a characteristic look in their eyes, no matter how gay they acted: a look of bitter steel. The incompleteness of my own affair with Dennis was a minor illustration of how we medical people could distort our private lives, maybe because we are required to be so straight and effective with our patients.

But in fact, Amy doggedly pursued her career, and did not drop out. Somehow, she found enough persistence to keep on, taking her internship the following year at Grey's and finding a residency in a small county hospital about fifty miles away where the demands on her were not onerous. When she was finished, her husband bought her a small suburban practice. So far she hasn't had children, which surprises me; I expected her to capitulate to the implicit ideal of maternity. Her not having children, however, won't be an affirmative decision for her; she'll interpret it as another failure. But she is a doctor: that's what's admirable. Though no doubt she thinks something is wrong with her for persisting.

However, at the time we spoke I felt only dismay and sadness. Every time another complaint came up about her—there may have been four or five—some man would say, "I'm sorry to say it, but she's just the kind of doctor we worry about when we admit women."

"You ought to blame her husband!" I protested.

Nobody understood or believed me.

I had been waiting to work with Dr. Fallon ever since my pleasant encounter with him in the ER. One day I finally got to stand by him holding retractors for four hours during an orthopedic reconstruction performed on a patient who was awake, anesthetized only with an epidural.

Harley Snow was twenty-two. He'd developed arthritis at an early age. His hip joints had deteriorated so severely that the femoral heads, the round ends that cap the long thighbones and fit into the hip socket, had to be replaced. His arthritis was so severe that he couldn't bend his head back for the endotracheal tube needed to keep the airway open. He had to have an epidural.

Orthopedic operations have to be undertaken under especially sterile conditions: bone is exposed, and bone infections are especially difficult to eradicate since there is no blood supply. Four operating rooms in Grey's are equipped with a laminar air flow, a kind of curtain of filtered air surrounding the center of the room that moves in such a way that it whisks any foreign particles or bacteria down to the floor. Walking through it feels like passing through a breeze. The surgeons have to wear a kind of spacesuit, which itself keeps vacuuming them, in effect.

This operation was impressive because it was radical surgery, in which each leg was almost amputated before being re-formed, but it was at the same time rather crude: they sawed off the femoral head, replaced it with a metal ball fixed to the thighbone with a pin, and remolded the hip socket to fit the new joint.

Everything was ready. Harley Snow was drowsily lying on the table on his side, the tubing of the anesthetic going into his spine, draped around the operating field of the hip with green sterile cloths.

"Do you feel this?" asked Dr. Fallon, as he pricked the skin of the hip.

"What?" asked the young man. "Hey, you doing somethin' already, man?" He opened his eyes and looked alert.

"No, no, nothing important yet, Harley. Just take it easy."

"I'm not the one's worried," he chuckled. "I'm just lyin' here."

"Yeah, and you keep your mouth shut, too," he was warned. "No criticisms."

"Swear to God."

During this brief conversation Dr. Fallon had sliced open the skin, and Tom McHale, the second-year resident, and I were in there with retractors.

Whenever I saw surgery on blacks, the memory of the statement of a fellow medical student flickered across my mind. As we worked on our cadavers, he told me that he had been very disappointed when he saw that his cadaver was a black man; he feared there were racial differences other than the color of the skin. I couldn't believe such an idea could survive high school biology. "Hell," he told me, "you take a bandage off a black, it comes off dirty, right?"

I'd countered, "A bandage takes off a little bit of anybody's skin, white or black. You just see a little bit of brown pigment."

326

He'd wondered, "You think they gave me this black man on purpose to test me?"

I told him to look around; he'd see that more than half of our cadavers were blacks. If it was a test, at least half of us needed it. Of course, every part of the black cadaver was like every part of the white cadaver; under the skin, the universal human colors are red, pink, yellow, and white.

Dr. Fallon was cutting and parting where possible, peeling the tendons back from the head of the bone to expose it. The femoral head looked ragged from the arthritis. Becoming absorbed in the drama of such a large procedure, Dr. Fallon was commenting, describing, and giving directions in a steady flow of explicit detail.

Poor Harley Snow had to hear it all.

"You feel okay?" the anesthetist asked him.

"Oh, man," he moaned, "I feel something there in my hip."

"Hurts?" Immediately the anesthetist gave him more medication, even as he spoke.

"No, just feels like somebody pushin' on me."

"It will be better."

"Yeah?"

Dr. Fallon said, "Now. The saw." The bone saw was an electrical one with a thin blade. The sound of it cutting into bone was high and shrill. Dr. Fallon quickly and loudly sawed the bulbous end of the femur off and lifted it out of the wound. It filled his palm. It was placed on a cloth in a receiving pan on the nurse's table.

Fitting the prosthesis to the femur required grinding and some drilling to shape and prepare the bone end. The operating room was full of the high-pitched whines of the tools. It sounded like a dentist's office, which is familiar enough, but we don't associate these sounds with surgical procedures on a body. I found myself gritting my teeth as if a nail were scratching a blackboard. The pelvic socket, being rough, also had to be molded to fit the new ball.

It took them two hours to complete the left hip and

327

get it sewn up again. Then there was a short pause. Dr. Fallon spoke to Harley, who seemed to be dozing. "You all right?"

The young man sighed shallowly and opened his eyes. "You all finished?" he asked wearily.

"Ah, no, sorry. Got the other side to do. We'll turn you over in a sec. Your muscles are going to be a mite weary," Dr. Fallon told him jocularly, "from lying in one position all this time, flexed like this, but you won't feel much in the bones themselves, I think."

"Gee, that's a relief," Harley Snow said, with an ambiguous little smile. He observed, "Say, you bone jockeys sure make a lot of noise in your line of work."

"Yep, yep, well, tools of the trade, you know. I'll give you a sight of them some other time."

"You do that. Jeesh, it's a good thing I work on my car so much, you talkin' 'bout what you doin' and all that noise. Otherwise I could get sick."

"Oh, ha-ha," Dr. Fallon laughed quickly. "Sorry. I get carried away."

On the second leg, Dr. Fallon did not talk so much about what he was doing. In fact, he didn't even talk to me after the case, as I had hoped he would.

After the operation, Harley Snow recuperated swiftly. He was a contagiously cheerful patient on the floor and was especially devoted to Dr. Fallon. Dr. Fallon seemed to have a good understanding with young men, I realized, remembering the dislocated shoulder case in the ER.

Harley began to teach me about cars and tried to get Fallon to help. But after two failures to get Fallon and me to discover a shared passion for Michelin tires, I sensed an absence of response. It was too bad. He had a happy manner with his patients that I found very appealing. It wasn't condescending to think of him as a sweet man. Not only did I like and respect him, but he was physically good-looking, too. I was definitely attracted to him.

Harley Snow, bless his soul, didn't give up trying to get us together the whole time I was on Surgery. The

328

day before I left for Ped., I brought Harley a model kit of an old Reo, which I wasn't sure he'd like.

"Something to pass the time," I said.

"You think I'm old-fashion', huh? Matchmakin' you two."

"You're too young for any of that," I kidded him.

"I musta lost my touch." He pretended to be disconsolate, then he brightened up. "Hey, I got an idea! I got an article here on diesel engines. The doctor is really interested. I can let you read it, you get all . . ."

I interrupted him. "Harley Snow!"

"That's the only way you gonna catch him."

"Listen here, buddy, I'm gonna teach you not to have such sexist thoughts!"

He touched his forehead in a salute of acknowledgment and grinned.

The simple fact was that Fallon was not attracted to me. After being amazed, I laughed to myself. I guessed it wasn't possible for me to have everything I wanted.

Harley Snow was in the hospital for three weeks after his operation and recovered excellently. Soon he was able to walk again. I could see in his early attempts with the physical therapist what would soon become his expressive, irrepressible swagger.

32

Mrs. Dolan was my patient for a probable mastectomy.

Her first name was Alberta, and she was called Bert. Forty-eight, a widow with four grown children, perimenopausal—that is, having periods still, but irregularly—she was a woman with a high risk of breast cancer: it was not only her age, but also her family history. Her mother had died of breast cancer, and her sister had already had a breast removed.

The sister, Evelyn Giacasso, accompanied her. Though they were ten years apart in age, Evelyn being older, they still looked like sisters. Short women with middle-aged shapes, not sloppy but neatly thickened about the middle, they both had blue eyes and wore decorated plastic-framed glasses, and had the same distinctive voice, pleasant and slightly husky.

They came in one afternoon to the Admitting Office, where I greeted them and interviewed Mrs. Dolan. Mrs. Giacasso sat in front of the desk quietly, nodding as her sister answered, helping when she forgot something.

"You noticed the lump yourself?" I asked.

"Oh, yes," Mrs. Dolan replied. "I always check very carefully for lumps."

"I see," I said in answer to the matter-of-fact starkness of her statement.

She paused, then told me about discovering it. Tears came to her eyes. She looked at her sister, who smiled fondly at her.

"Evelyn and I both know what it's like to die of breast cancer," she said simply. "Mother died a long time ago, thirty years, before there was much talk about it. She was a very modest woman. She'd never show her body to anyone, so no one knew for the longest time. One day while Evelyn was visiting, she noticed Mum was short-tempered with the grandchildren, and she seemed to be in pain.

"I'd just come back from school when Evelyn called me in to Mum's bedroom and made me look at her, too. She just had a big dimple on her breast. Neither Evelyn nor I had ever seen anything like it, and we didn't know what it was. Mum had had it for years. Now her hip and stomach hurt and had hurt for months. You see, the cancer had spread." Her voice was quiet.

She turned to her sister, who continued, "Mum didn't

330

want to die in a hospital. Our people didn't in those days. We didn't want her to either. Mostly Bert took care of her. I had my family, so I couldn't do it, but I'd come over to spell Bert. We got morphine to give her, but by the end the pain could hardly be relieved. She smelled bad, too. She was rotting inside."

We sat silent.

Finally I asked, "How old was she when she died?"

"Fifty-two."

"And, Mrs. Giacasso," I asked the elder sister, "when you did discover you had the disease?"

She said, "I found a lump fifteen years ago. It was cancer, and I had the whole breast removed, all the muscles and everything."

I don't know whether I'll ever get over the shock of hearing that a woman has had or will have to have a classic radical mastectomy. Involuntarily my eyes went to her bosom. "Which breast?" I asked.

"Oh. The left one." She smiled cheerfully. "You can't tell, can you?"

"No, I can't." The prosthesis matched her other breast perfectly.

"Here, feel it," she said. "See if you can tell which is which."

I was reluctant to do so.

"Come," she coaxed me. "I don't mind."

I got up and leaned over the desk to press one finger lightly onto the upper side of her left breast. It felt natural enough—somewhat springy, like real flesh.

"Now the other," she offered.

So I felt the other breast, and I could tell a difference, but it was so slight as to be unimportant. "It's amazing," I said, relieved to be finished.

"My sister," Mrs. Giacasso said proudly, "wouldn't be upset to have her own breast removed, because she's seen it's not so bad after all." She shook her head. "It was not the end of *my* life, I mean in my feelings about myself. And here I am, fit as a fiddle." She sat erect, her breasts uplifted by a good, healthy breath, her head nodding in tiny enthusiastic nods.

"Any recurrence?" I asked.

331

She closed her lips and shook her head triumphantly.

Though Mrs. Dolan was aided by her sister's confidence, she was apprehensive nevertheless. I might have been suspicious if she hadn't been. When I examined her, she was quiet and tight.

Afterward I told her what the next two days would hold: the bone scan, bone x rays, and blood tests, to see if the cancer had spread to her bones or liver. If it had spread, only the lump itself would be removed, and, ironically, she would keep her breast and be treated generally with radiation and chemotherapy. If the cancer was still localized, however, she had given permission for the doctors to take the breast. She was very clear about it. Some women prefer the biopsy and possible mastectomy to be two separate operations in order to make the decision themselves. The chance that Mrs. Dolan's lump was cancer was so high that she had already decided.

"Can my sister go with me to the tests?" she asked in a small voice.

"I don't see why not. She'll have to wait for you each place instead of coming in with you, but, yes, she can go with you."

"Thank you," she whispered.

Mrs. Dolan's tests were all negative, suggesting that the cancer had probably not spread. She signed the form allowing the surgeon to take the breast. Referred to the surgical ward by her gynecologist, she was going to be operated on by the chief surgical resident, Dr. Norton, and me.

She grasped her sister's hands fiercely before she was carted from the room that morning, and I walked with her to the OR area before I scrubbed. Then I caressed her forearm briefly. "You'll be all right," I said. She smiled wearily. The shots she'd been given that morning had made her drowsy.

When I went in to scrub, Norton was already there. "Good morning, Phyllis," he said briskly. "I want you to do the easy parts today, everything except under

332

the arm." I was appalled. With his face masked his eyes looked steadily at me, then he nodded and led the way into the operating room.

Mrs. Dolan was already on the table, asleep, her head intubated and back and her body draped. The one breast was exposed, scrubbed, and painted red-orange. Dr. Norton and I stepped up to the table on opposite sides. He made a small incision in the lower middle of the breast, quickly found the small lump in the wound, cut it out, and sliced it once. "It's gritty," he curtly said. That suggested cancer.

The circulating nurse prepared the sample for a quick-frozen section and gave it to the messenger outside, while Norton put several loose stitches over the incision. Pathology, which in this case meant a small lab just down the hall from the operating suites, took about fifteen minutes to make its findings, time Norton and the circulating nurse whiled away by discussing Norton's preschooler and how his social skills had changed in the last year. In a distant part of myself I was interested, but I couldn't contribute to the animated discussion they were having.

The circulating and scrub nurses were women. The nurse-anesthetist was a woman. I was struck by the unusual fact that the only man there was the surgeon.

The Pathology report came back: cancer.

I sighed. Norton looked at me across the table and said warningly, "Never falter."

I made the long incision. The red line that the nurse followed with her gauze sponge started under the upraised arm, passed around the upper limit of the breast, and ended below the breastbone. Then I made another line, beginning at the same place and tracing the underside of the breast, coming around and meeting the first incision. A wedge of skin was removed, then the whole breast was gathered up and cleaned off down to the muscle by scraping off the distinctive fatty tissue. The breast was placed in the waste bowl to be sent to Pathology.

Then Dr. Norton dissected out the axillary nodes,

the lymph nodes in the underarm, and added them to the waste bowl.

The sight of a whole breast, its skin smooth and with the nipple perched on top, the yellow fat visible, and what look like pebbles—the axillary nodes—on or beside it, being carried away on a silver salver will always cause me a moment of terror.

Dr. Norton wiped his fingers dry of grease before he cleaned any breast tissue off the skin flaps. "Everything out?" he asked the nurse, who counted the instruments and sponges and gave us the go-ahead. He told me I could close. I stitched the two flaps of skin together.

"First time you've seen major breast surgery?" he asked curiously.

"Not really," I replied, "but the first I've done."

He raised his eyes to me as I finished the stitching. "It's brutal," he said, and he blinked.

Dr. Norton then inserted the drains to collect blood under the wound, bandaged it, and ordered the other breast prepped and draped. There is a 10 to 20 per cent chance that the other breast will have cancer and in the same place, so he biopsied the same location in the other breast. I'd forgotten that Mrs. Dolan had given permission for a double mastectomy if necessary, and I waited with horror for the Path. report that said the tissue was normal. Relieved and breathing normally once again, I was glad to finish.

The breast tissue also could be tested for estrogen and progesterone receptors. If metastasis occurred later in a woman whose tissue tested positive, then she'd have a 60 per cent chance of responding to adrenalectomy and oophorectomy, because hormones produced by these organs may be stimulants to breast cancer. The removal of the hormone-secreting adrenal glands and ovaries may aid the regression of the cancer. If there were no estrogen receptors, then the operation would probably not work and might not be attempted. This recently devised test may be a better guide than menopause in deciding whether to do the operation; it promises to be a very useful prognostic tool.

Mrs. Dolan's tissue tested negative; she would not be a candidate for adrenalectomy and oophorectomy. Suddenly I realized that Stella's tissue could not have been tested, for the test had come into use more recently than Stella's mastectomy had been done. Chilled, I wondered if that was an ominous fact.

Violently I jammed the paper surgical gown into its receptacle. "Shit!" I muttered.

Dr. Norton said, "We can't just do nothing."

"Of course not," I replied irritably.

He led me down the hall to the lounge.

"You're upset," he said, handing me some coffee. "You have some problem with these sex operations, don't you?" he observed.

"No, I don't!" I hotly denied, realizing that it was true, seeing Stella's scar, Natalie's castration, the vag. hys., Stella's hysterectomy, the penis dissection, and just then Mrs. Dolan's mastectomy. For a moment I wondered why I should be more vulnerable to the impact of these operations than other—male—doctors seemed to be, and then I remembered their bravado about circumcision or the penis operation . . .

Dr. Norton was going on warningly. "Mastectomies and hysterectomies are an occupational hazard for a woman in medicine."

"The cure rate for breast cancer hasn't changed in forty years!" I charged. "*Forty* years. And mastectomy as the treatment of breast cancer hasn't changed. If there's no change in the cure rate and no change in the treatment, we might begin to wonder, mightn't we?"

"Some centers have a cure rate of eighty per cent now," he pointed out.

"*Some* centers. What are the overall statistics?"

"All right," he responded. "If you find a lump in a woman under thirty-five, there's a ninety per cent chance it's not cancer; if you find a lump in the breast of a woman over forty-five, there's a ninety per cent chance it *is* cancer. One out of fifteen women will develop breast cancer, and women with a family history of breast cancer have a fivefold increase in the risk. But forty per cent of the breast cancers we catch early will be cured—of course, that depends on how early—and the patient will be cancer-free for ten years."

"Only forty per cent," I observed. "Pretty awful."

"Look, Phyllis," he said, "don't think so much about it. Let the researchers worry. Just do your job. You mother your patients too much."

"You don't make it sound like a compliment." I smiled.

"You can't afford to get so deeply involved in your patients' lives."

"How can you help it? They come in in crisis . . ."

"That's right, and you intervene in the crisis, and that's it."

"Hm."

"Don't mistake yourself for anyone but a doctor."

"Hm," I said, struck by the turn of his argument.

"That's my advice," he finished.

"I'll think about it," I said.

Dr. Norton left. I slouched in the chair for a moment, gazing at the Surgeons' Lounge. It was grubby. The corner wastebasket overflowed, the ashtrays reeked of stubbed-out cigarettes and cigars, rings of coffee stained the tables. Around midnight one of the janitors, faithful Harry, maybe, would clean. The Doctors' would be cleaned up after, as usual.

I didn't like the way I kept remembering Stella and worrying about her. She'd become a talisman to me, in a way. Though interns, next to nurses, were the most intimately acquainted with death, I wasn't able to cover myself over with a shell when I was with her, to think of her simply as a Grey's prep, a problem in electrolyte balance.

She made me think of Mrs. Macklin, my kidney patient, and the woman who'd committed suicide, and Al Whittaker, and all my cancer patients—of whom there were so many—and Pete Witowski, who'd prepared himself to die.

But she'd promised me she wouldn't die!

I sat for a moment as though a silent bell had struck and vibrated horribly within my body—*my* body that I used so efficiently, often so pleasurably.

I looked around the lounge and imagined doctors speculating about their own suicides. I'd often heard such discussions, for doctors knew what happened to terminal patients, knew without any possibility of denial the deterioration of the body, and even the mind, and knew the pain. I'd heard them say that if they discovered they had an incurable disease, they'd commit suicide. I'd listened to them discuss alternative methods of committing suicide—for this too they could know and could do.

I sat alone in the very room where such speculations, such vows had been made. There was a closet of drugs nearby. When the time came, I could step into that closet and close the door, the short way to die. Or I could walk into a narrowing, darkening hall where there were faint disturbing echoes, vagrant smells, sharp points.

In a kind of dream, superstitiously, I got up and walked into the hall. And, of course, it was the corridor that led past the operating rooms, and there were staff people here going about their business.

Mrs. Dolan and her sister were a strong team. As soon as it was appropriate, they called in the prosthesis people to make a fitting for a new breast. Mrs. Dolan was eager to use her arm, and she boasted each day of being able to brush her own hair. It's painful to use muscles that have been scraped like that, but she did it.

"Do you feel bad about losing your breast?" I asked.

She smiled wisely. "Oh, my dear," she answered, "yes. Yes, I do. But maybe I already went through it before, with Evelyn, when she had to lose hers." She sighed. "Oh, we're women past out prime anyway, and somehow this just makes it clear. We're no longer youthful.

"So," she laughed, "what else is new, as they say? People have been growing old since people began. The important thing is to live your life! Let me tell you, Evelyn and I intend to do it!"

Mrs. Giacasso put in, "Next fall we're going on a cruise of the Greek islands!"

"The Greek islands seem to be very popular," I murmured.

"Then the next year," she continued eagerly, "we're going to Brazil. We've already been to Mexico and Jamaica. I want to see Hawaii after that."

"I'm more interested in the Holy Land," Mrs. Dolan reproved her.

"Well, we'll just have to wait and see which place we agree on," answered Mrs. Giacasso perkily.

I said, "Send me a postcard no matter where you go."

Mrs. Dolan left the hospital in a week, beaming with hope that her disease had been stopped, accompanied by her sister who'd been disease-free now for fifteen years. In the fall a postcard was forwarded to me. It showed an azure sea below a brilliant, rocky coast, and the greeting said they were having a marvelous time and that the captain was flirting with both of them.

PART VII

May and June

Pediatrics

33

By April I'd begun to fear that my internship would never be over. I'd spent my whole life running head-long; whenever I changed direction I'd turn a corner at full speed, dangerously. I began to feel that I'd lost control of my speed. If I didn't pull over I'd go faster and faster until I cracked up. I was looking forward with all my heart to moving, to getting away from the hospital and into the lab, to taking a kind of rest.

I was ambivalent toward my last rotation, Pediat-rics. I'm not the kind of woman who feels an inevita-ble warmth toward little babies. Children seem like foreigners to me. I couldn't stand teen-agers when I was one, and I could see no reason to change my at-titude. A Pediatrics stint was standard for a rotating internship like mine, but increasingly I was eager to get to work on the oncological, or cancer, research of the lab.

On the other hand, on Pediatrics my chief resident would be Annabelle Zabriskie, and I was curious and eager to work under her. She had the reputation of being brilliant. I'd already seen, on two occasions—with the rape victim and with the hydrocephalic baby's parents—how emotionally capable and calm she was. Also, the nicest doctors I'd met in the hospital were in Pediatrics. I expected to enjoy working with them.

When I first came on, I had to fill in for a week in a nursery. Well newborns were in nurseries on the postpartum floor. Pediatrics had an ICU nursery as well as a pediatric ICU. In isolettes in the Nursery were newborns up to six months old with such conditions as congenital deficiencies and who needed special care—like transfusions for a rare platelet deficiency which one newborn was getting.

I was awkward with the infants. Infants are entirely different as patients, since they are so tiny. I had to take blood from a foot; I had to learn to find a thread-sized vein in a head for transfusion. In the week I was there, I couldn't get used to handling a patient who weighed something like ten pounds. It amazed me to think of dealing with tiny newborns weighing only four. The nurses were so attentive, capable, and loving that I was appalled, in one sense. The babies who survived benefited from their warmth; yet the nurses' open hearts made each death painful. It was a mystery to me how they could keep it up and not harden themselves.

While I was on the nursery the five-month-old Antonin baby came in. He was the hydrocephalic baby who'd been born when I was on OB.

Mr. and Mrs. Antonin had noticed that Georgie was irritable and sleepy, and one day it was clear that the shunt was no longer working. So he'd come in to have the first of a number of revisions necessitated by his growth.

The shunt is the tube that drains the cerebrovascular fluid from the ventricular cavity inside the brain and sends it to the heart, where it mingles and is harmlessly diluted with blood. The tubing runs down the neck, and a valve is just under the skin in back of the ear. Mrs. Antonin had been taught how to check the shunt by pressing on it. If it was easy to press and swelled, it was working.

I admitted Georgie. Mrs. Antonin proudly told me the details of his first holding his head up, lifting his upper body, and of his grasping something he'd just seen. Annabelle Zabriskie examined him. Most babies cry when laid on their backs and handled by a stranger, and Georgie did, too. Dr. Zabriskie smiled, watched the baby and talked to him, and when he opened his eyes to take another breath in his crying he saw an attentive face.

Mrs. Antonin, nervously hovering where her baby

could see her as well, said, "He always cries, and he never lets up!"

When Annabelle was finished, she let Mrs. Antonin dress the baby. When Georgie saw his mother at her accustomed angle before him, he stopped sobbing and smiled. He'd grown into a good-looking baby, normal in shape, with lots of red hair. Both of his parents had light brown hair, though Mr. Antonin's had a light reddish cast to it. Mrs. Antonin smiled so warmly at Georgie that he laughed in response, and with a caressing voice she talked to him completely un-self-consciously as she dressed him. When I left, I found that I had a little smile on my own face. I was surprised that the sweetness of the baby food ads had some basis in reality.

Whenever Mrs. Antonin was allowed to, she was with the baby. She seemed to communicate not anxiety, but a great tenderness. When Mr. Antonin came in the evening, he too was happy-looking. It was obvious that the baby could have no more advantageous an environment. He recovered quickly from the surgical procedure and was able to go home in three days.

Parents of children who are patients are encouraged to stay with them at Grey's. We had plenty of cots, so a parent could even stay the night. In the Nursery or in Isolation, however, a parent could not be with the patient overnight, but slept on a cot where there was room. Babies under ten months don't really need a parent here, but from then on, to prevent the all-too-common traumas of childhood hospitalization, a parent stays as close as possible.

It has been found that young patients should be with people, so we had a good many three- and four-bed wards and several six-bed wards. I've seen one or two parents get upset because their child has three other children in his room, and they ask why there isn't at least a lower rate for the room. I explain that sick children can perceive isolation as abandonment, so the more friends they have the better, while the greater skills we need to deal with young patients are reflected in a regular room rate.

I was fascinated to watch Dr. Zabriskie, whose reputation throughout the hospital was extremely high. It was said that she was one of the most brilliant residents they'd ever had. I'd even heard her introduced as "Dr. Zabriskie, one of our brightest doctors," which intrigued me, since I couldn't remember ever hearing a man introduced as "one of our brightest."

She had a habit of rushing into the room where a parent was waiting to see her and apologizing breathlessly, "I'm sorry I'm late. I've just been presenting a terribly complicated case," or "I just came from a very difficult case."

Since I knew often that she hadn't just come from any such thing, I wondered whether the testimonials she'd heard about herself had gone to her head. I asked her once, "Do you always refer to your previous case, Doctor?"

She glanced at me and blushed. "I guess I can tell you," she said. "I do that on purpose to impress the parent with my competence. Otherwise they are often skeptical."

"Surely that's not a problem for *you!*" I said ingenuously.

She laughed. "Phyllis, that'll be a problem for every woman doctor until society rearranges itself. You might find a trick like that very useful. I learned it myself from a woman gynecologist. A grand old lady, she was in the generation of woman doctors who had to sacrifice everything and become tough to get a medical education. She told me she often did it. She'd walk in with a firm, brisk step and say, coolly, 'I'm very sorry. I've just done a very difficult hysterectomy.'"

Annabelle had drawn herself up as though she were six feet tall instead of five feet two, and she delivered the explanation in a curt, businesslike voice. I liked her. A quiet woman, she seemed to have no illusions about herself or the world, but she didn't seem bitter. She seemed amused.

Once, several minutes after I heard a doctor introduce her to someone by saying, "Don't let her size fool you! She's bright, very bright!" I said to her, "How can you stand to hear yourself described as intelligent all the time?"

She smiled. "Why else am I chief resident?"

For a moment I thought she was either very conceited or else extraordinarily matter-of-fact about her genius, then I saw her raise her eyebrows satirically. "Aha," I said, "I see." While an intelligent man could be chief resident, a woman had to be brilliant. Otherwise men working under her could not tolerate their being subordinate.

"It's all to my benefit," she said. "You're considered bright yourself."

I knew that was true, but since I also knew that I wasn't extraordinarily intelligent I'd ignored the patently false compliments.

"Do you think you've been appointed chief because you're a woman?" I asked, conscious of the kind of privilege a solitary woman might enjoy.

"Perhaps."

"Do you think that's fair?"

"Phyllis, don't be naive," she replied. "If I *didn't* get the job, *that* would be because I'm a woman. I'd rather be rewarded than penalized for being one. In the meantime, I try not to burden myself with outrage or guilt. There's better work for me to do."

I nodded. In effect, I stepped back to watch her, for she was very impressive. It was unfortunate that there were not more Annabelle Zabriskies to teach me and the other women who are now coming through medical school. I enjoyed working with her so much that if I'd been more enchanted with children, I might have gone into Pediatrics just because of her. She herself had a marvelous way with children, as though there were no barrier between her and them. She looked straight at them, talked to them directly, and they responded right back to her. She was comforting without embarrassment or effusiveness.

A teen-aged girl named Ellen Tracy came in. She was tall and lanky and, like most adolescents, had acne and greasy-looking hair. What a painful, unattractive time of life! Her injury must have been very embarrassing to her. It was a very large vulvar hematoma she had received playing basketball. She was a star player at a girls' school that took the sport so seriously that they practiced in weighted shoes, and somebody had kicked her in the crotch by accident. The poor girl was in great pain. Her vulva and the surrounding tissues were swollen to at least three times their normal size, and they were filled with blood. It would be painful for her to urinate. Hardly able to sit in the wheelchair, she slouched back to prevent any pressure on the bruise. With cold packs, and Demerol for the pain, she might be in the hospital for three days.

She kept flushing, perhaps with embarrassment or discomfort, and was decidedly nervous. By this time, I knew that one question I ought to ask any patient was: "Is there anything that worries you?"

"Uh . . . Am I . . ." she began, and gulped, and stopped.

I waited, not prodding her.

She tried again, not looking at me so I wouldn't see the tears that had sprung to her eyes. "Am I . . . Oh . . . Will this bother me when I get married?"

"Ah," I said. "No, this won't have any effect on your sexual development or your sexual ability. It's not even close to an injury to your reproductive system, so it won't affect your fertility or your ability to deliver a baby." I made such an extensive denial in order to try to cover whatever it was she was asking.

She looked confused and embarrassed.

"Did I answer your question?" I asked. "Or did I answer too much?"

"Maybe too much," she whispered, blushing. She still wouldn't look at me.

"Tell you what," I offered, "I'll check with your mother first and then see if I can find a book I can let you borrow. I'll let you have it while you're in the hospital, and you can ask me any questions after you've had a chance to look it over. Okay?"

346

"Oh. Okay." She didn't sound enthusiastic. Whether she was actually disguising her eagerness, I couldn't tell.

Ellen settled in silently, paying very little attention to her mother's attempts to organize the bedside table and her belongings. When that was all done, I suggested that she let her daughter sleep and come with me to the waiting room.

In her forties, Mrs. Tracy was conservatively dressed in a dark maroon suit. She looked anxious, and the lines in her forehead and around her mouth suggested that she felt anxious much of the time.

"Sit down, please, Mrs. Tracy. I'd like to explain your daughter's injury to you and ask your permission for a little sex education for her."

"Oh, certainly," she said timidly and vaguely.

"The bruise in the genital area is so large because that area is richly supplied with blood vessels. Your daughter is in such pain because there's also a network of nerves in the area. I don't want you to worry. The hematoma is not far up the vagina, and the blood in the hematoma will be reabsorbed slowly.

"Now, I'm not sure how much your daughter understands about her genitals and sexual development," I said in an inquiring tone.

"Oh, I don't know," Mrs. Tracy mumbled, looking anxiously at me.

"I thought it might be useful if I could explain all that to her if it doesn't interfere with what you have told her," I suggested tentatively.

"Oh." She blushed, but seemed relieved. "Well, frankly, we don't seem able to talk very much together anyway these days. I think . . . Well, I think it would be just fine for you to teach those things."

It occurred to me that a nursing text might have drawings of normal sexual characteristics. When I asked Donna Puckett, a nurse on the floor, for a nursing text that included the reproductive system, she stared at me and then laughed. "Hey!" she exclaimed. "Didn't your mommy tell you?"

"Oh, yeah," I replied, "she did her best, but what

347

I'm looking for now are the pictures to go with it!"

When I gave the book to Ellen that evening, she was feeling much better and was able to sit up in bed. Her appetite had not been affected, and she was asking for seconds even though she was on a soft diet. It looked as though she'd made friends in her room, and I was well pleased with her condition.

When I made rounds the next morning with Larry Berman, the second-year resident on my team, three of the other girls were clustered around Ellen's bed giggling. The other two were in their beds, teasing to be shown the pictures.

The minute we stepped into the room there were shrieks; three girls scampered to their beds, leaped in, and looked innocent, embarrassed, and thrilled.

"Well," said Larry, "what's the attraction?" He looked at Ellen for information, but she was leaning against whatever she'd stuffed behind her back. There was a lot of giggling.

"They found your journal, Dr. Berman," I said, "the one you kept when you were in high school." Dr. Berman was a happily married man who lived far out of town on a kind of farm and had four adopted children.

He grinned sheepishly. "Oh, no," he groaned. "Girls, don't read that!" There were more giggles. "Wait a minute, now. If you're serious about that kind of research, I'll have to scrounge around in my bureau and find Dr. Donnan's diary for you."

"Uh-oh," I said.

They calmed down. Willing to be kidded about Dr. Berman, they seemed uncomfortable with the notion of my having a sex life. Nevertheless, when I came back in later in the day Ellen was interested enough to ask me questions, and everybody else listened. I answered them as meekly and moderately as I could.

I found that I liked Ellen Tracy despite my antiadolescent prejudice. I guess it's an example of hating mankind but liking Tom, Dick, and Harry.

34

I was disposing of my tray after breakfast when a medical intern named Talcott stopped me. "I admitted a former patient of yours last night," he said. His face was grim.

I stopped abruptly. "Who?"

"Stella Black," he said.

With his words I felt pain. I didn't say a thing.

Talcott looked closely at me. "She came in in septic shock," he said.

I could visualize her, thin but bloated from Cortisone, yellow-skinned from liver damage, being wheeled in on a stretcher. Her cancer had not been sensitive to removing the ovaries and adrenal glands after all. I could imagine Talcott's immediate realization that she was dying, not wanting her to die on him, doing a Grey's prep on her; that is, getting her into electrolyte balance, with all of her chemicals normal.

"You did everything you could," I stated.

"She's not dead yet."

"Where is she?"

"K 540."

"I'll stop by later."

I went up to Ped, and into the first conference room. At the window I looked out. It was the middle of May and already hot. I opened the window. The sounds and smells of the street came up. For a moment I watched the people. I could see the entrance to the parking garage and the pause of each car as the driver reached over to take a ticket from the machine. I could see the main entrance of Grey's and people walking toward the columned porch and disappearing into its shadow. I could not see very much of the long red façade of Levering, where I was, but on the bulky skyscraper of Kinderkopf the curtains and shades made a random pattern.

I took a deep breath of hot, exhaust-filled air and closed the window.

I got to rounds late, which Annabelle commented on. "A patient of mine has been admitted to Medicine, dying," I explained. I can't remember a single thing that was said on rounds. As soon as I could, I asked for a half-hour break.

I crossed the threshold of Stella's room. Under control, I went up to her bed and stood there a moment in the silence. No machines were hooked up; there was just the quiet sliding of fluids into her. I touched her arm. She made no response. "Stella," I whispered.

She opened her eyes. The eyeballs were tinged yellow. She tried to see me. Then she smiled weakly.

"Do you know me, Stella?" I asked, wanting to grab her by the shoulders and make her sit up, to animate her.

"Phyllis," she murmured. Then she clutched my hand and said, "I don't want to die. I can't die yet. I'm not ready."

"All right," I answered.

"You mean it?"

"Yes."

It was a lie. I was grimly sad that Stella had to have a lie. She ought to speak about her death as clearly as before. If I'd had to prepare myself for her death, I thought, she should also. Now she awoke in me the impulse to save her, which I knew would be impossible, and again and too painfully I wanted her to live forever.

"I'm not ready yet," she repeated insistently.

"Do you think you could be ready sometime, Stella?" I asked.

"Oh," she moaned. She was silent for a moment. Then she said, "I'm afraid."

"What do you fear?" I asked her quietly.

After a long time, and with dread and longing, she whispered, "I wish I had my parts."

I'd expected her to fear annihilation and loss of identity. I was surprised at this primitive desire to be physically whole, as I interpreted it. "Oh, my dear Stella," I said, "I wish I could help you."

"Where are they?" she asked more clearly. "My breast, my uterus and ovaries, my glands?"

"They . . . they're gone."

"Where?"

"They were all destroyed, Stella, soon after the operations."

Her mouth twisted into a kind of smile. Then she whispered, "I was afraid . . . I had these nightmares, like old movies I used to go to all the time when I was a kid . . ."

She had fantasized macabre images of brains kept alive in nutrients, organs saved by a madman, hands crawling vengefully up the stairs. "Oh, Stella, Stella," I shook my head. "You don't have to worry."

I said, "It's you, dear woman, you are still you."

She sighed lightly. "I wonder for how long."

We were silent. Then I sensed that someone had come and I looked up. Stella's daughter Rags was studying me.

"Your daughter is here," I said to Stella, and it hurt when she immediately looked away from me to the door with a glad cry.

The girl came in to her mother's bedside. "Hi, Mom," she said softly.

"Miranda," Stella murmured.

"I'll come back later, Stella," I said.

Stella looked back at me and smiled. "Phyllis, my dear," she said, and her inclusion of me was sweet. "Can't you stay a while?"

Miranda was looking at me. I couldn't see hostility any longer, but there was no real welcome, either. It was as though she were willing for anything her mother wanted.

"No," I said, "I'll leave you two alone."

Then I went away.

I called Dr. Speir. His voice made me feel better. At one point in the past I'd thought his cheerfulness deluded his patients. Now I wondered whether his treatment of his dying patients was in fact subtle and appropriate. He told me, in his calm way, that her infection was overwhelming and she was too debilitated to wage any of the fight against it herself. The bone destruction was exceedingly painful and also made it impossible for the marrow to synthesize new cells and fight infection. "We are giving her supportive care," he said, "but there will be no heroic measures."

He meant that if her heart stopped, if her breathing stopped, she would not be resuscitated.

"I don't want you to get yourself involved in her case again," he warned. "You're on a different service now. I don't think she ought to be your patient when she dies."

"I can visit her," I said.

"Of course."

"All right, Dr. Speir, thanks," I said, and hung up.

It wasn't until about ten o'clock that night that I was able to go back to Stella. I went quietly down the hall, conscious of the evening sounds: nurses getting the juice glasses back, checking the medications cart from which they'd just dispensed the drugs, patients getting ready for bed after their visitors left at 9:30. I could hear water turned on and off in some rooms, other patients were padding down the hall to the bathroom or asking the nurse at the last minute for a sleeping pill or a painkiller. It was closing-the-day activity, quiet and slow.

I came to Stella's room and looked in at her lying on the bed in the dim light.

"Stella?" I called softly.

There was no reply. Then a figure by the window stirred. It was Mr. Black. He spoke quietly to me, his voice tight. "She's in a coma," he said.

352

"Oh, no!" I cried. I'd missed her, I was too late. I'd missed my last chance to talk to her.

I turned around abruptly and left. Remembering, I caught myself and turned back for a moment to say goodnight to him. Then I quickly left the hospital.

I walked.

I was full of self-recrimination. Had I unconsciously delayed coming back to Stella? Had I been still jealous of Miranda and punished Stella by not coming back in time?

As I walked, I gradually calmed myself. It had been a privilege to know Stella. We had become tender friends, and my love and care had been dignified by her response. I should have no regrets. As I walked in the darkness I wept.

Before I was due on rounds the next morning, I stopped by Stella's floor to see if there had been any change. The nurse told me she'd come out of the coma into a delirious state only to go back into the coma.

As I came into the room her son, Jeff, who had apparently taken over the vigil so that Mr. Black could have breakfast, looked up at me. His face had looked scared, but then relief and hope flooded it. I was conscious of pitying him for his ignorance, hoping he would be able to learn to grieve. I nodded silently to him; he looked away as if embarrassed.

I walked over to Stella's figure and lifted her hand, noticing as I did that it was swelling and that she'd need another intravenous site.

"Stella!" I called her again as I'd done before. "Stella!"

She opened her eyes. "Swimming," she said.

Haltingly, she mumbled, "Carried . . . Tourniquet . . . He put her . . . Novocain, stitches . . . By my neck . . . Scream so loud in my ear . . ." Stella murmured, with saliva gathering at the corners of her mouth. "Cut. She cut her foot."

"Yes," I said, when she finished. "Do you know me?"

She closed her eyes. "I think I'll call her Miranda," she mused.

353

"That's beautiful," I said. I stood silently watching her. Her hand was very hot.

"Is she in pain?" Jeff asked.

"Not right now, I don't think. Is Dr. Speir coming in today?"

"Yes. At least, I think Dad said so."

"All right. I'll stop back in when I can," I promised.

"I'll tell Dad," he replied.

I went back to work.

Dr. Speir told me that Stella's case was going to be presented at Tumor Rounds the second day after she went into her coma and delirium. I felt compelled to be there.

Dr. Speir was very impressive. I'd said that of many doctors before when I referred to their intellect or powerful presentation, but this time I meant a kind of clarity, calm, and simplicity. I felt I could depend on him. I felt very warmly toward him.

Stella's metastasis had proceeded to the lungs and the kidneys as well. Her kidneys were in bad shape and perhaps on the verge of shutting down. Since her bones had been invaded by the cancer, she would have been in excruciating pain if it were not for the massive doses of morphine she was getting. I hoped the cancer might have spread to encompass an artery, where, if it penetrated, she could bleed out—that is, die when her blood was pumped under high pressure into whatever cavity the artery passed through—in two or three minutes, painlessly.

"Morphine in that high a dose," argued a medical student whom I could have strangled, "can make somebody a drug addict!"

They talked interminably about whether that was true or not.

Finally Dr. Speir walked forward a little from his position of leaning against the door jamb and said, "The patient is going to die."

There was a shocked silence and I thought I heard

a nervous giggle. But there was no more discussion.

A day later Talcott, the intern, stopped me in the hall. "Well," he said, "your patient died."

My thoughts raced down the corridors of Pediatrics checking on each patient, for none had been near dying. "What patient?" I demanded, outraged.

"That patient of yours, Mrs. Black," he insisted. For a moment I was intensely relieved.

He went on, "God, I hate to have them die on me."

As I heard him, I realized what he had told me: Stella had finally died. "Oh, no," I said at last.

"You know what I mean," he responded defensively. "I don't like to have to ask the family for an autopsy. They didn't give permission, of course."

I interrupted him by putting my hand on his arm and instinctively patting it, saying "That's all right, don't worry about it." Then I walked away.

I was at Stella's door suddenly, not having gone up in the elevator or passed through the intervening halls, it seemed, for I saw nothing in between. Mr. Black was in the room, looking ashen and weary. A nurse asked him to leave while the attendants wrapped the body and put it on the cart to take down to the hospital morgue where the undertakers could pick it up. Jeff, who I think had been there when she actually died, had disappeared. I had passed Miranda standing just outside the door, crying. Her chin was crinkled; her face was wet and red.

I put out my hand and automatically Mr. Black shook it. Then we stood in the hall outside, leaning against the wall, not speaking. When they brought Stella's body out and started to wheel it off, Miranda gasped out a louder cry, turned, and sobbed against her father's chest.

I could hear her sobs and the sounds of patients talking, the soft swish of a nurse's nylon thighs as she passed, the rattle of the bloods cart down at another end of the hall, the elevator doors opening and closing, and somebody's beeper going off.

35

Henry Elkins, a sixteen-year-old patient with a soft, unlined face, had had rheumatic heart disease some time ago, which had enlarged his heart. Now he kept having fevers. He said, "They just keep coming back and coming back. My shrink sent me to the clinic and the clinic told me and my mom I might as well come in to find out what it was." He looked at me with a most trusting expression when he said, "You'll find out."

I grunted noncommittally, but he smiled.

His heart was as big as half his chest. When he stripped, I thought I could see a flutter, and when I put my hand on it, I felt the heart's heavy throb. I stood for a moment feeling the sensation, realizing what it must be like to have a heartbeat so insistent, a heart so large that its volume and motion dominated a large portion of the interior space. I wondered if it made him feel crowded or even crowded out, or whether he got used to it, just as one's own pulse, detectable at times, can be ignored.

He was very cooperative during the examination, but when I prepared to take blood he showed nervousness, and he whimpered when I stuck him. His other hand hovered in the air, threatening to hold the arm I was getting the blood from, and I had to tell him sharply to get his hand out of the way. We suspected he had a bacterial infection of the heart, and in order to discover the origin of his fever I had to draw blood several times a day. Each time it was more difficult until, by the third try on the second day, he was trembling and whimpering, "No, oh, don't do it, please don't . . ."

The bloods kept coming out negative, so we had to do a spinal tap. When he heard that, he was inconsolable. Larry Berman and I tried, but Henry just wouldn't stay curved into the proper position, which exposed as much space between two vertebrae as possible. Annabelle suggested that I shouldn't do the tap but should hold him. When I tried putting my arms over his shoulders and drawn-up legs, talking soothingly to him, he stayed as quiet as we could expect for him. He groaned when the needle went in and moaned as it drew up the fluid. It's not a painful procedure or a long one, and I told him that it would be over in five minutes. He fussed anyway.

Since he was so young and his complaint was mysterious, he became a focus for teaching. In the morning during rounds, the attending always stopped at his bed, and we were always having to wake him up. He would roll over and groan. "Oh, Doctors," he would reprove us. "Why can't you let a boy sleep?" Henry seemed to drift back to sleep while we stood there discussing his case, but I suspected that he heard everything. We decided to see whether he had any disease of the bowel, and scheduled him for a barium enema and fluoroscope series. He seemed to sink deeper into his bed, though he didn't move a muscle. I looked at him carefully and saw him quickly shut his eyes.

Later in the day I got a call from Radiology, telling me they hadn't taken the series on Elkins and asking why I hadn't told them he was diabetic.

"What do you mean? He's no diabetic," I answered.

"He said he was having an insulin reaction. He was very convincing."

I could just imagine him crying out: "Oh, I'm having an insulin reaction! I've got to get some orange juice!" and running out quickly in panic. I myself didn't think the fluoroscope series was necessary, since I thought his bacterial infection would show up eventually on the cultures. Nevertheless, my job was to get

357

it done, and I told him he'd have to go through with it.

Though I promised to stay with him and let him hold on to me, as he had done for the spinal tap, he refused. I knew he was serious. He just shook his head no, his lips closed tightly, and tears gathered in his eyes.

When I told Annabelle, she said, "Well, you can't physically force him to undergo it. I suggest you hypnotize him."

"I can't do that!"

"Why not?"

"But . . . take over his mind?"

She smiled. "I don't think you'll find it's that powerful, Phyllis. Why don't you talk to his psychiatrist?"

Henry had been a psychiatric clinic patient for six weeks. His psychiatrist was a rotund man and had a dark brown handlebar mustache that seemed the typical style of men that size and shape. "Yeah, certainly," he said, "he'll respond to hypnosis. He giving you any trouble? I've hypnotized him many times to relax him, and you can do it, too."

"He's been cooperative until this refusal. He's actually very meek and dependent."

The psychiatrist smiled. "He's actually able to manipulate you very well, I'd guess."

"Oh."

"Now this enema," he went on with a twinkle, "is often associated with homosexual fears. I think your hypnotizing him is an excellent idea."

"But how do I do it? I've never hypnotized anyone in my life!"

"You've seen it done, haven't you, as a medical student?"

"Yes."

"Well, just be scrupulous and keep to the task, and you'll find hypnosis the easiest thing in the world. Just count backward from a hundred out loud. A regular, slow count. At eighty-five, talk about a field . . ."

"What field?"

"There's a field he used to like to go to. Just a field with wildflowers."

"Any animals?"

"No, just a field. Tell him he's in the field. Tell him he'll know what's going on in the room, but it won't trouble him. Remind him once in a while about the field, and I'll bet you'll have no trouble at all."

"Why don't you do it?"

He smiled. "Come on, Doctor, don't be chicken."

I realized that I was fascinated by the possibility. Perhaps I wouldn't have hesitated except that Henry Elkins seemed so dependent on me that I feared complete control over his mind; I feared that I would be corrupted by it. Then I realized that the whole issue of being someone's powerful doctor was symbolized in this transaction.

I replied, "You're right. Who's a chicken?"

The next day, having told Henry what would happen, I went to Radiology with him. He was nervous but surprisingly willing. He took my hand and said, "I'll be all right, won't I?" with hardly a trace of question in his voice.

I had him lie down sideways on the table. Then I stood beside him.

"Hold my hand," he whispered. I did.

I said, "I'm going to count backward now, and you'll feel more and more relaxed, Henry."

I did as I had been instructed, and at eighty-five I said, "You're in the field now, Henry. You're in the field."

"Yes," he murmured. "Yes." I was astonished.

The enema was given and the machinery pulled into place. While the series was being fluoroscoped he said, "I'd like to know what's happening to my body. Please bring me back to the room, but don't keep me here."

Startled by his clarity, I didn't know what to do—whether he could be in two "places" at once, whether I was supposed to let him "be" here for just a minute and tell him to go back to the field then, or what. I said, "I don't know what to do with you."

He said, "Just keep telling me it won't matter what they're doing to me, and tell me I can go both places if I want to."

I couldn't believe he was in a hypnotic state, but I did what he suggested. I could tell when he was attentive to his body and when he was abstracted. By the time I brought him out of hypnosis I was sweating, but I was also exhilarated and amazed. To be hypnotized seemed to make Henry more competent than he usually was, rather than less. My stereotype of someone hypnotized was his being passive and helpless.

His cultures came back positive; he did have subacute bacterial endocarditis requiring antibiotic therapy. It was unfortunate for Henry that he became so dependent on me. In the long run it was medically bad. He would watch for me to enter the room each morning. Awake and waiting, he would smile a soft little smile when he saw me. It was an unmistakable crush, and I started getting kidded about robbing the cradle. When he developed irregular heartbeats and had to be put into the ICU, he became very anxious. He insisted that I stay with him all the time, which I couldn't and wouldn't do. I did keep track of him, and checked in on him whenever I could at least once a day, but it didn't satisfy him.

In his worsened condition he wanted my care more, which was impossible. No amount of talking with me or with his psychiatrist, no substitute nursing, no reassurances or even hypnosis would convince him that it was important for him to be in the ICU, that I was being as attentive as I could, and that he was safe. He became more and more depressed until, hopelessly, he allowed his mother to sign him out.

There wasn't anything we could do to prevent it. We could, and did, arrange for home nursing service to make sure he took his antibiotics.

Perhaps I'll never completely accept a patient's

signing himself out AMA but my perspective on Henry Elkins was very different from the limited one I'd had on the other patient, Mr. Foley. For Henry I'd been able to do everything that was possible for me to do, and I knew and did not reproach myself for the fact that I couldn't do everything.

I found myself sitting next to a very attractive man named Joe Bensinger at a dinner party. He looked about forty, with thick brown hair and a neat brown beard, and was a lawyer in the firm that did the hospital's business. He made sure we got our marital status clear right away.

"Are you married?" he asked.

"No, are you?" I replied.

He laughed quickly. "Just divorced," he announced, as though it were the Purple Heart, modestly and boastfully at the same time.

I was pleased to be sitting next to someone with whom a conversation wouldn't develop into medical shoptalk, and we spent the whole evening, during dinner and afterward, engrossed in discussing movies and plays (only a few of which I'd seen), vacations and resorts, and trips we had taken. We were both feeling relaxed, as though we'd been on a vacation that evening, by the time we left the party, and I was not surprised when he suggested we sleep together that night.

"I'd like to," I answered.

"Whoopee! Where then, my place or yours?" he said eagerly.

I said his. My associations with sex at my apartment were still a little painful, apparently.

"Good."

When we got there, I was amused to see that after his divorce he'd regressed to American playboy. His apartment, a one-bedroom, had a red shag carpet, a sheepskin scatter rug, and white furniture. The bedroom had a waterbed with a fake fur coverlet and a mirror-tiled ceiling. It too was red and white.

"Come here, baby," he said, and pulled me backward to him and placed both hands on my breasts.

I hoped he'd calm down as I wondered whether I was the first woman he'd gone to bed with since his divorce. There was a valiant bravado in his whole manner that I sympathized with. It was my telling him that I used a diaphragm, however, that I didn't have with me, so he'd have to use a condom, that snapped him out of his falseness.

He looked startled and disappointed. "But I haven't used a condom since high school!"

"Do you have any?"

We searched the bathroom, the bedside tables, and the closet. By the time he found a packet, among some camping supplies, he was amused and relaxed. We had to make sure they weren't old and brittle, so he took one out, unrolled it, and filled it with water like a balloon. It didn't leak.

It was then that I grabbed it and spilled it all over him.

Scooping me up with laughter, he carried me to the bedroom and dropped me on the bed. He undressed himself and me and pulled back the covers. Caressing me, he stretched out my arms and legs and kept caressing me until I felt gloriously exposed and open. He stroked me again and again all over, murmuring things, breathily kissing me, and when I said, "Let me make love to you," he told me no, he wanted to love me, and after a time of delicious tingling, he came into me and began rocking me, rocking me, rocking me to sleep.

The next morning we awoke in one another's arms. "Mmmm," he murmured into my hair. "You're nice."

"You're nice, too," I said, remembering the gentle rings of sensation that had risen in me last night and wanting to bring them back.

After we made love again, he said, "I'm glad I found you. When can we do this again?"

I stretched pleasurably, glad to be secure with him and in myself. "We won't have much more time," I said. "I'm going to be moving in a couple of weeks."

His face fell. He'd thought he'd found another wife, I think.

I told him where I'd be and what I'd be doing. My mind and body were all smiles as I heard myself saying that I'd be going into cancer research, and I knew that my next year could be used in the final specialty I would work out in Oncology.

"Maybe my work will bring me to the city," he said hopefully. "Can I see you when I do?"

"Yes. I'd love that."

36

I had never heard such an uproar in a hospital corridor, unless it had been an argument I was having with a male chauvinist. All the way down the hall in the third wing of Pediatrics, it sounded like a flash flood. Hurrying, I turned the corner to see a group of people clogging the hallway, almost pinning the other intern, Alan Radcliffe, to the wall, and two nurses clinging to the edges of the group.

"Shut up!" Alan yelled. He was so mild-mannered, it was unusual for him to raise his voice. The furor did not die down. He caught sight of me. "Hey, Phyllis!" he called, as if I could save him from sinking.

The whole group of people turned as one to stare at me, several heavy-set men dressed in workclothes and a number of equally dark-skinned women. One woman called to me in heavily accented English, "Shoo! Shoo some norse? Shoo don't touch my baby. Nobody touch baby. We decide!" With a defiant shake of her whole body, she turned her back on me.

"Alan," I called over the bobbing heads and the

hubbub, "come over here and tell me what's happening."

He sidled around the group, grabbed my elbow, and swiftly steered me around the corner.

"They look like Gypsies," I observed.

He scraped the sweat off his forehead with a finger. "They *are* Gypsies," he said breathlessly.

"Really?" I said excitedly. "I've never met any. I never knew they really existed. I just thought they hung around old Jennifer Jones movies on the late show."

"Har, har," he said sarcastically. "Boy, am I glad you're here. Maybe you can deal with them!" He took me into the room behind the nurses' station where we could consult. "They brought a little girl in. She'd been having convulsions, and now she's in a coma."

"Aha. Suspicious," I said.

"Yeah. But they won't let me get near her for even an ENT check." That was an ear, nose, and throat exam, the first step in a diagnosis. "We have to deal with the whole tribe," he continued in exasperation. "We have to try to explain to them and then get permission from the whole bunch for everything! The whole tribe is her family!"

"Oh, no."

We looked at one another. We couldn't tell what the convulsions had done to her or what they meant. As she lay in a coma quietly breathing, we should be doing all sorts of things, but the Gypsies wouldn't let us at her.

"Where is she?" I asked.

"They commandeered the stretcher from the orderly and just wheeled her down the hall, opening doors and looking in each room until they came to one that didn't have anybody in it. They took her in there. Right in the middle of C wing and several psychosomatic kids! I can't think of a worse place!"

"Well, look, Alan, we should get Annabelle in on this. Maybe they'll listen to her."

Alan groaned. "I did try to get her, but she's in the OR watching an operation right now. Won't be out for another couple of hours. I called the visit, but he can't be here for fifteen minutes. Until he gets here, it's up to you and me, Phyllis. And if anybody can cope with Gypsies, it ought to be you."

"Thanks," I said dryly.

We sat there for a minute. Alan was frustrated and demoralized. I was intrigued. "Listen, Alan," I said, "tell you what let's do. Call for Deacon." He was a hulking man, the most popular orderly on the children's ward. "Get him to bring out a portable EEG. You get the crash cart, we'll both load ourselves down with gleaming hardware like stethoscopes and oto-scopes and wrap a lot of tubing around our necks. I'll get the bloods cart and the spinal paraphernalia, and we'll see if we can intimidate them with all our weaponry."

"That won't work. It's exactly what they don't want."

"Frankly, I doubt that. Come on. It won't hurt to get everything ready anyway." I had already gone to call Deacon on the phone. Alan reluctantly went along with me. Maybe I could instinctively deal with them like a steamroller. Deacon arrived and nodded agreement to the scheme.

"I seen Gypsies before," he said. "You better nail everything down."

I recruited two of the nurses, and we set off down the hall like a phalanx, five of us garbed impressively in white, pushing rattling machinery and looking as efficient as a television medical team.

We rounded the corner noisily and the Gypsies fell silent.

We pulled up to them and I stepped in front of my cart. "Silence!" I commanded majestically and un-necessarily, raising my arm. There were murmurs. "Silence!" I repeated sternly. "These are only some of the tools this great hospital can use to make your child well. You will give your permission for the first of these tools to be used immediately!"

There was an uproar of protest. I stood unflinchingly. "Now," I called, "who speaks English? I don't speak Spanish."

One woman said impressively, "We are not speaking Spanish!"

"Pardon me. Would you come here, please?" I said to her.

I took her hand and placed the otoscope in it. "Now look in my ear." She started to step back, but I guided her hand with the lighted instrument in it so she could get a glance into my ear. They questioned her and she answered in their language. "Now let me do it to the child," I said. She glowered at me. Then she nodded. I took it to mean permission.

"There will have to be several tools," I announced.

"No! Only one thing at a time!" a large man yelled.

"Yes!" I insisted.

"No! We decide one at a time." He stepped up to me and glared. He was almost exactly my height, but seemed to bulk twice as large.

I gave in. "Very well, but we doctors will make you decide fast. Do you understand?"

Reluctantly, they agreed. They insisted that a man and a woman be in the girl's room during all of our procedures. Emergency teams always seem like a crowd around somebody, and with two threatening spectators in the room with us, it would be like doing a procedure in the middle of a subway station, but I conceded. We did the ENT very quickly, and found that pus was leaking from her ear.

I whipped around in a theatrical manner and demanded permission for taking blood. The man and woman conferred, then the man scurried out to the corridor where I impatiently heard a new hubbub as they discussed the next step. He came in and nodded yes.

When I prepared her arm and the needle, I heard some kind of protest behind me, but before the Gypsy could interfere, I plunged the needle into her vein and began drawing dark blood into the syringe. After a moment I was able to pay attention to the loud noises I had subconsciously heard.

It had been the man's hoarse voice, a scrabbling, and a big thump. When I turned, I saw his body crumpled on the floor. He had just fainted. The woman was bending over him, and one of the nurses had broken open a vial of ammonia salts, and was waving the ampule under the man's nose. The Gypsy woman squatted beside him by the bureau. When he was recovering and she was sure he was awake to see it, she spat on the floor in disgust.

"Hey! Cut that out!" I yelled. "You're making this room septic enough as it is!"

She glared, then said, "The man don't know what suffering is. *He* should have the babies!" Grimly, she turned to him as he was regaining consciousness and prodded him to get up. He sagged against the wall.

When I began to undress the girl for the routine physical check and then the spinal tap, the woman insisted that only women be in the room. The Gypsy man and Alan Radcliffe had to leave. Deacon was already gone.

She was a pretty little girl, about nine or ten, with the dark skin of her race. She was what is genetically called mosaic, with one blue eye and one brown one. I wondered whether she was considered a freak, or special, because of it. Her hair was nearly black. Her bones seemed straight enough, she was a little malnourished, maybe, but clean, but her teeth were in terrible condition. I doubt that she'd ever seen a dentist. Poor kid, she'd lose several teeth before she was twenty, I was afraid. Maybe I could get permission for a dental consultation on her once she recovered. I thought probably her front teeth could be saved.

Our main findings were pus coming from the ear and white cells in her spinal fluid.

It seemed like hours because the process was so complicated, but it must have been only a short while before Dr. Macintosh, the visit, arrived. He was an old-fashioned pediatrician, an impressive, dignified man who must have seemed to his young patients like a somewhat distant but reliable grandfather. Under his Victorian patriarchal exterior, however, he had a mind like a steel trap. He had a reputation for never letting a diagnosis get away from him. I felt sure that the Gypsies would respect his type.

They did, but he could not get them to break up camp in the corridor. They settled in.

Jennifer Landau, one of the young patients in that wing, was waiting for me as I emerged from the room. She popped out from behind a cart where she'd lain in wait. A slim pale thirteen-year-old, she was in the hospital for severe dysmenorrhea. Very painful menstruation is not uncommon during adolescence, but Jennifer had been fainting from the pain since the onset of menses a year ago. There was a distinct possibility that her emotional situation—a cold, withholding father whom she desperately adored—contributed to the severity of her complaint, and she was also under psychiatric observation. But the physical problem had to be dealt with as well, so we put her on the birth control pill. She had to stay for a couple of days while we checked her for psychiatric problems.

"Dr. Donnan!" she whispered urgently, coming swiftly up to me as if she would like to catch my hand —and then not doing it, as was her way.

"What is it, Jennifer?" I said, stopping so that she knew I was listening to her, then starting to walk along again.

"Do you know what I saw one of those Gypsies do?" she asked breathlessly and wide-eyed.

"What?"

"Well." She gulped before she began her story. "You know those carts? Somebody was bringing up a whole lot of supplies, like bandages and stuff, you know? And the cart went right by one of those Gypsies, and a little box got brushed off, maybe it was pickpocketed, because she bent down and picked it up, and kept it!" Jennifer was amazed and excited to have witnessed a crime.

"What was it, do you know?"

"Well, I saw them open it afterward, and you know

368

those long flat sticks like they use to look in your throat?"

I nodded.

"Well, it was that. *And they kept them!*"

I smiled. I almost laughed, but I didn't want to disturb Jennifer's seriousness. What could a bunch of Gypsies find to do with a bunch of tongue depressors, I wondered.

"Thank you, Jennifer," I said. "I'll take it up with them; though certainly it's not a loss of great value. Do the Gypsies interest you?" I took a different tack.

"Oh, yes," she said enthusiastically. "Well, kind of."

"Would you be interested to talk to them?" I asked.

"Oh, no!" she breathed. "I wouldn't dare!"

By this time we'd come to Jennifer's room. The other three girls in the room were staring agog at us. "What did she say? What did she say?" they asked. I was struck by the eager, simple excitement I saw in these girls' faces, a child's excitement not often visible in them. They were having an adventure, and it was doing them good.

"So, you all know, huh?" I said.

They all nodded, flushed and happy.

"Well, I think you might try even closer observation." I made my voice serious though not portentous, I hoped. "See if you can . . . uh . . . talk to a Gypsy. I'm sure if you keep an eye on them for us, we'll appreciate it very much."

"Oh!" one girl squealed. They were all delighted. "Yes, of course we will. Oh!" The room instantly became a collaboration unit.

Later in the day, after doctors from Neurology and ENT had come over to see her, the Gypsy girl, Maria, was still in a coma, being watched and monitored. She had good heart action, so she was not in terrible danger, but her case was puzzling. Annabelle, Dr. Macintosh, Alan, the doctors from Neurology and ENT and I all sat around a conference table looking at her chart, graphs, and x rays, trying to diagnose her. Dr. Macintosh sat back in his chair, his white jacket folded open over his vest, and listened to all of our theories.

Finally he said, "I'm betting it's a mastoid infection."

If the mastoid, the sinus between the skull and the brain behind the ear and above the neck, becomes infected and is not drained, the infection will sooner or later penetrate the covering of the brain, and even be fatal. A mastoid infection is very unusual now. It used to be common because bacterial infections could hang on, migrate to many sites, and not be controlled so easily as they can today with penicillin and other drugs. I'd never myself seen mastoiditis, and I was ready to bet that even my chief resident hadn't seen one, because she was looking as skeptical as I was surprised.

"I don't see any evidence of it on the plates," Annabelle objected, referring to the skull x rays.

"The films weren't made with mastoid infection in mind, Doctor," Dr. Macintosh replied mildly. He meant that the angle might have disguised any evidence.

"We've palpated the area," Dr. Zabriskie challenged.

"Yes, of course. I have, too. No swelling detectable. There may be some warmth, but that, of course, might be subjective." Macintosh wasn't going to claim anything he couldn't back up.

"Well, Doctor," began Annabelle argumentatively, "you may have seen many mastoids in your day . . ."

"I have, indeed," said Macintosh genially, accepting the implication of his age.

"But they simply do not turn up nowadays," she insisted.

"You forget, Doctor," Macintosh said, very quietly, very gently, "that this child is not a nowadays child."

Dr. Zabriskie was silenced.

Macintosh got up and walked to the door purposefully. He turned before he went out and said, "You stain the pus from her ears, Doctor, and I'll bet you'll find red snappers!" Red snappers are tubercular bacilli that stain bright red.

Macintosh had made a brilliant diagnosis of tubercular mastoiditis.

"Gentlemen," he said, including me and Annabelle in this group, "this afternoon ENT will operate. Dr. Zabriskie, you may observe. The child stays in Isolation, and you get whoever's got TB in that tribe out of here and into a sanitarium." With this pronouncement, he regally left the room.

"Who in the hell is going to get permission for this operation?" Annabelle muttered. It was a good question. Dr. Macintosh was enough on his dignity not to reappear until after the operation itself had proven him right. The Gypsies didn't know Annabelle. They didn't trust Alan Radcliffe. It was me who was going to have to get their permission to cut into the girl's skull to let the pus drain out.

Fat chance, I thought.

Surprisingly, the Gypsy queen accepted me as an authority and gave me permission quite readily. The operation itself was very simple and turned out as Dr. Macintosh had claimed. We found out that the girl's grandmother had recently died of TB. We checked everybody by tine test and x ray and were able to get her aunt to go to a sanitarium. When Maria was out of the acute stage, she too would have to go to a sanitarium. Annabelle acknowledged Dr. Macintosh's diagnosis very gracefully.

The news of the spy mission Jennifer Landau and her roommates had instituted spread through the whole wing, as I had guessed it might, and of the twenty children who were ambulatory, probably about eighteen were soon out and around in the halls or in the lounge, at first shyly, then more openly, trying to observe those Gypsies who were allowed to wait in the hospital with Maria's mother.

I overheard one boy ask an elderly black-clothed woman sitting on the floor in the lounge with her back to the wall, "Where do you come from?"

371

The woman looked up from her knitting and smiled, nodding.

"Where are you from?" the boy repeated politely.

The old woman nodded as if she were deaf, then patted the place beside her, so Frank obediently sat down with his back against the wall, too. She laid aside her knitting, reached inside a voluminous cloth about her waist, and took out a handful of musically tinkling jacks and a red rubber ball. "Oh, that's a girl's game," he protested, but she nodded and started playing the ancient game of jacks, until he was fascinated and gladly took his turn. I left them together with the jingling sound of the jacks being tossed on the floor and then the little bounce of the ball.

I met Alan Radcliffe just around the corner. He had a worried expression on his face. "Phyllis!" he cried upon seeing me, "what *is* that funny noise?"

"Uh, I think it's called fraternizing," I said.

There were about seven or eight Gypsies who came and went in the lounge or the corridor outside Maria's Isolation room. They had an irrepressible habit of cadging orange juice and ginger ale for one another. A Gypsy would never ask for it for himself or herself, always for someone else, someone who was desperately thirsty, had a bad heart, needed something on her stomach all the time or she got terrible gas pains. And the consumption of crackers on that wing doubled. But contrary to Deacon's warning nothing was stolen —except perhaps the notorious tongue depressors. When Maria recovered consciousness after the operation, they cheered and broke out a bottle of wine. They were good-natured, though noisy, additions to the service. The women moved swirlingly. Until the nurses and doctors told them not to, the men tried to carry things for us. Best of all, the children on that wing were having a marvelous time. Soon they were all learning games from long ago.

"Ho!" Vanda, the Gypsy queen, called to me the day before Maria was scheduled to be transferred to a TB hospital. "Joo, voman doctorrr! Doctorrr Donnan!" She was standing arms akimbo in the doorway of the lounge. She was wearing crimson taffeta, purple velvet, and a black, embroidered shawl. With her dyed-blond hair in a beehive hairdo like a crown, she was a striking, if not to say commanding, figure.

Behind her, I could see that the blinds in the lounge had been pulled, making the place dark.

In her thick accent she explained to me that in gratitude for Maria's recovery, the two most expert fortunetellers of the tribe were telling fortunes free. "It is a big expense," she told me gravely, implying that the women made a significant income from fortunetelling.

She led me into the chamber. The old woman of the tribe sat in the darkness wearing her black clothes. "You choose," said Vanda. "It is important you choose who will read your cards." The other woman looked ominous, so I chose Vanda. Taking my arm, she led me to a chair. Seating herself and shaking out her arms from her shawl, she lit two fat candles that she'd placed in ashtrays.

Then she picked up a thick deck of big cards. Though familiar with T.S. Eliot's mention of Tarot, I'd never seen anyone using a whole pack. I was fascinated, and the longer she continued the more fascinated I became, leaning forward in the glow of the two candles and listening to her read the cards and me.

She handed me four queens she'd removed from the pack. "You choose ones you like best," she said, smiling ferociously as I took them. I chose something that looked like wands first, then swords, then I said I was not certain whether I preferred cups or coins.

"Aha!" she rumbled, narrowing her eyes. She took the four queens from me and began to shuffle them back into the pack. "You ask yourself a question you want to know," she said, shuffling with a swift motion. "Do not tell me what your question is!"

The first question that popped into my mind was: "Is she serious?" I decided to let it stand. Skeptically I received the pack from her. As she had told me, I cut it into three piles three different times. Returning them to her, I waited, amused by her intensity. An ambulance had drawn up outside, blasting us with a sudden shriek for help, but she hadn't harkened.

"I will do Solomon's Seal for you!" She laid out seven cards face down in a pattern I couldn't decipher. It looked like a medallion. She turned up the first one, a queen upside down, a queen of the cups suit. Well, I thought facetiously, an upside-down woman is certainly appropriate to me.

"There was someone like a mother . . . your mother?" she asked, "who was ill or is recently been ill. She was troubled."

I was shocked. Stella!

"She is loving woman, she helps others. She has the gift of prophecy maybe but she was in trouble."

I was stunned. Suddenly it was not an issue of science or superstition. No doubt anyone my age could have had experience with a female relative or friend in trouble; what woman can live to her thirties and not suffer? Or Vanda simply knew that a doctor would have encountered *some* woman in pain. Yet my rationalizations disappeared before the vivid question I had to know about Stella: was she willing to die? I had to know whether finally she was willing to die.

I almost blurted out the question, but Vanda was turning up the next card, an eight of the wands things, and saying, "Mmmm. You are intelligent, yes, but you are impulsive. Too impulsive. You do not always have respect, yes? You want your own way." The next card, on the other side, was a two of cups. She smiled. "You will have love," she said, "and interesting work. Yes," she continued, as she turned over a five of coins on the bottom of the medallion, "you can make much money."

Of course, I thought, critically again, any doctor can.

She turned up a five of swords and sucked in her breath. "This is interesting," she said, glancing at me. "You must realize things do not go smooth for you, not just because you fight, but because the world fights you, too." When she turned up a nine of swords on the other side, she sat back for a moment, gazing at the cards and frowning. She tapped those two swords cards with her red fingernails, one after the other, and looked at the whole arrangement again, with all the cards now revealed except the central one.

She looked at me. "You be doctor, is all right you help babies come. Woman only should do that. No men!" She frowned fiercely in condemnation of contemporary obstetrical practice. "But I think there is danger you will not be a safe woman doctor. See! You will have trouble, yes, very much trouble with men. You stay what you are doing, and you will have trouble with men!" She nodded grimly.

At last she picked up the central card and turned it over. It was a man in a window, holding a scimitar behind him and a wand-like thing in front. "The Seventh Arcana!" she whispered with a kind of delight. Then she looked over all the cards again. "Sorrow, yes, you have had—you will have more sorrow. You have to fight, you have to struggle. Anything you get, even love, you will have only by conquer. Never will you have a quiet life." Then she shook her head. "You don't worry about it, though. You are a strong woman!"

Good Vanda, I hope she was right.

Afterword

The idea of a book about the internship of a woman doctor occurred to Florence Haseltine when she was a resident in Obstetrics and Gynecology at the Boston Hospital for Women. Patricia Gercik, her sister-in-law, introduced her to Yvonne Yaw, a professor of English and a professional writer. Florence taped and transcribed the lively anecdotes she told so well, and, with them as a basis, Yvonne wrote a documentary with fictional elements.

Most of the incidents in the book actually happened, and the sex bias and its manifestations are real. Names, sexes, even illnesses have been changed to protect those involved, and the characters as they appear here, including Dr. Phyllis Donnan—her motivations, thoughts, and many of her actions—as well as the working of the incidents themselves, are fictional. In advance, and while she was writing, Yvonne discussed issues and effects with Florence. They often compromised and always finally agreed. Florence made suggestions for the manuscript and checked it thoroughly for medical accuracy.

They believe this synthesis of documentary realism and imagination faithfully represents what actually occurs in hospitals, yet preserves the privacy not only of the patients and staff but also of Florence Haseltine herself.